The Humility and Glory of the Lamb

The Humility and Glory of the Lamb

Toward a Robust Apocalyptic Christology

JEFFREY R. DICKSON

WIPF & STOCK · Eugene, Oregon

THE HUMILITY AND GLORY OF THE LAMB
Toward a Robust Apocalyptic Christology

Copyright © 2018 Jeffrey R. Dickson. All rights reserved. Except for brief quotations in critical publications or reviews, no part of this book may be reproduced in any manner without prior written permission from the publisher. Write: Permissions, Wipf and Stock Publishers, 199 W. 8th Ave., Suite 3, Eugene, OR 97401.

Wipf & Stock
An Imprint of Wipf and Stock Publishers
199 W. 8th Ave., Suite 3
Eugene, OR 97401

www.wipfandstock.com

PAPERBACK ISBN: 978-1-5326-5110-6
HARDCOVER ISBN: 978-1-5326-5111-3
EBOOK ISBN: 978-1-5326-5112-0

Manufactured in the U.S.A.   08/23/18

"Scripture quotations taken from the New American Standard Bible® (NASB), Copyright © 1960, 1962, 1963, 1968, 1971, 1972, 1973, 1975, 1977, 1995 by The Lockman Foundation. Used by permission. www.Lockman.org»

To my wife and children
May the humility and glory of the Lamb always serve
as our greatest inspiration

With special thanks to
Dr. Ed Hindson, Dr. Leo Percer, and Dr. Daniel Mitchell
along with
Joyce Williams and Debbie Dickson

Contents

Abbreviations | viii

1 Introduction | 1
2 A Brief Historical Survey of Apocalyptic Christology Studies | 19
3 Contemporary Johannine Christology with Special Attention to the Apocalyptic Lamb | 62
4 The Humble and Glorious Lamb of Revelation | 85
5 John's Christological Use of Lamb in Revelation | 106
6 Conclusion | 123

Appendix A: A Word on Revelation's Date and Authorship in Connection with the Apocalyptic Lamb | 137
Appendix B: Diagrammatical Analysis of Revelation 5:6–10 | 149

Bibliography | 155

Abbreviations

1 Apol.—Apologia i
Carn. Chr.—De carne Christi
Cels.—Contra Celsum
Comm. Jo.—Commentarii in evangelium Joannis
Decr.—De decretis
Dial.—Dialogus cum Tryphone
Dom.—Domitianus
Ep.—Epistulae
Haer.—De haeresibius
Hist. eccl.—Historia ecclasiastica
LXX—Septuagint
NT—New Testament
Or. Bas.—Oratio in laudem Basilii
OT—Old Testament
Princ.—De principiis
Prax.—Adversus Praxean
Quis div.—Quis dives salvetur
Res.—De resurrectione carnis
Trin.—De Trinitate

1

Introduction

AN ACUTE APPRECIATION FOR the person of Christ has rightly preoccupied a panoply of scholars and debates throughout Christendom ever since Jesus of Nazareth emerged onto the scene, so much so that a much larger work would be required to review how christological studies have evolved to their current form. However, this introduction will briefly survey the current discussions underway in this integral subset of theology in an effort to draw attention to a pressing need for further investigation—a clearing in the Christological forest. Thereafter, this introduction will outline the argument of this book that, if proven, will help satisfy the need that is revealed, particularly as it pertains to the christological presentation of the Lamb in the Apocalypse of John. Ultimately, this project will stipulate that John's unique use of Lamb (ἀρνίον—*arníon*) throughout his Apocalypse paves the way for a multifaceted christological presentation of Jesus Christ that is dependent on the paradoxical theme of glory in humility. After this argument is introduced in this opening chapter, a presentation of how this work is organized will betray exactly what the reader can expect from this study as it pertains to its scope and aim.

The Humility and Glory of the Lamb
Identifying the Clearing in the Christological Forest
Contemporary Christological Scholarship

Most christological works today fit one of three categories: (1) they study the person of Jesus on a more general level by perusing the New Testament (NT) for pertinent passages and presentations,[1] (2) they choose to focus on one Christo-centric book (most often of Johannine origin or one of the synoptics) or a divine characteristic of Christ in an effort to exhaust one of his many important attributes, accolades, or activities,[2] or (3) they investigate Christology on a historical level in an effort to yield why and how the church worshipped Jesus immediately following his earthly ministry.[3] The strength of each of these approaches is easily identified by enlisting the help of a popular analogy. The first approach (what might be called the general approach) is able to survey the entire landscape of the christological forest (the NT) and take into account as many of the trees (pertinent passages) therein. The second (the focused approach) zeroes in on one magnificent tree (important christological passage), or grouping of trees, thereby eliciting a deep appreciation of one specimen belonging to a much larger biome. The third (the historical approach) helps explain how the christological forest emerged in the first place as it traces the many individual considerations back to their roots (which, in this case, involves Jesus' original socio-historical localization). This illustration demonstrates both the variety of ways to study Jesus and what each of these methodologies is uniquely capable of yielding as it concerns his identity and ministry.

That said, it is incumbent upon this introduction to identify the gaps in the research that exist in today's christological scholarship—clearings within the forest in need of cultivation—so that a more complete and, by proxy, more sophisticated understanding of Christ can be achieved. To this end, it must first be acknowledged that most christological studies

---

1. See Hurst and Wright, *Glory of Christ*; Witherington, *The Christology of Jesus*; and Longenecker, *Contours of Christology*.

2. See Anderson, *Christology of the Fourth Gospel*; Gathercole, *Pre-existent Son*; and Johns, *Lamb Christology*, for three examples. The first delimits the study of Christ to how he is portrayed in the book of John. The second makes a compelling case for Jesus' self-proclaimed preexistence and subsequent divinity. The third seeks to discover why the apostle John uses "Lamb" in the book of Revelation and applies his findings to the christological implications contained within the apocalypse.

3. See Dunn, *Unity and Diversity*; Marshall, *Origins*; Hurtado, *Lord Jesus Christ*; Ehrman, *How Jesus Became God*; and Bauckham, *Jesus and the God of Israel*.

Introduction

conducted on a more general level—that is, those taking into consideration what the entire Canon or New Testament (NT) reveals—build their cases by making much use of what may be called "christologically rich" or "christologically inclined" books/passages.[4] This trend is witnessed in *Contours of Christology in the NT*, edited by Richard N. Longenecker.[5] Therein the contributors betray exactly what they believe to be of most value in christological study by means of the order in which they organize their chapters and how much space is devoted to each section (synoptics, Pauline literature, other). It is clear from their choices that Mark is deemed most valuable as it comes first in the canonical presentation.[6] This no doubt comes as a result of two phenomena: historical-critical scholars have assigned Mark an early date[7] and source-critics believe content in Mark is fundamental to both Matthew and Luke.[8] For these reasons, many like Simon Gathercole[9] argue that any Christology that can be yielded from Mark is especially compelling to skeptical critics as it is an early reflection of what Jesus said about himself and what the church believed.[10] Therefore, it is little wonder why so much christological cultivation has been conducted on Mark in recent years.[11]

However, similar attention is spent on the other synoptic gospels, the tension between the three, and the distinct portrayals of Jesus contained within them.[12] For reasons similar to what has already been said of Mark, many believe that much can be yielded from these similar and yet distinct

---

4. The synoptics, John, and to some degree, Paul's letters (in that order).

5. See Longenecker, *Contours of Christology*. See also Hall, *Jesus Christ Today*, and Francesca Murphy, *Oxford Handbook of Christology*.

6. Hooker, "'Who Can This Be?,'" 79–99.

7. Crossley, *Date of Mark's Gospel*. This work dates the composition of Mark's gospel sometime between the mid to late 30s and the mid-40s of the first century. Even though Bart Ehrman gives the gospel of Mark a later date of 65–70, he concedes that this is the best that one has in studying the historical Jesus. See also Ehrman, *How Jesus Became God*, 87–90.

8. Ehrman, *Did Jesus Exist?*, 69–71. See also Ehrman, *How Jesus Became God*.

9. Gathercole, *Pre-existent Son*.

10. See Robbins, "Christology of Mark"; Jackson, "Christology of Mark"; Conley, "Christology of the Gospel of Mark"; Kingsbury, *Christology of Mark's Gospel*; and Henderson, *Christology and Discipleship*.

11. Although this is generally the case, some still lend priority to the Gospel of Matthew.

12. See W. Blevins, "The Demand Motif"; Boring, *Sayings of the Risen Jesus*; Gruenler, *New Approaches*; Donaldson, "Vindicated Son," 100–121; Marshall, "Christology of Luke's Gospel and Acts," 122–147; Grindheim, *Christology in the Synoptic Gospels*.

The Humility and Glory of the Lamb

accounts of Jesus and his activity on the earth. Parallels and contrasts within these works and their comparison to Mark afford much information concerning who Jesus was believed to be. One helpful survey of the distinctions and similarities between the synoptics and what they say about Christ is found in Witherington's *The Christology of Jesus*, in which he parses the historical Jesus by means of his interactions with others,[13] his deeds,[14] and his message as presented in his recorded teachings.[15] As Jesus' life and ministry occupy the majority of these works, it is no wonder why the synoptics are pursued by many scholars in order to understand their shared principle character.

However, some of Paul's letters were written even before the synoptic gospels. Because of their early date and critical acceptance,[16] Pauline literature is yet another field that many scholars believe contain more christologically rich soil.[17] Inasmuch as Paul's letters to the church are didactic, many have concluded that to know what Paul says about Christ is to know what the early church was taught to believe about Christ. Everything from instructive materials to the early creeds Paul endorses[18] provide the kind of literary nutrients in which a high Christology can naturally grow. Not only that, but the prominent place Paul gives to the resurrection of Jesus[19] and the apostle's personal testimony render his work uniquely qualified for christological investigation.

In addition to christological studies conducted on the synoptics and Paul's letters are the multitudinous studies of John's presentation of Jesus

---

13. Witherington, *Christology of Jesus*, 33ff. Here, Witherington believes that much can be learned of Christ by examining his interactions with John the Baptist, the Pharisees, revolutionaries, the Romans, and his disciples.

14. Witherington, *Christology of Jesus*, 145ff. These include but are not limited to his miracles and resurrection.

15. Witherington, *Christology of Jesus*, 179ff. Especially as it pertains to the contents of his many sermons, his predictions of the kingdom of God, and his pervasive use of "the Son of Man."

16. Most date 1 Corinthians around AD 55. However, the creed found in 1 Cor 15:3b–6a, 7 is dated by some at AD 35. See Macgregor, "1 Corinthians 15:3b–6a, 7," 225–34.

17. Abbott, "Paul's Christology in Romans"; Wright, *Climax of the Covenant*; Moo, "Christology of the Early Pauline Letters," 169–192; Martin, "Christology of the Prison Epistles," 193–218; Towner, "Christology in the Letters to Timothy and Titus," 219–246; Fee, *Pauline Christology*; and Tilling, *Paul's Divine Christology*.

18. See 1 Cor 8:6; 12:3; Phil 2:6–11; Rom 1:3–4; 10:9, 13.

19. See 1 Cor 15:12ff; Acts 9; 1 Tim 1:15ff.

Introduction

as found in his gospel.[20] John has long been an epicenter for christological studies because of its explicit Christo-centric content. In no other place in the NT is there a more direct claim of the divinity of Christ than in John. John not only quotes Jesus saying as much about himself, but he organizes his book in a way that argues that Jesus is, in fact, God made flesh. In so doing, John betrays his two-fold agenda: legitimizing the church's new faith in the God-Man and persuading those outside the faith (the Roman world in general and the Judaizers in particular) of his unique identity.[21] Therefore, its explicit content, literary structure, and ecclesiological and apologetic value render John a wellspring of christological discussion. However, due to its late authorship and dissimilarity with the synoptics, whatever the Gospel of John yields, especially as it pertains to its presentation of Jesus, is met with skepticism among historical-critical scholars.[22]

For similar reasons, many, even of an evangelical persuasion, have failed to treat the Apocalypse of John with the same christological interest. There is little doubt that while much work has been done on what the synoptics, Paul's letters, and John's gospel have to say about Jesus, Revelation has remained largely underappreciated for its explicit christological content.[23] Its later date[24] and the ongoing debates concerning the authorship,[25] genre,[26] and eschatological content[27] render the interpretation of this book

---

20. See Anderson, *Christology of the Fourth Gospel*. See also Fennema, "Jesus and God according to John"; Willieett, *Wisdom Christology*; J. McGrath, *John's Apologetic Christology*; Bauckham, "Monotheism and Christology," 148–168; van Belle, Van der Watt, and Maritz, *Theology and Christology*; Rainbow, *Johannine Theology*.

21. See J. McGrath, *John's Apologetic Christology*.

22. Ehrman, *Did Jesus Exist?*, 76. See also D. Smith, *John Among the Gospels*.

23. Christological content includes but is not limited to Revelation's many descriptions of Christ (1:13–18; 5:6–10; 7:17; 14:1–4; 17:14; 19:11–16; 21:23; 22:5) titles used ("Alpha and Omega" [1:7–8]; "Lion" [5:5]; "Lamb" [5:6]; "Faithful and Truth" [19:11], "Word of God" [19:13]) and worship thereof (4:8, 11; 5:9, 12–13; 15:3–4; 19:5).

24. Most conservatives place the date of Revelation at AD 90–95 while critical scholars place its authorship well into the second century.

25. Potential authors include but are not limited to the following: the apostle John, John the Elder, a Johannine community, John the Baptist, or a combination of several authors.

26. Scholars typically fall into one of three categories concerning the genre of Revelation. Either they concede that Revelation is a letter, prophecy, apocalyptic, or some combination of the three.

27. Debates concerning the prophetic content are most easily illustrated in the bifurcation between futurists, preterists, or historicists and the millennial views associated with each.

tenuous. Thus, understanding what it has to say about its central character proves difficult.[28] For these reasons and more, little has been done to explicate what Revelation has to say about Jesus, especially when compared to what has already been said about similar studies of other NT works. Might this be a clearing in the christological forest in need of cultivation? Does Revelation possess the kind of soil that might offer something of christological significance, something that has gone largely unnoticed? For answers to these inquiries, a brief survey of how current scholarship treats the Apocalypse of John must be provided.

Contemporary Revelation Scholarship

Eschatological concerns dominate the discussion surrounding Revelation on both a popular and scholarly level.[29] This is witnessed in everything from pervasive interpretative debates concerning its contents to fictional works that have occupied places of prominence on the *New York Times* bestseller list. No doubt this eschatological proclivity stems from the relatively obscure and symbolic language that is used throughout this work, raising several questions in need of answers: to what do John's visions refer? What is literal? What is figurative? When does this all take place?

These questions explain why so much energy is spent in critical studies on the authorship, potential source(s), and genre of this literary anomaly. That the apostle John authored this book is difficult for some to concede for the following reasons: (1) the author never claims apostleship, (2) the gospel events are not mentioned, (3) nowhere does the author indicate that he had a special relationship with Christ, (4) there are striking theological differences between Revelation and John's gospel and epistles,[30] and (5)

---

28. Aune, "Stories of Jesus," 292. "Theological claims are intentionally embedded in the narratives and descriptions of the Apocalypse, as they are in the Gospels and Acts. But stories and descriptions cannot easily be translated into the ideas—nor is that translation necessarily desirable."

29. Carson and Moo, *Introduction*, 721, "if, as we have argued, Revelation focuses on the end of history, then it is in the area of eschatology that it makes its most important contribution." Though Carson and Moo identify the high Christology in Revelation, they do very little to delineate it. See also Lea and Black, *New Testament*. In presenting their "purpose" of Revelation they conclude, "Revelation presented a broad, sweeping portrait of future events (1:3) in order to strengthen the church, promote endurance in the face of trials, and encourage suffering believers."

30. Perceived theological differences include, but are not limited to, the following: God is depicted as a majestic deity of cosmic judgment in Revelation while he is

Introduction

copious stylistic discrepancies exist between the Gospel of John and this later work.[31] However, skeptical scholars reach this conclusion by neglecting the testimony of the second century that nearly universally concedes Johannine authorship (that is, the apostle John)[32] and the internal evidence suggesting the same.[33]

Questions surrounding authorship have given source-critics much fodder in their pursuit of preexistent works/stages that the author(s) used to create this masterpiece. In the nineteenth and twentieth centuries, scholars speculated that any number of authors and potential sources were used to yield the finished product that is known today as the Apocalypse of John.[34] However, these same scholars make little mention of the pervasive use of the Old Testament (OT) that is consistent throughout.[35] Also, these rarely entertain what the book claims concerning how the information presented was provided (i.e., dictation in chapters 2 and 3 and a vision thereafter) as a possible reason why its content is so unique. Therefore, one might con-

---

portrayed in the Gospel as a God of love, Christ is described as a revealer/redeemer in John while a warrior/ruler in the Apocalypse, and John's earlier work is an example of "realized eschatology" while Revelation reveals things yet to come. See Carson and Moo, *Introduction*, 703.

31. R. H. Charles has even stated the following in reference to the Greek found in Revelation, saying, it "is unlike any Greek that was ever penned by mortal man." Charles, *Revelation of St. John*, xliv. Beasley confirms as much and concludes along with Dionysius that the same person could not have written both John's gospel and Revelation. Beasley, *Book of Revelation*, 35–36.

32. See Justin, Milito, Bishop of Sardis, Eusebius, Irenaeus, and the Muratorian Canon. These conceded Johannine authorship while Marcion and Dionysius called it into question.

33. Revelation's claim to be written by "John" (1:1, 4, 9; 22:8), his address to his readers as "your brother and companion in the suffering and kingdom and patient endurance that are ours in Jesus" (1:9), the literary similarities and thematic connections John's gospel and his apocalypse share.

34. Charles, *Revelation*, lxxxiii–lxxxvi. Therein, Charles suggests that the original writer not only depended on other sources for his material, he died before he finished the text, leaving another to pen Rev 20:4–22:21. J. Massyngberde Ford argues that chapters 4–11 stem from John the Baptist, and 12–22 from a disciple of John, with 1–3; 22:16a, 20b; 21 being added by a Jewish–Christian disciple, *Revelation*, 3–37. See also Aune, *Revelation 1–5*, cv–wwwiv. Here, Aune makes the case that Revelation was formed in two stages—a first edition of the book, containing 1:7–12a and 4:1–22:5 was penned around AD 70 with a strong apocalyptic flair while the remaining sections and other edits were completed much later.

35. Revelation is said by some to allude to the OT more often than any other book in the NT. For a complete analysis, see Beale, *Old Testament in Revelation*.

clude that source-critical analysis, especially in the last one hundred years, has complicated the study of Revelation and further destabilized other considerations.

For instance, reaching any broad consensus on the genre of the book of Revelation has also proven difficult.[36] Some read "apocalypse" in verse 1 ("Ἀποκάλυψις Ἰησοῦ Χριστοῦ") and conclude that the book is primarily apocalyptic. These are quick to cite the unveiling nature of Revelation along with its symbolism, angelic mediums, episodes of cosmic catastrophe, showdown between good and evil, and figurative nature as evidences in favor of this position.[37] However, many who are fearful of opening the door to subjectivism that they believe is inherent in the apocalyptic genre believe that John's Apocalypse might be better understood as primarily prophetic (see "prophecy" in Rev 1:3, "Μακάριος ὁ ἀναγινώσκων καὶ οἱ ἀκούοντες τοὺς λόγους τῆς προφητείας"). These cite as their evidence the similarities this work shares with Daniel and other OT prophets and the eschatological/moral nuances therein.[38] Still others believe it is an epistle because of its named authorship and clearly defined addressees in chapters 1–3.[39]

Perhaps this is why most contemporary scholars suggest a broader definition of Revelation's genre. For example, Everett Harrison concludes that Revelation "is apocalypse with respect to its contents, a prophecy in its essential spirit and message, and an epistle in its form."[40] Robert L. Thomas agrees with Eugene Boring when he says that a view that leaves "no room for an apocalyptic document such as Revelation to be considered also as a genuinely prophetic document directly concerned with the realities of political history" is tenuous.[41] Therefore, the conclusion Carson and Moo reach—that "elements of prophecy, apocalypse, and letter are combined in a way that has no close parallel in other literature"—not only seems to be the current representative view endorsed by most scholars, but the most responsible understanding of the text's form.[42]

36. J. Blevins, "Genre of Revelation," 396.

37 See discussion of the apocalyptic genre in Lea and Black, *The NT*, 583, and Harris, "Apocalyptic Genre," 241ff. For a proponent of this view see Rowland, *The Open Heaven*, 14, 21, 356–57.

38. Hellholm, "Problem of Apocalyptic," 164–65.

39. See Karrer, *Die Johannesoffenbarung als Brief*, and Lucke, *Die Offenbarung Des Johannes*.

40. Harrison, *Introduction*, 458.

41. Thomas, *Revelation*, 29 and Boring, "Theology of Revelation," 261.

42. Carson and Moo, *Introduction*, 716. See also Baukham, *The Theology*, 1–17;

Introduction

These background and literary investigations yield any number of interpretations concerning the contents of John's Apocalypse, especially as they pertain to its eschatology. Approaches to the prophetic phrases in Revelation stretch the gamut of theological persuasion and are defended, albeit with varying degrees of promise, in sophisticated theological and text-specific ways. Preterists insist that John's description in Revelation is a vivid report of events that took place among historical people and countries in his own day. Those adopting a historicist approach believe that Revelation provides an outline that illustrates what will take place throughout the centuries until the end of time. Futurists, on the other hand, conclude that everything in Revelation 4–22 will be fulfilled in the very last days. Still others (idealists) believe that Revelation is not as concerned with events as it is with the character of God and overarching principles according to which God's people are called to live. With this large variety of possible interpretations brought on by the myriad of investigations into Revelation's authorship, potential sources, and genre, it is no wonder why many critical scholars and many more on a popular level often underappreciate the contents and message of this work.

Something must be done in order to bring Revelation back from the brink of slipping further into a skeptical oblivion at the hands of critical scholarship or becoming so narrowly defined that it loses its practical relevance as a result of uninhibited and irresponsible eschatological dogma. Thankfully, according to D. A. Carson and Douglas Moo, "Scholarship in Revelation, in keeping with NT scholarship generally, has moved away from a concern with sources and historical background to a concern with the final literary product."[43] Additionally, interest in John's use of Greek in the Apocalypse has recently grown, opening the door to a greater appreciation for the authorial intent of John's last work (assuming Johannine authorship)[44] and the high Christology that nearly everyone acknowledges and yet so many fail to fully appreciate.[45] These studies demonstrate that

---

Michaels, *Interpreting the Book*, 29–33; Roloff, *Revelation of John*, 5–8; Beale, *Book of Revelation*, 37–43.

43. Carson and Moo, *Introduction*, 719. See also, Fiorenza, *Book of Revelation*, and Paulien, "Recent Developments," 159–70.

44. Mussies, *Morphology*. See also Johns, *Lamb Christology*. See also Gerhard Maier's useful survey of the history of interpretation of Revelation in the church. Therein, he provides information supporting the apostolic origin and canonical status of Revelation. *Die Johannesoffenbarung*.

45. To be discussed later.

there is more to Revelation than parsing prophetic predictions or conducting one's historical/source-critical investigations into its contents. One could say, given the current lay of the land, that Revelation's place in Christendom might be redeemed, in part, by cultivating the clearing in the forest instead of adding to the densest areas of brush where so many are already tangled up in matters that ultimately prove tangential to understanding the essential message of the book.

This brief investigation into the currents of Revelation studies has indicated that much work still needs to be done, especially as it concerns John's eschatological Christology. While analysis of all christological considerations in Revelation is something that this work is not prepared to tackle, this project has chosen to delineate one christologically charged term found in John's apocalypse—the "Lamb" (ἀρνίον). This theologically heavy locution just so happens to be the most prolific word for Christ in the Apocalypse of John and as such, might prove to be a literary key that will help unlock John's greater christological presentation. However, before an argument can be framed, one must survey the myriad of studies given to the lamb motif found in the Scriptures and identify whether or not there is a void in the literature.

Contemporary Lamb Scholarship

The lamb is one of the most beloved and pervasive symbols used in the Canon. Mentioned roughly 750 times in the Bible by a variety of terms,[46] this symbol is deserving of the attention it has received throughout the centuries and in more current scholarship. Most OT references to lambs are literal and found in contexts concerning sacrifice (i.e., burnt offerings in the temple,[47] Passover,[48] and offerings for purification and reparation).[49] For most of these passages, *kebeś* is used to describe a ewe that was less than a year old and qualified to serve in this capacity.[50] The connection these

---

46. These include but are not limited to *kebeś, kibśâ, tāleh,* and *immar* in the OT and ἀμνός (*amnós*), ἀρνός (*arnós*), and ἀρνίον in the NT.

47. Num 15:1–13.

48. Exod 12:3–4.

49. Lev 4:32; Num 6:12.

50. Lev 17:30; 1 Sam 17:34; Isa 11:6; 65:25.

Introduction

literal lambs maintain with the sacrifice traditions "prove(s) . . . that the lamb was available as a metaphor to the ancient Israelite literary mind."[51]

One example of this use is the Passover lamb. In Exodus 12, at God's instruction, the Israelites slay a lamb and paint its blood on their lintels so that the Lord would "pass over" their homes when the angel of death moved through Egypt to slay the firstborn of the land. Here, the lamb is more than just an animal, it serves as an instrument that is capable of providing a right relationship with God as its blood staves off his judgment. From this point on, God's covenant with Israel is maintained in part by the sacrifice of lambs and other livestock at various times, including the annual commemoration of the Passover itself. These sacrifices reiterate the people's need for an offering in order to remain in right relationship with God (safe from much-deserved wrath).

From a literal lamb, to Passover lamb, to sacrificial lamb, the lamb motif in the OT is developed even further elsewhere. In Isaiah 53:6–7 the lamb is depicted as a suffering surrogate—a vicarious victim—that takes the place of someone else. While figurative associations of the lamb elsewhere are tethered to literal livestock and the sacrifice thereof, here, there lamb potentially refers to something else entirely—a person. This is also the case in passages like Psalm 23 in which the Lord God is depicted as a shepherd and his people are understood indirectly as his sheep.[52] Though examples of more figurative uses of lamb do exist in the OT, it is important to acknowledge that it is most commonly used with literal sheep in mind.

While nearly all of the OT passages that mention lamb use this term literally (referring to the pastoral animal)[53] "practically all references in the NT are metaphors comparing the relationship of Christ and his followers to that of the shepherd and his flock."[54] This is nowhere more clearly witnessed than in John the Baptist's introduction of Christ in John 1:29 and 36 when he refers to Jesus as the "Lamb (ἀμνός) of God who takes away the sins of the world." Many believe that this is most likely a reference to the many sacrificial lambs used throughout the OT for a sin offering to appease the

---

51. Freedman, *Anchor Bible Dictionary*, 4:132.

52. See also Ezek 37:24.

53. With the exception perhaps of its metaphorical use in describing the suffering or death of innocence on behalf of others in 2 Sam 12:1–6; Isa 53:7, and indirectly in Ps 23:1.

54. Kohler-Rollesfson, "Sheep," 1008; Hylen, "Lamb," 563, and Elwell, *Baker Encyclopedia*, "Lamb of God," 1299.

wrath of God.[55] The phrase "that takes away the sins of the world" appears to confirm as much.[56] Further evidence that ἀμνός is understood here as a figurative allusion to the many sacrificial types that proliferate the OT is found in its use in Acts 8:32[57] and 1 Peter 1:19.[58] That said, there is a complementary image of the suffering servant intended with the direct reference in the former passage to Isaiah 53.

Others believe that the Baptist's use of ἀμνός here refers instead to the Passover lamb, citing the prominent role the Jewish festivals play in John's gospel as support.[59] However, typically when people wanted to refer to the Passover victim, they would use what Paul implements in 1 Corinthians 5:7—πάσχα (*pascha*)—instead. In fact, the Passover victim was not always nor necessarily a lamb. Still others hold that the Baptist's statement is more accurately understood as an allusion to Isaiah 53, which uses ἀμνός in the Septuagint (LXX), arguing that both passages are a direct reference to the Messiah as suffering servant. However, that the "lamb" of Isaiah 53 was prophetic or popularly understood as messianic was probably not common until after Jesus' ministry.[60]

Regardless of the translation, it is clear that "Lamb of God" has received much attention in contemporary scholarship, and rightfully so, for this phrase introduces the person of Christ in what is believed by many to be the most exhaustive christological treatise available—John's gospel. However, this is not the only time a word for Lamb is used in the NT. Ἀμνός is also used for Jesus in Acts 8:32 when Philip quotes Isaiah 53:7–8 (from the LXX) saying, "a sheep is brought to the slaughterhouse, and as a lamb

---

55. It is described by some as a "general term used by John the Baptist to show that Christ would fulfill what the OT sacrifices pointed to." Elwell, *Baker Encyclopedia*, 1299.

56. "Lamb of God," Douglas, *New Bible Dictionary*, 670. Hylen, "Lamb," 563. "The role of lambs in OT sacrifice has been important for interpreters of these metaphors, many of whom have associated Jesus' designation as a lamb with the Jewish sacrifices of atonement. In this understanding, the death of the lamb, Jesus, eradicated the sins of his followers."

57. "He was led as a sheep to slaughter; and as a lamb before its shearer is silent, so He does not open His mouth."

58. "But with precious blood, as of a lamb unblemished and spotless, *the blood of Christ*."

59. Hoskins, "Deliverance from Death," 285–99.

60. Elwell, *Baker Encyclopedia*, 1300, "unless people general were in the habit of calling the Messiah a 'lamb,' the first suggestion will not stand up, and there is no evidence for this. Moreover, it is hard to believe that the well-known phrase "the Servant of the Lord" would have been translated by such an unusual expression as 'the Lamb of God.'"

Introduction

(ἀμνός) before its shearer is silent, thus he did not open his mouth." First Peter 1:18–19 uses of the same word when it says, "by means of the valuable blood of Christ, like that of a lamb (ἀμνός) without defect or blemish." These references, as in John 1, appear to communicate something about the atonement of sin that is accomplished by a sacrifice. Also, as mentioned earlier, Paul uses πάσχα with the Passover lamb in mind.[61] Still another occurrence of lamb is found in Luke 10:3 where ἀρήν is employed—"Go; behold, I send you out as lambs (ἄρνας, plural of ἀρήν) in the midst of wolves"—to speak of Jesus' followers.

However, the very work in which the Lamb image proves most concentrated in the NT is the same work where the least amount of study has been executed as to its meaning. The word "Lamb" is found twenty-nine times in the Book of Revelation by means of Greek word that has not yet been mentioned— ἀρνίον. Though one might assume that many would award this term special attention because of its frequency and near-exclusive use in Revelation, many quickly conclude that John must mean the same thing in Revelation that he does in his gospel. For instance, in an article devoted to the use of ἀρνίον in John's apocalypse, Donald Guthrie delimits his interpretation to the sacrificial lamb saying, "there can be no question that the sacrificial lamb must be in mind."[62] Paul Rainbow endorses the same lean interpretation of this prolific word when he says "that for John the lamb was an image of atoning sacrifice is confirmed by its use in the Apocalypse (ἀρνίον)."[63] In a note Rainbow continues, "in the NT ἀρνίον occurs only in John's writings . . . where it is synonymous with probation."[64] However, little to no analysis is given in defense of this one-dimensional interpretation.

Just about the only thorough treatment of ἀρνίον and its meaning in Revelation is found in Loren Johns's *The Lamb Christology of the Apocalypse of John*. Therein Johns provides a rigorous linguistic–historical–rhetorical–critical analysis of this most pervasive term for Christ in the book of Revelation. He argues that every time ἀρνίον is used in the LXX, vulnerability and innocence is suggested and then makes the case that for the apostle John to choose this particular word and endorse it every time he refers to

---

61. See 1 Cor 5:7. Clean out the old leaven so that you may be a new lump, just as you are *in fact* unleavened. For Christ our Passover [πάσχα] also has been sacrificed."

62. Guthrie, "The Lamb in the Structure," 71. On this interpretation, Guthrie concludes, "This link it at once with the words of John the Baptist concerning Jesus in John 1:19."

63. Rainbow, *Johannine Theology*, 183.

64. Rainbow, *Johannine Theology*, 183.

The Humility and Glory of the Lamb

Christ as the Lamb in Revelation, especially given the linguistic and historical–critical case to be made, the Apocalypse is adopting the same meaning in every occurrence. Although vulnerability, as Johns admits, might prove an unnatural association with the victorious eschatological Christ, he reassures his readers by saying, "if vulnerability is in view, it can only be a gutsy, costly, and effective kind of vulnerability and an apocalyptic challenge to the usual meaning and value of these nouns and adjectives."[65]

Is this true? Is this complete? If two occurrences of "Lamb of God" as found in the relatively straightforward context of John 1 and the rigorous study thereof have yielded a myriad of interpretations, might one assume that twenty-nine occurrences of ἀρνίον in a far more figurative context like Revelation require more attention than they have been given and yield far more than what has been achieved? If christological studies are missing something from Revelation (which is at present preoccupied with eschatological and author/source/genre debates) and the Apocalypse's christological language (especially its use of ἀρνίον) is not being cultivated to its fullest potential, there is a potential theological clearing in need of cultivation. Ultimately, terms like ἀρνίον in Revelation deserve more attention. This is the tree that this work intends to plant in the blank space that, as already argued, exists in the greater christological forest.

Statement of Thesis

Though Revelation is best known for its graphic prophecies of mysterious characters and epic battles set against the backdrop of cataclysmic tribulation, many, as stated earlier, fail to recognize the sophisticated and altogether brilliant christological presentation that is witnessed within this unique piece of inspired literature. Substantial work must be done to elucidate the eschatological view (and therefore more complete view)[66] of Christ—his

---

65. Johns, *Lamb Christology*, 149.

66. Pannenberg, "Dogmatic Theses," 139, 144. If history's end is the goal of all that is taking place, Jesus Christ and his earthly ministry is the midpoint and climax. According to Pannenberg's view, the end of all events is anticipated in the fate of Jesus Christ. In Jesus' earthly work (especially in the resurrection), the end is not only witnessed ahead of time, but it is experienced by means of a foretaste. Although, as already stated, the whole of history alone can demonstrate the deity of God, and this only at the end of all history, the Christ event, insofar as it anticipates the end of history is one particular event that has absolute meaning as the revelation of God. In its relation to mankind, so long as mankind is heading toward the future, the Christ event is not overtaken by any

Introduction

person, work, and ministry—that is recorded in John's Apocalypse. What John witnesses in his vision is both a peek behind the curtain, where heaven and its glory is currently veiled to the world and where Jesus currently occupies his place at the right hand of God, and a trailer of the major events that will one day take place on the world's stage. Therefore, as John has witnessed this vision of the end times and because he was moved by the Spirit to share this preview with the church, disclosing what was previously veiled/hidden but now, although incompletely, unveiled, it is both appropriate and fruitful for readers to investigate this work in an effort to understand something of Revelation's greatest and most central character—Christ.

The primary way in which John constructs his Christology in the book of Revelation is through the use of elegantly crafted descriptions of Jesus. These take advantage of image-rich language in order to elucidate something about who Jesus is, as witnessed in both what he has already accomplished and what he will one day complete. These include, but are not limited to, the following: the "Alpha and the Omega,"[67] descriptive passages of Christ's appearance,[68] the Lamb,[69] and a juxtaposition between Christ and his foil—the Antichrist.[70] However, this study has chosen to delineate John's use of ἀρνίον in an effort to begin the process of developing a more complete apocalyptic Christology than what already exists.[71]

To this end, this work will argue that John's unique choice of ἀρνίον and the way in which he endorses this term throughout his Apocalypse

---

later event and remains superior to all other concepts as the anticipation of the end. Also, the Christ event culminating in the resurrection satisfies the eschatological character of history as it projects a future state yet to be experienced. See also Vanhoozer, *Is There Meaning*, 303, "In the final analysis, the ideal of the single correct interpretation must remain an eschatological goal."

67. Rev 1:7–8; 22:13.

68. Rev 1:13–18; 19:11–16.

69. Rev 5:6; 7:17; 14:1–4; 17:14; 21:23; 22:1; 22:5,

70. See especially Rev 12; 17–19.

71. "A study of the names of Jesus has always been central to an understanding of the person and work of Christ . . . in the Apocalypse one name stands out above all the rest. Jesus is supremely 'the Lamb.' In chap. 5 it is the Lamb alone who is worthy to unroll the scroll of human destiny. In chap. 7 he stands before the great multitude which has passed through the tribulation and receives their adulation. In chap. 19 he is the victorious avenger who in the cause of righteousness smites the nations with a sharp sword and treads the winepress of the fury of the wrath of God . . . Chap. 21 presents him in joyous reunion with his bride, the people of God." Mounce, "Christology of the Apocalypse," 42.

yields a robust and multifaceted christological presentation of Jesus Christ that is dependent on a radical paradox of glory in humility. This paradox affords John the freedom to demonstrate several important christological themes: (1) his worthiness to receive worship, (2) his ability to judge, (3) his leadership capabilities, and (4) his capacity to illuminate the presence of God.

Design of the Argument

Before this argument can be made, a brief survey of Revelation's use in christological development will be provided in chapter 2 with special attention paid to any consideration of the Lamb. Ultimately this review will demonstrate that on a historical level, understanding apocalyptic Christology in general and Revelation's Lamb Christology in particular has not proven to be a priority. Charting the evolution of Revelation's use in christological considerations will provide an adequate foundation upon which to yield an adequately nuanced understanding of the current theological *sitz im leben* and the shortcomings therein (the lack of an adequate understanding of and appreciation for ἀρνίον in Revelation) in chapter 3.

Following a review of how many have decided to interpret the Lamb of Revelation today, chapter 3 will award special consideration to the work of Loren Johns and his more recent and exhaustive work on the subject. A critical analysis of Johns's recent work in *Lamb Christology* will demonstrate that while there is much to be gleaned from this project—hard data, linguistic analysis, and historical insight—the conclusions reached by means of these insights are inadequate. Analysis of his work will also reveal that Johns's interpretation of the Lamb is more in keeping with his own presuppositions than it is with what is found in Revelation itself. It will be argued that Johns's failure to adequately delineate ἀρνίον in a responsible way stems from issues concerning the design of his case, which, as it is a more deductive approach, succeeds in discoloring the connotation of the word in question prior to its reconfiguration into its original context. A better, more inductive and canonically-contoured approach would reverse Johns's program, allowing for the authorial intent to guide the meaning of the term and its implications within the context of the apocalypse itself first and then check what is yielded against linguistic and historical analysis.

Such an approach will preoccupy the remainder of this work. The shortcomings that will inevitably surface in chapter 3 will be answered in

Introduction

chapter 4. Following a brief comment on the genre of Revelation, a contextual–grammatical–canonical–historical analysis of Revelation 5:6–10 will be offered. In this pivotal passage—which might be likened to the downbeat that begins the major eschatological movement of Revelation—Jesus is cast as a brilliant paradox that accentuates not only his matchless glory but his uncompromising humility. The words used (particularly ἀρνίον), descriptions offered, worship witnessed, precedent given (in both the OT and NT), and even the extra-biblical usage of similar language support these claims. The unique genre of the context in which this is provided—apocalyptic prophecy—allows John the literary freedom to accomplish this goal (equal parts eschatological/predictive and metaphorical/creative)—a presentation of a humble and therefore glorious Christ that he endorses no less than twenty-eight additional times throughout the remainder of this letter to the Church. This study will reveal that what John intends when he uses ἀρνίον may not be limited to what has already been assumed by so many.[72] Proving this to be true will help crack open the door leading to more complete understanding of how Christ is understood and portrayed in the other passages that use this same label.

This more polysemous interpretation of ἀρνίον (centered on the paradox of humility and glory that is established in Revelation 5) will be further evidenced by an overview of this term's use in the remainder of Revelation in chapter 5. As ἀρνίον is endorsed in worship, judgment, leadership, and heavenly contexts present in the Apocalypse of John, it proves itself to be a flexible term that can be applied in any number of ways and in any number of contexts to convey any number of christological truths (in part because of its more general and overarching connotations that are bracketed between the themes of humility and glory witnessed upon Christ's initial emergence earlier in Revelation). Ultimately, what is sought is an understanding of John's use of ἀρνίον and, by proxy, a robust eschatological Christology that is textually rooted, contextually informed, and historically nuanced (in that order).

Finally, chapter 6 will discuss the integral christological implications of the study that has been provided in chapters 1–5. Space will also be devoted to demonstrating how this argument adds value to Revelation studies by drawing attention to what has gone undeveloped/underdeveloped. Choosing to acknowledge the dynamic and wondrous Christology

---

72. That is, that "Lamb" exclusively to the idea of sacrifice, the Passover lamb, the suffering servant, or a vulnerable example.

The Humility and Glory of the Lamb

contained in Revelation, even as it pertains to this single symbol, provides further impetus for both critical scholars and popular audiences to read and study this amazing work: apprehending and celebrating who Christ is now and anticipating who he will one day prove to be in the end.

2

A Brief Historical Survey of Apocalyptic Christology Studies

THE FIRST TASK OF this project is proving that there is, in fact, a clearing in the christological forest in need of cultivation. Is there something that is either missing or largely insufficient in christological studies on a historic level? This present chapter seeks to answer this inquiry by providing a survey of christological consideration and its investigation (if any) of Revelation and/or the Lamb therein. Ultimately, the survey contained in this chapter will reveal two things: (1) that on a historical level, the Apocalypse of John has been largely neglected for its christological content, especially as it pertains to John's use of Lamb, and (2) that reasons for this are copious and vary depending on the discussions taking place, debates had, and distractions present in specific socio-historical localizations.

From the Resurrection to Revelation: The Glorified and Multidimensional Christ

In order to understand the Christology of the first Christians, one must first be willing to understand the primitive Jewish Christian community.[1] A fiercely monotheistic Jewish worldview was not designed to immediately endorse the addition of Jesus—a man—into the Godhead. After all, the idea of a Godhead may have even proven foreign to the followers of

---

1. Grillmeier, *Christ in Christian Tradition*, 9–10.

The Humility and Glory of the Lamb

Yahweh. So how did this happen? Charles H. Talbert suggests that there are two approaches to understanding how Christology evolved in Christianity's earliest years. First, there are those who understand christological development as a logically backward process[2] in which Christ was imbued with more and more exceptional and divine qualities as reports of Jesus' were being produced in the second half of the first century.[3] Second, there are those who insist on a high Christology very early (pre-Pauline) that was then promulgated throughout the known world via the NT.[4] Those belonging to this second group believe that major christological developments came in the first four or five years after Jesus' death as a result of the disciples' experiences that were connected to the resurrection and what transpired thereafter.[5] Though, as Talbert claims, "neither perspective on Christology's development . . . is able to claim consensus status,"[6] the latter coincides with what has been discovered about the Jews during this period.

Larry Hurtado and Richard Bauckham recognize a dramatic shift/"mutation" in the religious practices of the earliest Jewish/Gentile Christians away from what these scholars refer to as "strict monotheism" toward what they call "the binitarian shape of early Christian worship."[7] Guided in large part by the *šemą* and the first two commandments of Moses, Jewish worship was defined by the conviction that the God of Israel was the one and only God and creator of all things. Because of this, God alone was worthy of worship. That these ideas comprised the theological

---

2. See W. L. Knox, *St. Paul and the Church*, 90; Brown, *Birth of the Messiah*; and Casey, *From Jewish Prophet to Gentile God*.

3. This evolutionary progress is described by Talbert as follows: "(1) At the earliest stage in Christian thought, the *parousia* was regarded as the point when God would reveal Jesus as the Christ. (2) In a pre-Gospel period (Paul and the speeches in Acts), the resurrection was the chief moment associated with the divine proclamation of the identity of Jesus (Acts 2:32, 36; 13:32–33; Rom. 1:3–4; Phil. 2:8–9) . . . (3) Mark tells the reader that at Jesus' *baptism* Jesus was declared Son of God (1:11). (4) Matthew and Luke push the question of Jesus' identity back to his miraculous *conception*. (5) In John the question is pressed back to the *pre-existence* prior to creation. Christological development has been conceived in this way for a long time." Talbert, *Development of Christology*, 4.

4. Fuller, *Foundations*, and Hahn, *Titles of Jesus*.

5. Hurtado, *Lord Jesus Christ*.

6. Talbert, *Development of Christology*, 4.

7. Hurtado, *At the Origins*, 63ff, *How on Earth Did Jesus Become a God?*, 111–51, *Lord Jesus Christ*, 42ff, *One God, One Lord*, 99–123; Bauckham, *Jesus and the God of Israel*, 140ff.

A Brief Historical Survey of Apocalyptic Christology Studies

cornerstone of the Jewish faith is demonstrated in both linguistic studies on the OT and analysis of first-century Jewish worship.

In his dissertation titled "Monotheism and Christology in 1 Corinthians 8:4–6," Paul Rainbow compiles over 200 phrases that represent the monotheism inherent in Jewish worship (25 of which occur in the NT). These include but are not limited to divine titles accompanied by "one," "only," "sole," and "alone." Jews also described God as a monarch over all, explicitly denied all other gods, claimed Yahweh was without a rival, and restricted their worship to him.[8] Hurtado and E. P. Sanders agree that this rhetoric asserts God's universal sovereignty and his utter uniqueness as true, real, and compelling in contrast to the false, unreal, and counterfeit gods offered in other worldviews.[9]

This exclusive rhetoric is reiterated in the worship practices of first-century Judaism. For instance, the copious sacrifices offered in the NT were always and only offered to the God of Israel.[10] Not only that, but Carol Newsom believes that all available evidence suggests that the religious devotion witnessed in the synagogue focused on Yahweh and his Torah.[11] This is observed in the prominence given to the Decalogue and the recitation of the šemą. Both of these practices were used in first-century liturgy to accentuate God's distinctiveness.[12] What was seen in the sacrifices, studied in the synagogue, and recited in the liturgy could also be found in the prayers many first-century Jews offered. After analyzing Jewish prayers preserved in Second-Temple Jewish literature, N. B. Johnson reveals that all the prayers in these writings were offered to the God of Israel alone.[13]

These historical trends demonstrate that the first-century religion of Jerusalem was a thoroughgoing monotheistic worldview firmly rooted in OT theology. Such a rigid and streamlined system was not prepared for theological amendment, especially of the type that endorsed worship of Jesus in addition to Yahweh. However, this is exactly what happened. Hurtado reveals the following,

---

8. See chapter 4 of Rainbow, "Monotheism and Christology." See also Rainbow, "Jewish Monotheism," 78–91. See also M. Smith, "The Common Theology," 135–147.

9. Hurtado, *How on Earth Did Jesus Become a God?*, 120; E. P. Sanders, *Judaism: Practice and Belief*, 241–51. See also Bauckham, *Jesus and the God of Israel*, 115–16.

10. Hurtado, *How on Earth Did Jesus Become a God?*, 123.

11. Newsom, *Songs of the Sabbath Sacrifice*.

12. See Albright, "A Biblical Fragment," 145–76.

13. N. B. Johnson, *Prayer in the Apocrypha*.

The Humility and Glory of the Lamb

"Given that the religious attitudes of earliest Christians were much shaped by biblical/Jewish scruples about avoiding the cultic worship of other gods, humans, angels, and any figures other than the one true God of the biblical tradition, the explicit and programmatic inclusion of Christ in their devotional practice is interesting, even striking."[14]

From very early on, Jesus was worshipped by the young Christian movement and understood to be equal to God. The posture people took toward Jesus as demonstrated in the gospels[15] and the pervasive use of προσκυνέω in contexts involving Christ (especially in Matthew) each in their own way prove the early worship of Christ and, by proxy, an early Christology.[16]

That a high view of Christ was endorsed by many in the infant Christian movement is illustrated in some of the oldest first-century works available to biblical scholars today—recorded creeds, confessions, and sermon material.[17] The major theological shifts described in these works demonstrate how the resurrection of Christ precludes the dramatic change in the preaching material, doctrinal content, and worship practices that can be witnessed among those in this transitional epoch. O. C. Edwards argues from the NT that the first Christian congregations did not understand themselves as part of a new religion, but rather as Jewish synagogues differing from their more traditional counterparts in their affirmation of Jesus as Messiah.[18] If this is true, then similarities between worship in the

---

14. Hurtado, *At the Origins*, 70. See also Hurtado, "First-Century Jewish Monotheism," 3–26.

15. See words/phrases like πίπτω, γονυπετέω, and τίθημι τὰ γόνατα. Each of these words/phrases describe the physical posture of falling down before someone either on the knees or fully prostrate.

16. Hurtado, *How on Earth Did Jesus Become a God?*, 146. "The term προσκυνέω is a recurrent feature of Matthew's narrative vocabulary, with thirteen occurrences, a frequency exceeded only by the twenty-four uses in Revelation among the NT writings. Moreover, ten of these Matthean occurrences describe homage offered to Jesus, which makes it Matthew's favorite word to Designate the reverence given to Jesus by people." Hurtado also points out the total number of uses in other NT writings: Mark (2), Luke (3), John (10), Acts (4), 1 Corinthians (1), Hebrews (2), and Revelation (24).

17. Most of the creedal material is believed to have surfaced between 30 and 50 AD and is therefore very compelling evidence for what many believed about Christ at the earliest stages of church history. NT examples of creedal statements can be found in the following passages: Luke 24:34; Acts 2; Rom 1:3–4, 10:9–10; 1 Cor 8:6, 15:5–7; Phil 2; Col 1, 1 Tim 3:16; 2 Tim 2:11–13.

18. Edwards, *History of Preaching*, 8.

A Brief Historical Survey of Apocalyptic Christology Studies

synagogue and in early Christianity would be expected. However, each would differ in focus.

For instance, many believe that both Judaism and those faiths that stem from the Torah (Christianity and Islam) are unique in their commitment to homilies in their corporate worship settings.[19] However, in analyzing the characteristics of the typical first-century synagogue sermon, one is immediately struck by the differences between Jewish and Christian preaching. Richard Stegner identifies the following elements that were involved in a typical Jewish sermon:

1. The sermon begins with a statement of the first verse of the passage or several words from the first verse.
2. A key word or words are explained and emphasized throughout the sermon.
3. Other words and phrases from the whole passage (not just the initial verse) are explained and repeated.
4. Other biblical verses are cited for purposes of illustration or for developing side points.
5. Illustration are drawn from Scripture or contemporary life.
6. Scriptural illustrations are used, the biblical story is frequently retold with imaginative additions to the text.
7. In the conclusion a word or words from the opening verse are repeated to indicate the sermon is ended.
8. The main thrust of the sermon is summarized.[20]

There is little to no question that the content of these sermons was dominated by readings from the Torah and the prophets as found in the Hebrew Scriptures.[21]

---

19. "Only Judaism and its descendants, Christianity and Islam, have given room to the specific interpreting of religious truth as a normal element in their services of worship. Judaism long ago lost its priests, with the loss of the Jerusalem Temple, but it has kept its rabbis. Christianity had preachers before it had priests of its own, and for many centuries it has had both, usually in the same person. Islam has no priests properly so called, but long has depended upon the imam, the divinely inspired teacher or preacher." Hedley, *Christian Worship*, 164. See also Beckelhymer, "Place of Preaching in Worship," 277–289.

20. Stegner, "Ancient Jewish Synagogue Homily," 58–62.

21. Edwards, *A History of Preaching*, 9. In fact, that this is so is even witnessed in the

The Humility and Glory of the Lamb

However, this was not what preoccupied the sermons of the early church following Christ's earthly ministry. Instead, acute variations in style, approach, and design are witnessed in the sermons that populate the NT. Peter's sermon in Acts 2 and Stephen's sermon in Acts 7 make great use of the OT. Still others like Paul on Mars Hill in Acts 17 use very little if any of the OT. Length as well as use of language also varies. However, one thing that all of the sermons of Acts have in common is the report of the resurrection of Jesus Christ.[22] Therefore, instead of a preoccupation with the Torah and prophets, homilies in the first-century church became more fascinated with the person and work of Jesus. In fact, most if not all of the sermons represented in Acts and elsewhere reveal that the decisive message of the gospels is that which comes at the end—the message of the resurrection of Jesus and the implications thereof.[23]

That the topic of the resurrection transcends multiple preachers and multiple genres of preaching (i.e., multiple attestation of sources and forms) lends more credence to the centrality of the resurrection of Jesus as witnessed in these sermons. Whether a sermon was primarily missional/hortatory,[24] prophetic,[25] didactic,[26] or interpretative,[27] most if not all of the homilies that are preserved in the NT endorse a high Christology. That Christ in general and his resurrection in particular usurped the formalized homilies on the Torah in the early church and that Jewish monotheism appears to have made room for Jesus in the Godhead suggests that Bauckham is right to conclude that earliest Christians claimed Jesus as God.[28]

This view is validated by the worship practices endorsed by the first-century saints. In addition to the sophistication of monotheism witnessed in the early church and the change in the preaching content, many new corporate worship trends were introduced at the genesis of the Christian movement that demonstrate an unusually early and high Christology. The first of these involves the use of hymns in worship. As evidenced by their

---

gospels themselves as they give an account of the young Jesus in Luke 2 and witnessed in the Sermon on the Mount in Matt 5–7.

22. See Acts 1:21–22; 2:22–36; 4:8–10; 5:29–32; 10:39–43; 13:28–31; 17:1–3, 30–31.
23 Dahl, *Jesus in the Memory*, 27.
24. See Acts 2; Phil 2:1–11.
25. See 1 Thess 4:13ff; Rev 1.
26. See 1 Cor 15.
27. Acts 7.
28. Bauckham, *Jesus and the God of Israel*, vii–viii.

A Brief Historical Survey of Apocalyptic Christology Studies

presence in the NT[29] and the variety of genres in which they are found,[30] these hymns demonstrate a devotion to the person and work of Jesus that most believe arose "from the religious experiences of the first generation of believers."[31] Though both Christian and preceding Jewish worship services incorporated the use of hymns,[32] the preoccupation with Christ "does not seem to have a parallel in any other sect of Judaism known to us from antiquity."[33]

Prayer also evolved in the early church. Although (as witnessed in Pauline literature) early Christianity kept the tradition of addressing prayer to God the Father,[34] other references indicate that Jesus was also directly addressed [35] In fact, as the church continued to develop, evidence shows that Jesus was consistently invoked in prayer.[36] Along with the innovations made in hymns/doxologies, addressing Jesus in prayer is further evidence of the exaltation of Christ following the revelation given on the first Easter morning.

The observance of the Lord's Supper, especially as witnessed in 1 Cor. 11:23–26, also reveals that from very early, this ceremony both appreciated Christ's death and anticipated his return and the subsequent eschatological victory thereafter. For Hurtado, this suggests that "among the earliest we have, of the corporate gatherings of Jewish Christians [we witness]

---

29. See John 1:1–18; Col 1:15–20; Phil 2:5–11; Eph 2:14–16; 5:5:14; 1 Tim 3:16; 1 Pet 3:18–22; Heb 1:3; Rev 4;8, 11; 5:9–10, 13–14; 15:3–4.

30. Bauckham, *Jesus and the God of Israel*, 133. "The commonest form was a doxology to Christ alone, of which three examples occur in the NT, though in relatively late NT documents (2 Tim 4:18; 2 Pet 3:18; Rev 1:5–6). . . . The three clear NT examples are from different geographical areas and theological traditions and so presuppose a common Christian practice going back some time before the writing of these works."

31. Hurtado, *One God, One Lord*, 102.

32. Deichgraber, *Gotteshymnus und Christushymnus*, 25–27. See also Bauckham, *Jude, 2 Peter*, 119–20. Both of these works argue that there is little doubt that the early Christian use of doxologies/hymns derive from Judaism.

33. Hurtado, *One God, One Lord*, 102. This preoccupation is also witnessed in the frequency of the hymns preserved. Though it is the case that hymns/doxologies were typically used by both Jews and Christian as a conclusion to a prayer, sermon, or letter, in extant Jewish literature they are rarely preserved. This is not so in the NT where many songs from many sources and in many contexts are preserved—all magnifying Jesus Christ because of what he has accomplished.

34. Rom 1:8–10; 1 Cor 1:4; 2 Cor 1:3–4; Phil 1:3–5; 1 Thess 1:2–3; Phlm 4.

35 Acts 1:24; 7:59–60; 2 Cor 12:2–20; etc.

36. Hurtado, *One God, One Lord*, 107.

another example of the prominent place of the risen Christ in their devotional practice."[37] Though common meals were shared in earlier Jewish tradition,[38] there is no historic parallel for the Lord's Supper and its focus on Christ.

The unprecedented theological innovation witnessed among first-century Jewish Christians, specifically pertaining to the nature of the Godhead (as witnessed in what has been called a "binitarian shift"), and the homiletical and ecclesiological implications thereof (i.e., the content of sermons, the hymns sung, prayers prayed, and Lord's Supper observed) is most adequately explained by the resurrection of Jesus and the high Christology that resulted. This conclusion is supported by what is discovered in the book of Revelation itself. Therein, toward the lattermost part of the first century, a sophisticated and representative view of the nature of Christ is both revealed and applied eschatologically. However, because of pervasive preoccupation with what is earliest and, by proxy, most credible,[39] understanding how the Apocalypse of John helped shape and/or articulate Christology in its own socio-historical localization has been studied less. This is unfortunate as the presentation of Christ in Revelation brilliantly confirms and expands what is said of him elsewhere in the NT (albeit in more colorful ways).

For example, Talbert has compiled a list of theologically charged titles that are ascribed to Jesus in John's Apocalypse. These betray a multilayered Christology that is, in some ways, rooted in works that precede Revelation. They include the following:

1. Lord (Rev 11:8; 14:13; 22:20, 21; see also Rom 10:9; Phil 2:11; Acts 2:36)

2. The Messiah/Christ (Rev 11:15; 12:10; 20:4, 6; see also Mark 8:29; John 20:31; Acts. 2:36)

3. The Son of God (Rev 2:18; see also John 20:31; 1 John 3:8; 4:15; 5:13)

4. The Faithful witness/martyr (Rev 1:5; 3:14; 19:11; see also 1 Tim 6:13)

---

37. Hurtado, *One God, One Lord*, 112. For more exhaustive discussions on the nature and impetus behind the Lord's Supper, see Marshall, *Last Supper*, and Kodell, *Eucharist*.

38. For an overview of the prevalence of the sacred meal, see Lietzmann, *Mass and Lord's Supper*.

39. That is, hymns, sermon reports, Paul's letters, Mark, and Matthew. See also chapter 1.

A Brief Historical Survey of Apocalyptic Christology Studies

5. The Firstborn of the dead (Rev 1:5; see also Rom 8:29; 1 Cor 15:20; Col 1:18; Heb 12:23)

6. The Ruler of the kings of the earth (Rev 1:5; 3:14; 19:16 see also 3 Macc 5:25; 1 Enoch 9:4)

7. The First and the Last (Rev 1:17; 2:8; 22:13; see also Isa 44:6; 48:12–13)

8. The Living One (Rev 1:18; 2:8; see also Deut 5:26; Josh 3:10; Isa 37:4)

9. The Holy One (Rev 3:7; see also Mark 1:24)

10. The True One (Rev 3:7; 19:11; see also John 14:6)

11. The One who has the key of David (Rev 3:7; see also Isa 22:22)

12. The Amen (Rev 3:14; see also 2 Cor 1:20)

13. The ἀρχή (Ruler) of God's creation (Rev 3:14; see also Neh 9:17)

14. The Beginning and the End/Alpha and Omega (Rev 22:13; see also Josephus, A.J., 8.280)

15. The Lion of the tribe of Judah (Rev 5:5; see also Gen 49:9)

16. The Root of David (Rev 5:5; see also Rom 15:12)

17. The Lamb (Rev 5:6, 8, 12, 13; 6:1, 16; 7:9, 10, 14, 17; 12:11; 13:8; 14:1, 4, 10; 15:3; 17:14; 19:7, 9; 21:9, 14, 22, 23, 27; 22:1, 3; see also Exod 10:12–15, 21–23; 12:6, 7; 15:1, 18; 19:6)

18. The Word of God (Rev 19:13; see also John 1)

19. The bright morning Star (Rev 22:16; Num 24:17)

20. The One who has the sharp, two-edged sword (Rev 1:16; 2:12; 19:15; see also Wis 18:15–16).[40]

Such titles affirm the following: (1) an awareness of symbols and names used in ancient Judaism,[41] (2) a willingness to use what is found in Christian and extra-biblical literature,[42] and (3) an appreciation for the multiple functions that Christ is capable of performing.[43] These titles also prove

---

40. Talbert, *Development of Christology*, 144ff.

41. See "Lord," "Messiah/Christ," "Son of God," "Lamb," and "Bright and morning Star" and corresponding references above.

42. See "Lord," and "Rulers of the kings of earth" and corresponding references above.

43. See "Ruler," "Beginning and End," and "Lamb" and corresponding references above.

The Humility and Glory of the Lamb

that a sophisticated appreciation for the person of Christ was present by the end of the first century. Added to this, Talbert concludes that "by speaking of Jesus Christ as eternal (the first and last)[44] and by depicting him as a legitimate object of worship,[45] the author of the apocalypse clearly locates him on the side of deity rather than on the side of creatures."[46]

As lofty and divine as some of these titles are, John depicts Christ as both heavenly *and* human,[47] holy *and* humble. While his holiness is emphasized in titles like "Lord," "Son of God," "Holy One," "Beginning and End," and "word of God," his humility is confirmed in designations such as "faithful witness" and "Firstborn of the dead." Interestingly, the most prolific title used of Jesus in Revelation—the "Lamb"—marries these two "faces" into one incredible symbol. Inasmuch as lambs intended for sacrifice were chosen for their uniquely pure and especially blameless qualities and yet were, in and of themselves, humble creatures and nearly defenseless on their own against predator and priest alike, there are few images John could have endorsed that would have better juxtaposed these two ideas (holiness and humility) for the central figure in his apocalypse.

The characteristics of first-century Christology—the changes in theology (from strict monotheism to binitarian considerations), titles used (emphasizing both Jesus' humility and divinity), and worship practices (preaching, hymns, and prayer content)—demonstrate that Jesus was celebrated in sophisticated ways in the period between his resurrection and the writing of Revelation. What began as a high Christology following the resurrection grew into a multifaceted appreciation for the God-Man at the close of the Canon (as evidenced by the many theologically weighty titles ascribed to Jesus and pervasive use of προσκυνέω in places like Matthew and Revelation).[48] Grillmeier concludes the following of this early Christology:

> "Within the limits marked out on the one hand by the synoptists and on the other by John and Paul, the Christology of the NT itself already displays considerable diversity. . . Common to all sources is a firm recognition of Jesus' transcendence and his central position

---

44. See Rev 22:13.

45. See Rev 4–5.

46. Talbert, *Development of Christology*, 159.

47. These categories are adopted from Weber, *Way of the Lamb*. See also Talbert, *Development of Christology*, 149.

48. For more on the worship of Jesus in Revelation, see Bauckham, "Worship of Jesus," 322–41; Freedman, *Anchor Bible Dictionary*, 3:812–19; Bauckham, *Climax of Prophecy*, 118–49; and Grillmeier, *Christ in Christian Tradition*, 33.

in salvation history. This clearly rests on living experience (primarily of the resurrection, but also quite simply of the words and actions of the Lord), and finds its climax in belief in the lordship of God and the divinity of Christ. This single recognition, or this single experience, is also the bond which links the post-apostolic and the apostolic age."[49]

It is to this post-apostolic age that this historical survey of Christology now turns.

From Revelation to Chalcedon: The Orthodox Christ

In the first five hundred years of the church, theological formulation was predominately concerned about the nature of God, especially as it pertained to understanding the Trinity and Christology.[50] These discussions were no doubt most clearly witnessed in their proximity to the early debates between Gnosticism and Docetism. Though many interjected their respective contributions to the debates entertained between these two poles, "what united the orthodox development of Christology was the keeping together of the biblical teaching regarding the full deity and full humanity of Christ in one active subject."[51] This common theme can be traced in the major contributors of the period ranging from Ignatius to Nicaea.

Reacting in large part to Docetists who undermined the nature of the incarnation, Ignatius stressed the full humanity of Christ alongside his glory.[52] Wellum and Grillmeier both recognize the paradox in which Ignatius affirms statements about Christ in the flesh on the left and concedes his preexistence on the right.[53] This demonstrates that at this early post-apos-

---

49. Grillmeier, *Christ in Christian Tradition*, 33.

50. Wellum, *God the Son Incarnate*, 256ff.

51. Wellum, *God the Son Incarnate*, 269.

52. In support of his humanity, Ignatius writes, "Turn a deaf ear therefore when any one speaks to you apart from Jesus Christ, who . . . was really born, who both ate and drank; who really was persecuted under Pontius Pilate; who really was crucified and died . . . who, moreover, really was raised from the dead when his Father raised him up. . . . But if, as some atheists (that is, unbelievers) say, he suffered in appearance only . . . why am I in chains. And why do I want to fight with wild beasts? If that is the case, I die for no reason." Ignatius, *Epistle of Ignatius to the Trallians*, 9. Held alongside this commitment, Ignatius also affirmed the full deity and preexistence of the Son in *The Epistle to Ignatius to the Ephesians*, 7.

53. Wellum, *God the Son Incarnate*, 270. Grillmeier, *Christ in Christian Tradition*, 86–89. Here, Grillmeier states the following: "This theological understanding of the unity

tolic juncture, the full deity and humanity of Christ was conceded. Though Ignatius does not appear to endorse Revelation heavily to make this point (inasmuch as Revelation is not primarily concerned with the incarnation and therefore not immediately helpful as a rejoinder to Docetism) this brief description of Ignatius's major christological contribution demonstrates that like the Christology inherent within Revelation demonstrates (see discussion in the latter part of chapter 2), this early church father's understanding of Jesus was multivalent.

However, at least one early church father did endorse Revelation in his christological program—Justin Martyr. This Christian apologist sought to draw a connection between Hellenistic thought and Christianity by capitalizing on the apostle John's use of "Logos" (λόγος) for Jesus.[54] His apologetic method involved granting that even pagan philosophers possessed glimpses of the truth and could partially agree with Christian theology because of the longstanding Greek concept of a logos or universal reason that undergirds all reality. Christianity, for Justin, affirmed that this Logos was made flesh,[55] and argued that those who believe in him settle for the only philosophy that provides any real connection to the God of the universe.[56] The Logos made flesh serves as a mediator between God and the world and as such reveals the will of the Father to humanity. This he does both at his incarnation and in the "second *parousia*."[57] However, not only is the Logos present at the incarnation and at the *parousia*, he was also present at the beginning. "Now in this way Christ also becomes the 'Nomos' of the human race ... by him order is brought into world in which everything has been in confusion."[58] Order came out of cosmological chaos in Genesis 1,

---

in Christ finds its clearest expression in Ignatius in his use of the so-called 'exchange of predicates,' where the divine is predicated of the man Christ and the human of the Logos, while the distinction between the two kinds of being is clearly maintained. This way of speaking is possible only because the unity of the subject is recognized."

54. Wellum, *God the Son Incarnate*, 271. See also Parvis and Fosters, *Justin Martyr and His Worlds*.

55. See John 1:1–3, 14.

56. Using John's Gospel, Justin Martyr demonstrates that the eternal dunamiV of God, the Logos can himself beget his earthy existence from the virgin (thereby establishing the Logos's physical presence on the earth without stripping his divinity) (1 *Apol.*, 33). He backs this assertion by stressing the historical data of this earthly existence of the Word made flesh (1 *Apol.*, 13, 3; 35, 9).

57. This phrase was coined by Justin in 1 *Apol.*, 52–3, *Dial.*, 14, 8.

58. Grillmeier, *Christ in Christian Tradition*, 91. See also Justin, 1 *Apol.*, 40, 5ff; 39 and *Dial.*, 11–25.

order was made available out of moral chaos in John's gospel (by means of the salvific ministry of Jesus), and order will come out of global chaos at the end (see Revelation). In utilizing John 1 and passages like Revelation 1:8 and 4:8, Justin was able to establish the Logos at all of these historical junctures (past, present, and future) and argue that apart from Christ, all thought is incomplete.[59]

Later, Irenaeus helped correct the subordinationism that some believed was inherent in the Logos Christology of Justin Martyr by arguing "that the Logos has always existed as the One who reveals the Father and thereby is personally distinct from him."[60] Irenaeus also argued against the Gnostics' distinction between a divine Christ and an earthly Jesus saying "Jesus Christ is one and the same."[61] Similar to Ignatius before him, Irenaeus embraced the humanity and divinity of Jesus simultaneously. This he did by introducing two phrases: "The Son of God [has] become a son of Man" (*Filius dei filius hominis factus*) and "Jesus Christ, true man and true God" (*Jesus Christus vere home, vere deus*).[62] These phrases suggest that the redemptive work of Jesus "depends fully on the identity between his humanity and our humanity."[63]

Tertullian adopted the unity of the God-Man (as promoted by Irenaeus) in his own writings and affirmed that the incarnate one is the Logos who took on flesh (as argued by Justin Martyr).[64] However, Tertullian's unique christological contribution came when he insisted that Christ possessed a unique personhood within the Trinity[65] and that Jesus had a human soul.[66] Seeking to articulate exactly how this unity and diversity

---

59. See Justin's use of the phrase "who is, and was and is to come" in *Dial.*, 111, 2. See also discussion in Letham, *Holy Trinity*, 90–97 and Galot, *Who Is Christ?*, 220–223.

60. Wellum, *God the Son Incarnate*, 273: "One of the problems that Justin bequeaths later generations . . . is subordinationism, i.e., viewing the Logos as ontologically subordinate to the Father by making the procession of the Logos from the Father dependent on creation. This will open the door for some to say that there is no eternal preexistence of the Logos in a distinct personal existence—a door, sadly, that later Arian theology walks through," 272.

61. Irenaeus, *Haer.*, 3.16.2, 3.17.4.

62. Wellum, *God the Son Incarnate*, 274.

63. Wellum, *God the Son Incarnate*, 274.

64. Tertullian, *Prax,*, 8 and 27.

65. See Galot, *Who Is Christ?*, 226. Here Galot suggests that Tertullian argues Christ "is a single divine person who possesses a twofold state or twofold substance."

66. Tertullian, *Car. Chr.*, 13.

within the constitution of Christ is achieved, Origen mistakenly advocated for the preexistence of the soul. In the case of Christ, there was one soul in particular that was imbued with special qualities, rendering it suitable for union with the Logos. Once united, this ensouled Logos was joined together with an impeccable human body in the incarnation[67] (as a result, Origen opened to door to later heresies like Arianism that were answered in the councils of Nicaea and Chalcedon[68]). These considerations show up in Origen's comment on the Lamb standing as though slain in Revelation 4. Origen believed,

> "This is the lamb of God who takes away the sin of the world, from the standpoint of the dispensation itself of the bodily sojourn of the Son of God in the life of humankind, we will assume that the lamb is none other than his humanity... This lamb, indeed, which was slain in accordance with certain secret reasons, has become the expiation of the whole world. In accordance with the Father's love for humanity, he also submitted to slaughter on behalf of the world, purchasing us with his own blood from him who bought us when we had sold ourselves to sins."[69]

It would appear from this comment that Origen delimits the Lamb of Revelation to the atoning sacrificial lamb that provided satisfaction for the world. However, in so doing, Origen also bifurcates between Jesus' humanity and his divinity in ways that would be debated in christological discussions that would soon commence.

However, before this survey investigates Nicaea, Chalcedon, and the christologies thereof, it is important to identify why Revelation was only endorsed in a cursory way during this period of theological development. Though Justin Martyr made use of Revelation for his Logos Christology (especially Revelation 1:8; 4:8), it would appear that movements such as Montanism stifled a sweeping endorsement of the Apocalypse of John among these early thinkers. Growing in the fertile ground of early Asian Christianity, Montanism (or the "New Prophecy") was a diverse movement that focused on what many believed was the Holy Spirit's revelation for the present age.[70] These "revelations" presented as ecstatic prophecies that

---

67. Origen, *Princ.*, 1.2.13 and *Cels.*, 5.39.

68 See Wellum, *God the Son Incarnate*, 278. See also Grillmeier, *Christ in Christian Tradition*, I:147.

69. Origen, *Comm. Jo.*, 6.273–74.

70. Tabbernee and Imbler, *A Passion for Christian Unity*, 68.

A Brief Historical Survey of Apocalyptic Christology Studies

Montanists believed were messages from God. Adherents of this movement also believed that they were possessed by God during these episodes and in some cases spoke for God in the first person.[71] In its most radical form, Montanism also believed the following: (1) apostles had the power to forgive sins, (2) women could serves as bishops and presbyters, (3) asceticism was the ethical order, and (4) that new prophecy clarified ambiguities in Scripture.[72]

The Revelation of John in the hands of Montanists served as a kind of template for many of their prophetic practices. In fact, "the New Prophets . . . appealed to the Apocalypse as authoritative and inspired, this being a work also inextricably associated with prophecy."[73] After all, in its contents, a prophet uses the personal pronoun "I" to communicate God's revelation (something that Montanists were fond of doing). The Apocalypse also praises Christian zeal[74] and the ongoing activity of the Holy Spirit.[75] This boded well for the Montanist emphasis on ascetics and the third member of the Trinity.[76]

Though followers of the "New Prophecy" believed that Revelation justified their views and practices, Eusebius of Caesarea argued that this new movement departed from Church tradition. In his own comment on Montanus, Eusebius even said,

> "and he [Montanus] became beside himself, and being suddenly in a sort of frenzy and ecstasy, he raved and began to babble and utter strange things, prophesying in a manner contrary to the constant custom of the Church handed down by tradition from the beginning."[77]

Many in the church were also concerned about the "new scriptures" Montanists were producing and saw these works as unacceptable.[78] Therefore,

---

71. Tabbernee and Imbler, *A Passion for Christian Unity*, 12. This they did in keeping with the traditions of Greco-Roman oracles.

72. Tabbernee and Imbler, *A Passion for Christian Unity*, 111. See also Tertullian, *Res.*, 63.9.

73. Trevett, "Apocalypse, Ignatius, Montanism," 316.

74. Rev 3:10–12.

75. Rev 3:15ff.

76. Trevett, "Apocalypse, Ignatius, Montanism," 316.

77. Eusebius, *Hist. eccl.*, 5.16.

78. Eusebius, *Hist. eccl.*, 6.20, 3. See also Trevett, "Apocalypse, Ignatius, Montanism," 323. See also Eno, "Authority and Conflict," 47ff. "This initial clash between the authority

inasmuch as Montanists were preoccupied with Revelation and commandeered it for what many believed were unorthodox practices, it could very well be that the church was hesitant to depend on Revelation for something as important as christological formulation, even at this early juncture. Revelation's affiliation with the Montanist movement made it, in other words, unpopular to those who were trying to understand something as integral as the nature of Christ.

In addition to the Montanist distraction, much of what was being debated—namely the unity of the humanity and divinity of Christ—found clearer support in the synoptics and Paul's letters than it did in Revelation which, at least on the surface, seems to emphasize the glory and divinity of Christ. The plainer teachings and more historically situated presentations of Christ found elsewhere in the NT were no doubt more assessable to those building a compelling Christology than the highly figurative language of the Apocalypse of John—language that is still debated today. In fact, debating the language of Revelation would have to take a back seat to other more important christological debates in the fourth century.

One such debate was conducted between Arius and Athanasius. Arius and others like Eusebius sought to preserve the transcendence of God and his absolute unity. To keep the unity of God from being compromised, none could share his being with God the Father, not even the Son.[79] This meant, among other things, that both the Son and the Spirit had an origin and were therefore not worthy of divine worship.[80] Such a view was presented at the Council of Nicaea by Eusebius of Nicomendia before 318 bishops and was immediately denied. Thankfully, Athanasius opposed such heresies ("sometimes bitterly, always bravely, for the rest of his life"[81]) and

---

of Church officials who mediate the message of God from the past with the free spirit of the new, ongoing and uncontrolled 'revelation' was an instance of a fundamental type of conflict."

79. See Allison, *Historical Theology*, 368–371. See also Grillmeier, *Christ in Christian Tradition*, 219–228.

80. For a good summary of Arianism, see Letham, *Holy Trinity*, 113. There he provides a compendium of theological beliefs held by Arianism: (1) God was not always Father, for there was not always a Son; (2) the Son is a creature; (3) The Son is changeable by nature; (4) the Son's knowledge of God and of himself is imperfect; (5) the Son was created by God as an instrument by which he created the world; and (6) the Trinity, if we can even speak of such, is of unlike *hypostases*. See also Wellum, *God the Son Incarnate*, 280.

81. Hardy, "Athanasius," 49. See also Athanasius, *Inc.* 1–57. What many popularly refer to as the Nicene Creed today is an amalgamation of what was decided at the Council

stood for the true divinity of Christ as presented in the Nicene Creed. In the creed of Nicaea, the Son is said to be "of the substance (*ousia*) of the Father" (as it was no longer enough to say that the Son was "from God").[82] Also, the creed stressed that the Son was "begotten not made" and that the he was "true God of true God." These distinctions contrasted sharply with the Arians who believed that the Son had a beginning and was, as a result, not equal to God.[83] However, Athanasius did not carry this christological burden alone.

Two Cappadocian theologians, Gregory of Nazianzus and Gregory of Nyssa, strongly affirmed *homoousis* (same nature) "by insisting the full deity of the Son and the Spirit, including their eternal, personal distinctions from the Father."[84] In concert with Athanasius, the Cappadocian fathers made two crucial points: (1) God is singular in nature, possessing a single will, activity, and glory, and (2) God is a plurality/trinity of *hypostases* or "persons."[85] Interestingly, in articulating his argument, Gregory of Nazianzus makes use of Revelation 1:8 when he says,

> "Lord, King, He that is, the Almighty. 'The Lord rained down fire from the Lord'; and 'A scepter of righteousness is the scepter of thy kingdom'; Which is and was and is to come, the Almighty'—all which are clearly spoken of the Son, with all other passages of the same force, none of which is an afterthought, or added later to the Son or the Spirit, any more than to the Father himself. For their perfection is not affected by additions. There never was a time

---

of Nicaea in 325 and what would come later at Constantinople in 381. However, the original Nicene creed read as follows: "We believe in one God Father Almighty maker of all things, seen and unseen: and in one Lord Jesus Christ the Son of God, begotten as only-begotten of the Father, that is of the substance (*ousia*) of the Father, God of God, Light of Light, true God of true God, begotten not made, consubstantial with the Father, through whom all things came into existence, both things in heaven and things on earth; who for us men and for our salvation came down and was incarnate and became man, suffered and rose again the third day, ascended into the heavens, is coming to judge the living and the dead. And in the Holy Spirit. But those who say, 'There was a time when he did not exist,' and 'before being begotten he did not exist,' and that he came into being from non-existence, or who allege that the Son of God is of another *hypostasis* or *ousia*, or is alterable or changeable, these the Catholic and Apostolic Church condemns." See Letham, *Holy Trinity*, 115–116 and Hanson, *Search for the Christian Doctrine*, 163.

82. See the explanation of Athanasius in *Decr*, 5.19–21.

83. See discussion of significance in Wellum, *God the Son Incarnate*, 282.

84. Wellum, *God the Son Incarnate*, 287.

85. Wellum, *God the Son Incarnate*, 287ff. See also H. Brown, *Heresies*, 150–152 and Letham, *Holy Trinity*, 146–166.

when he was without the Word, or when he was not the Father, or when he was not true, or not wise, or not powerful, or devoid of life, or of splendor, or of goodness."[86]

This language unequivocally advocates for a high Christology and uses Revelation alongside other passages to this end. Later in his *Third Theological Oration on the Son*, Gregory of Nazianzus endorses other apocalyptic symbols for similar purposes when he states,

> "As a lamb he is silent, yet he is the Word, and is proclaimed by the voice of one crying in the wilderness. He is bruised and wounded, but he heals every disease and every infirmity. He is lifted up and nailed to the tree, but by the tree of life he restores us."[87]

Such language is sympathetic to the writings of the church fathers before him who, in their own way, sought to amalgamate the humility and the glory of Christ in appropriate ways.

From Nicaea to Chalcedon, the majority of the christological discussion was preoccupied with the following heresies: Apollinarianism, Nestorianism, and Monophysitism. Although Nicaea had formalized Christ's place within the Trinity, much work still needed to be done in order to articulate the nature of Christ himself, specifically as it concerned his divine–human constitution as witnessed in the incarnation. Apollinarius's view (otherwise known as the "Word-flesh" view) affirmed that Christ was consubstantial with God and, by proxy, fully God, and yet, as the incarnate Son, he took on himself an incomplete humanity. According to this view, Christ was devoid a human soul.[88] However, Gregory of Nazianzus and others rejected this view outright inasmuch as Christ could not have represented humanity completely and redeemed mankind totally had he not assumed a fully formed human nature.[89] Nestorianism was no better. Known by some as the "word-man" approach to Christology, his program sought

---

86. Gregory of Nazianzus, *Or. Bas.*, 3.17.

87. Gregory of Nazianzus, *Or. Bas.*, 20.

88. Wellum, *God the Son Incarnate*, 297. Apollinarius was a Trichotomist. According to his view, in the incarnation, the divine Logos displaced the human spirit (distinct from body and mind). Therefore, while Christ was fully God, he lacked a complete human nature such as we have. Such a view take John 1:14 in a narrowly literal way—"the Word became flesh." For Apollinarius, this meant that the Logos assumed a human body alone.

89. Gregory of Nazianzus once stated, "What is not assumed is not healed." "To Cledonius the Priest against Apollinarius," 218.

A Brief Historical Survey of Apocalyptic Christology Studies

to correct Apollinarius's tendency to erase Jesus' complete humanity by juxtaposing Christ's full humanity alongside his complete divinity.[90] However, Nestorius did very little to explain the unity of Christ and was criticized by many for teaching two persons in Christ who were only united in appearance.[91] Finally, Eutyches offered another approach—Monophysitism. This variation on the "Word-flesh" Christology of Apollinarius held that when the divine nature and the human nature mixed in the incarnation, the infinitely superior divine nature overwhelmed Jesus' humanity leaving a mostly divine Christ.[92] Such a view risked making Christ less than fully human, thereby rendering Monophysitism vulnerable to the same pitfalls as its Apollinarian cousin.

In contrast to these limited approaches to the person of Christ, Chalcedon sought to articulate a well-rounded understanding of Christ's identity.[93] Against Apollinarianism Chacedon confessed that Christ was "truly man of a reasonable soul and body . . . consubstantial with us according to his manhood."[94] Against, Nestorianism, it affirmed the unity of Christ as "one" and the "same" Son and "one" person and "one" substance.[95] Against monophysitism, "it confessed that in Christ there were two natures without confusion and without change."[96] Ultimately, what resulted from Chalcedon was a presentation of Christ that preserved his humanity and divinity

---

90. Wellum, *God the Son Incarnate*, 299.

91. Wellum, *God the Son Incarnate*, 299. See F. Sanders, "Chalcedonian Categories," 21. Here Sanders says of Nestorius's view, "The one person who is Jesus Christ seems to be, for Nestorisnism, the result of the incarnation or a way of talking about what these two vastly difference entities, God the Son and the man Jesus, are doing together." See also Barthellos, *Byzantive Christ*, 19. Here, Barthellos argues that Nestorian unity of Christ was an external unity only.

92. F. Sanders, "Chalcedonian Categories," 22. Here, Sanders argues that Autyches's view "does not produce a third substance equally identifiable as divine and human. Because divinity is infinitely larger than humanity, the result of the Eutychian mixing of natures is not an even compound, but a mostly divine Christ." See also MacLeod, "Christology of Chalcedon," 184.

93. Galot, *Who Is Christ?*, 243–44.

94. Chalcedonian creed excerpts taken from J. N. D. Kelly, *Early Christian Doctrines*, 339–340.

95. J. N. D. Kelly, *Early Christian Doctrines*, 339–40. See also Wellum, *God the Son Incarnate*, 305.

96. Wellum, *God the Son Incarnate*, 305.

in a radical unity. This allowed Christ the constitution necessary for serving as high priest, mediator, and savior of the whole human person.[97]

While references to Revelation in christological formulation are present in the period between the Apostles and Chalcedon,[98] these are scant at best. Reasons for this include but are not limited to the following: (1) a preoccupation with heresies[99] (heresies for which Revelation does not help to correct as clearly/directly as other NT works), and (2) skepticism of this work because of its precarious use by fringe groups.[100] That said, both the christological development of the first 500 years of Christianity and the Apocalypse of John appear to endorse an understanding of Christ that embraces the tension between his unity and diversity, particularly as it pertains to his humility and glory (or humanness and divinity).

Mediaeval Christology: The Incarnate, Crucified Christ

Following Chalcedon, other christological issues began to take shape. At the second Council of Nicaea (AD 787) a debate surrounding the use of icons emerged. Iconophile spokesmen claimed that depicting Christ visually had precedence in the first apostolic generation inasmuch as the disciples had to see Jesus before they heard and understood what he said.[101] Admonitions found in the Scriptures also suggest that activating faith presupposes a conduit through which revelation is made known in the first place.[102] This council concluded that in ways similar to the saints—albeit in a far greater and more perfect ways—while Christ is in glory, he retains his bodily form. Therefore if iconographers wanted to depict this glory in gold leaf or marble, they could without contravening the proper limits of representation (just as human language is employed to describe the indescribable and other-worldly in the Bible).[103] Applied to deeper christological consid-

---

97. Wellum, *God the Son Incarnate*, 305. See also Grillmeier, *Christ in Christian Tradition*, 547.

98. See the works of Justin Martyr and Gregory of Nazianzus used above.

99. See Docetism, Arianism, Apollinarianism, Nestorianism, Monophysitism, etc.

100. See discussion on Montanism above.

101. Nichols, "Image Christology," 173–75.

102. Nichols, "Image Christology," 173–78. See also Rom 10:17, "Faith comes by hearing."

103. Rom 10:17, "Faith comes by hearing." See also Mansi, *Sacrorum conciliorum*, 116 and Grikalis, *Images of the Divine*, 85.

A Brief Historical Survey of Apocalyptic Christology Studies

erations, Nicephorus of Constantinople contended that an icon of Christ is similar to the composite hypostasis of the incarnate Word. "If though, Christ in the visibility of his hypostasis, has 'form and character' . . . then an icon can characterize, represent, and depict him."[104] After this license to represent Christ visually was granted, the church took to illustrating Jesus, particularly his crucifixion, with far less inhibition. However, illustrating Christ responsibly was no easy task.

Chalcedon had agreed that Christ was a union of two complete natures—human and divine, "without confusion of substance, but by unity of person."[105] This was confirmed by Cyril, who believed that "what he was by nature, we might become by grace."[106] Depicting this unity in art became increasingly difficult, especially as iconography in the West was moving away from strictly theological representations of Christ to more natural and emotionally empathetic illustrations. Early medieval art represented Christ's passion experience in relatively tame tones (highlighting Christ's divinity over his humanity).[107] However, by the 1200s, many renderings demonstrated acute changes: (1) Christ's body on the cross was shown as bent; (2) his eyes, formerly opened, were now closed; (3) his fingers were made lifeless; (4) ribs were exposed through thin, yellowing skin; (5) and only one nail was shown holding both feet in place.[108] Later, as the Eu-

---

104. Nichols, "Image Christology," 179–180. See also Nicephorus's *Discourse Against the Iconoclasts I*, 46, 38 and Cameron, *Christianity and the Rhetoric*, 226. "The issue of representation was central: if Christianity could not be adequately expressed by logical means, resort must be had to image, and, where words failed, to the visual image. Thus the religious image, justified in the early stages as a way of educating the ignorant and illiterate, became the staple of Christian society and attracted its own sophisticated theology of representation."

105. Quote of Athanasius is found in Schaff, *Creeds of Christendom*, 69.

106. Cyril of Alexandria, *On the Unity of Christ*, 35. See also Milbank, "Seeing Double," 215. Here, Milbank states, "Throughout Cyril's essay . . . and despite his aim to question Nestorian separation of human and divine natures, he nevertheless keeps all the antitheses in play—passible/impassible; suffering/glory; divine/human; body/soul—while arguing that it is by assuming and integrating these antinomies that Christ saves humanity."

107. Milbank, "Seeing Double," 217. "In these early mediaeval images off the crucifixion, the eyes of Christ remain open, as if he were alive. His arms are actively outstretched upon the cross and the palms are often opened, so that he seems to be offering himself, rather than passively suffering. Indeed, often . . . his face is calm and peaceful." For examples of these early medieval depictions, see *Volto Sacro* by Lucca and Battlo's *Majesty*.

108. Milbank, "Seeing Double," 222. For an example, see Giotto di Bondone's *Crucifix* on painted wood.

charist grew in significance following the inclusion of the word "transubstantiation" in the Catholic *Articles of Faith*, Jesus' representation on the cross became even grimmer.[109] Just as the body and blood were exalted during the mass, a beaten and bloodied body became the norm in crucifixion images.[110] By the 1500s, pictures of Christ's crucifixion became even more grotesque. This is perhaps most appropriately encapsulated in the famous Isenheim altarpiece by Matthias Grunewald in which a gaunt Christ hangs lifeless before grieving spectators. In this depiction, Christ's hands are curled upward as though writhing in pain. Ultimately, this evolution of art suggests that the more macabre Jesus' death could be depicted, the more Christ could be appreciated. By elevating Christ's very human pain, these artists celebrated the divine love and grace he demonstrated.

While some were trying to connect to Christ through images, Anselm was trying to connect faith to reason and reason to faith in his christological program. For him,

> "Christology does not begin *tabula rasa* and proceed on the basis of reason any more than the existence and nature of God can be argued that way... Christian doctrine lives in the tension between the immanent and the transcendent. Faith is possible because it is reasonable, which is why probing the rationality of faith is vital; yet faith is also plausible because its divine object lies beyond human reason in the realm of the ineffable."

Ultimately, Anselm wanted to bring the intricacies of Christology to unbelievers of all stripes (atheists, Jews, and Muslims of his day). Simultaneously, Anselm wanted to edify the saints of his day, specifically by educating them on christological doctrine so that they might be able to "give satisfaction to all who ask the reason for the hope that is in [them]."[111] No work did this better in the Medieval period than Anselm's *Cur Deus Homo*, which provides an answer to the question, "Why did God become a man?"[112] Therein, Anselm begins by delineating the necessity of the incarnation,

---

109. Particularly the articles of faith of the Fourth Lateran Council of 1415.

110 This is witnessed in Master Frank's *Man of Sorrows* on painted wood. The name of this work comes from Isaiah 53:2–3, which says, "He is despised and rejected of men: a man of sorrows, and acquainted with grief." This image depicts a sickly Christ who is hoisted up by an angel and despondent, with blood pouring out of his side.

111. Davies and Evans, *Anselm of Canterbury*, 265.

112. Davies and Evans, *Anselm of Canterbury*, 355. Toward the end of this work, a discourse with Boso ends with Boso thanking Anselm for offering an argument "which would satisfy not only Jews, but even pagan."

A Brief Historical Survey of Apocalyptic Christology Studies

death, and resurrection of Christ—highlighting that both unbelievers and believers have difficulty understanding and explaining the implications of these events.[113] What is of greatest concern to Anselm as it pertains to Christ is that all people understand the nature of his atonement—Jesus is the Lamb of God who takes away the sin of the world. As such, Anselm's "theology of the atonement . . . touches the very heart of what matters most to the writers of the both the OT and NT"[114]—namely, the metanarrative of redemption. However, though Anselm glances at the contents of the book of Revelation to compare humanity's future constitution with that of the angels,[115] Anselm does not make much use of Revelation in his atonement Christology.

Christ is the center of redemption in Augustine's Christology also. For him, the incarnation involves God coming down to man in order to redeem the human person. Such a view contradicted the neo-platonism of Augustine's day that held a high view of man's capacity to ascend to God through human intellect. Instead of ascending to God, God came down in the person of Christ and revealed what had been previously hidden.[116] In other words, Christ's incarnation in Augustine's program has "a remedial, pedagogical function by demonstrating the humility of Christ that subverts human epistemoligical presumption."[117] Most of what concerned Augustine and informed his christological interest was the neo-platonism and pelagianism that undermined a complete understanding of the God-Man.[118] This is why he proved preoccupied with ontology,[119] Word theology,[120] and the Trinity[121] in his writings.

---

113. Davies and Evans, *Anselm of Canterbury*, 265.

114. Hogg, "Christology: The *Cur Deus Homo*," 211.

115. Davies and Evans, *Anselm of Canterbury*, 300–3. Here Davies and Evans says, "humans in that heavenly city . . . ought to be of like character to those who were there, whose substitutes they are to be, that is, the same in character as the good angels are now."

116. Augustine, *Trin*, 13.19.24, "our knowledge therefore, is Christ, and our wisdom is the same Christ. It is he who plants faith in us about temporal things, he who presents us with the truth about eternal things."

117. Ables, "Word in which All Things Are Spoken," 287. See also Augustine, *Trin*, 13.12.16–18.23.

118. See Lam, "Revelation, Christology and Grace," 131–149.

119. See Lyons, "Pursuing an Ontology," 179–196.

120. See Ables, "Word in which All Things Are Spoken," 13.12.16–18.23.

121. See K. E. Johnson, "Augustine, Eternal Generation," 141–163.

The Humility and Glory of the Lamb

However, Augustine also provides a comment on the Lamb of Revelation that helps discredit the neo-platonism of his day. For him, the Lion–Lamb juxtaposition of Revelation 4 argues for God's activity in both the spiritual and earthly realm.[122] Augustine continues his fascination with this leonine Lamb in a reflection on the death and resurrection of Christ. He believes that this salvific work is in many ways inherent in the Lamb and Lion motif that is present in Revelation 4. For Augustine, the Lamb of Revelation 4 is the same lamb referenced in Isaiah 53. After asking who the "lamb" of the latter passage is, he states,

> "Obviously the one about whom he goes on to say, 'In humility his judgment was taken away. His generation, who shall relate?'[123] I can see this model of such humility in a king of such power and authority. Because this one, who is like a lamb not opening its mouth in the presence of the shearer, is himself 'the Lion from the tribe of Judah.'"[124]

It is clear from this commentary that Augustine understood the apocalyptic Lamb to endorse a paradox of death (sacrificially upon the cross) and victory (resurrection from the tomb).[125]

Another exhaustive systematic presentation of Christ in this period came in the form of Thomas Aquinas's *Summa Theologie*. In the third part of this important work, Aquinas sets out to elucidate the incarnation of the Word, the place of Jesus in God's plan of redemption, and the sources of his teachings on Christ. Concerning the incarnation, Aquinas believes in the unity of two natures—the divine nature (Word) and the human nature (incarnate). This incarnate Word accomplishes the following: (1) he galvanizes the lost to faith in God, (2) provides a model for emulation, (3)

---

122. Augustine, "Sermon 263.2," 7:219–20. For Augustine the apocalyptic presence of the Lion calls to mind the victory that he achieved upon his incarnation, death, and resurrection when he says, "So the true victory of our Lord Jesus Christ was achieved when he rose again and ascended into heaven. Then was fulfilled what you heard when the Apocalypse was read, 'The Lion from the tribe of Judah has conquered'... And when this lamb was slain, he conquered by his death the lion 'who prowls around seeking whom he may devour.' Here, the Lion par excellence conquers lion that is Satan by taking on the likeness of a lamb and offering himself as the sacrifice for sin.

123. Isa 53:8.

124. Augustine, "Sermon 375," 10:330.

125. Augustine, "Sermon 375," 10:330, "Why a lamb in his passion? Because he underwent death without being guilty of any iniquity. Why a lion in his passion? Because in being slain he slew death. Why a lamb in his resurrection? Because his innocence is everlasting. Why a lion in his resurrection? Because everlasting also is his might."

announces the end of the journey, (4) warns against key sins, and (5) makes up for the sin that separates people from God by providing satisfaction.[126] Complimentary to this general presentation, Aquinas provides extensive comments on Christ's life, doctrine, miracles, Passion, and the resurrection/post-resurrection period.[127] This final category is of some significance to this present survey. Aquinas argues that Christ's own beatific vision (post-resurrection glorified self), in which the divine and human nature are shown together following the resurrection, points to and anticipates the unity that will come for others when they are made like Christ in the end.[128] In his answer to the question on whether it was necessary for Christ to rise again he says, "for the raising of our hope, since through seeing Christ, who is our head, rise again, we hope that we likewise shall rise again."[129] In fact, for Aquinas, the ontological union of the incarnation (in which divine and human natures are one) provides the foundation for the union of humans to the divine in the *eschaton*.

However, as Aquinas articulates this position and answers other eschatologically leaning questions,[130] he does not utilize the Apocalypse of John. Instead, in this portion of his christological presentation, Revelation is only used in a comment on Christ sitting at the right hand of the Father.

> "Further, Christ Himself says . . . *to him that shall overcome, I will give to sit with Me in My throne: as I also have overcome, and am set down with My Father in His throne*. But it is by sitting on His Father's throne that Christ is seated at His right hand. Therefore, others who overcome likewise, sit at the Father's right hand."

Though the Apocalypse may be used elsewhere in Aquinas's mammoth work, in his christological presentation, even in the areas that develop Jesus' identity and accomplishments, Revelation is largely underutilized.[131]

---

126. Wawrykow, "Christology of Thomas Aquinas," 235–6.

127. These discussion can be seen in questions 40–45, 46–52, and 53–59, respectively, in Aquinas's *Summa Theologica*, 2229–2338.

128 Wawrykow, "Christology of Thomas Aquinas," 246.

129. Aquinas, *Summa Theologica*, 2303. In supporting this point, Aquinas cites 1 Cor. 15, Job 19, and Rom. 6.

130. Aquinas, *Summa Theologica*, 2303. That is, the quality of Christ rising again (2307ff), the manifestation of the resurrection (2311ff), the causality of Christ's resurrection (2318ff), the ascension of Christ (2321ff), and Christ's sitting at the Right had of the Father (2327ff).

131. Interestingly, in his questions dealing with prophecy (questions 171–77 of part II), Revelation is also absent from most of the discussion.

The Humility and Glory of the Lamb

Reformation Christology: The Christ of Worship and Redemption

As the evolution of Christology confronted the Protestant Reformation, it donned a doxological tone. The works of Martin Luther betray his belief that "from it [Christology], through it, and to it all my theological thought flows and returns day and night."[132] This commitment no doubt betrays Luther's Augustinian training. For both Luther and Augustine, Christ is central and near (inasmuch as he has come down to save mankind when man could do nothing to reach God).[133] Nowhere was this more applied than in Luther's theology of worship. For Luther, Christ was not a distant deity to be revered from afar, he was close and involved in the worship of his people. Such a view became particularly important to Luther's understanding of the Eucharist. Evidence of Luther's fascination with Christ's presence at the altar is seen in the second generation of Wittenberg theologians that developed and used Luther's teachings.[134]

Luther believed that "we have only one single priest, Christ, who has sacrificed himself for us and all of us with him." As such, Jesus appeased the wrath of God and proves he is the mediator *par excellence* between God and man. Applied to the Eucharist, "the sacrament is not a work that gains forgiveness . . . but it can be said to be a sacrifice of praise and thanksgiving achieved through Christ's intercessory sacrifice."[135] Inasmuch as the exaltation of Christ as the highest high priest paves the way for and informs a more complete worship experience (particularly in the Lord's Supper), Luther's christological contribution is doxological. After all, this is the same Luther who celebrated Christ not only in written works, but in hymns.[136]

---

132. Luther, *Luther's Works*, 40.1:33.

133. Lugioyo, "Martin Luther's Eucharistic Christology," 268. "Luther's Christology was about worshipping a God who had come near and stayed near." See also Lam, "Revelation, Christology and Grace," 131–149.

134. See the *Formula of Concord* (1577). This work drew principally from Luther's *Confession Concerning Christ's Supper* (1528). In fact, the former cites the latter no less than ten times. See *Book of Concord*, 616–35.

135. Lugioyo, "Eucharistic Christology," 274.

136. For discussion on this, see Burba, *Die Christologie* and Leaver, *Luther's Liturgical Music*. One hymn that celebrates both the eucharistic and doxological elements of Luther's Christology is "Jesus Christ, Our God and Savior," which begins, "Jesus Christ, our God and Savior, turned away God's wrath forever, by his bitter agony helped us out of hell's misery. That we never should forget it, gave he us his flesh to eat it, hidden in this bit of bread, And to drink gave us his blood."

A Brief Historical Survey of Apocalyptic Christology Studies

Interestingly, though both Luther and the Apocalypse of John endorse the worship of God and Christ in hymnic form and secure a prominent place for the Lord's Supper (Luther retrospectively and John eschatologically),[137] Luther does not comment or endorse the hymns found in Revelation nor does he make use of the marriage supper of the Lamb in Revelation 19. Though one reason for this may be his emphasis on Christ's nearness and connection to the Lord's Supper, some of Luther's writings also suggest that he was not quick to embrace Revelation at all, let alone what it has to say about Jesus.

> "About this book of the Revelation of John, I leave everyone free to hold his own ideas, and would bind no man to my opinion or judgment; I say what I feel. I miss more than one thing in this book, and this makes me hold it to be neither apostolic nor prophetic. First and foremost, the Apostles do not deal with visions, but prophesy in clear, plain words, as do Peter and Paul, and Christ in the Gospel. For it befits the apostolic office to speak of Christ and His deeds without figures and visions; but there is no prophet in the OT, to say nothing of the New, who deals so out and out with visions and figures. And so I think of it almost as I do of the Fourth Book of Esdras, and can nohow detect that the Holy Spirit produced it."[138]

Quite surprisingly (and contrary to what this present work will articulate later), Luther did not endorse the Apocalypse of John because he saw very little of Christ in it, saying,

> "Finally, let everyone think of it as his own spirit gives him to think. My spirit cannot fit itself into this book. There is one sufficient reason for me not to think highly of it,-Christ is not taught or known in it; but to teach Christ is the thing which an apostle is bound, above all else, to do, as He says in Acts 1:8 'Ye shall be my witnesses.' Therefore I stick to the books which give me Christ, clearly and purely,"[139]

---

137. See Revelation 19 and its depiction of the marriage supper of the Lamb.

138. Luther, *Works of Martin Luther*, 488–489. This quote is taken from Luther's preface to the book of Revelation. Evidence of Luther's superficial association with Revelation is seen in his propensity to delimit his delineation of the last judgment to what happens to each individual at the hour of his/her death—excluding, in large part, any description of the "cosmic winnowing of humankind" that one finds in Revelation. See Strohl, "Luther's Eschatology," 356.

139. Luther, *Works of Martin Luther*, 488–89.

The Humility and Glory of the Lamb

Therefore, as Luther was unimpressed with what Revelation had to offer, it stands to reason that John's Apocalypse would not be mined for what it has to say either eschatologically or christologically among many of the Reformers. Much of Luther's eschatology and Christology is instead a construct of Pauline literature and the gospels.[140]

Calvin, for his part, "frames his understanding of the person and work of Christ in light of three sets of distinct but inseparable realities: (1) the self-revelation of God (first as Creator and then as Redeemer), (2) the self-disclosure of Jesus Christ (first in the Law given to Israel and then in the Gospel proclaimed to the nations), and (3) the knowledge of God and the knowledge of ourselves (as one can only know who Christ is and what he has done after one comes to know that she is a sinner and under God's wrath).[141] Calvin's high view of Christ is founded on his insistence that God has disclosed himself most perfectly through Jesus and this by means of Christ's humanity:[142] "Christ not only makes the invisible God somewhat visible in his humanity, but he may also be said to be the way the infinite God makes himself finite so that humanity can come to know God."[143]

According to Calvin, Christ's accomplishes this ministry in three different ways: (1) as a mediator, (2) in his office as Christ, and (3) in his demonstration of obedience.[144] Calvin concludes that in order to serve as the perfect mediator, Jesus had to be both truly God and human simultaneously. Likewise, if Christ is to fulfill the office of mediator, he must also be anointed by the Holy Spirit to accomplish the many tasks associated with

---

140. See Strohl, "Luther's Eschatology," 356ff.

141. Zachman, "Christology of John Calvin," 284.

142. "By this we are taught not only that by the Son's intercession do those things which the heavenly Father bestows come to us but that by mutual participation in power the Son himself is the author of them," Calvin, *Institutes of the Christian Religion*, 1:138. "For Christ, so far as his secret divinity, is not better known to us than the Father. But he is said to be the express image of God, because in him God has entirely revealed himself, inasmuch as his infinite goodness, wisdom and power appear in him substantially." See also *Calvin's New Testament Commentaries*, 5:78.

143. Categories taken from Zachman, "Christology of John Calvin," 285–86.

144. Zachman, "Christology of John Calvin," 288.

his office of Christ (prophet,[145] priest,[146] and king[147]). All of these offices and roles reach their zenith in the cross where Christ mediates as high priest on behalf of the world in a radical act of obedience that proclaims God's love for mankind and the kingdom that is to come. For Calvin, this act encapsulates the glory and humility of Christ,

> "The fact that the Son of God suffered himself to be reduced to such ignominy, yea, descended even to hell, is so far from obscuring, in any respect, his celestial glory, that is rather a bright mirror from which is reflected his unparalleled grace towards us."[148]

The grace manifested by Jesus on the cross led Calvin to conclude that "Christ is such a shining and remarkable proof of the divine love toward us that, whenever we look at him, he clearly confirms the doctrine that God is love."[149]

However, while the book of Revelation would reinforce Calvin's Christology on all points, his omission of a commentary on the Apocalypse of John betrays the fact that Revelation in general and apocalyptic Christology in particular is of little interest to this systematician. Though God will reveal himself again through Jesus at his second coming (providing more complete knowledge of who he is and what he did/will do), and though his offices of prophet, priest, and king are only fully realized in the *eschaton*, Calvin does not reflect on this. Instead, he is more concerned with what Jesus accomplished during his first advent. Such considerations along with the Eucharist would preoccupy christological discussions well into the seventeenth century.[150]

---

145. "[H]e received anointing, not only for himself that he might carry out the office of teaching, but for his whole body that the power of the Spirit might be present in the continuing preaching of the gospel," *Institutes*, 1:496.

146. *Institutes*, 1:502, "The priestly office belongs to Christ alone because by the sacrifice of his death be blotted out our own guilt and made satisfaction for our sins."

147. *Institutes*, 1:500, "For the Spirit has chosen Christ as his head, that from him might abundantly flow the heavenly riches of which we are in such need. The believers stand unconquered through the strength of their king, and his spiritual riches abound in them. Hence, they are justly called Christians."

148. Calvin, *Calvin's New Testament Commentaries*, 8:366

149. Calvin, *Calvin's New Testament Commentaries*, 5:290. See also Zachman, "Christology of John Calvin," 295.

150. See Elliott, "Christology in the Seventeenth Century," 297ff.

The Humility and Glory of the Lamb

From Kant to Harnack: The Personal and Historical Christ

Sometime following the Reformation, Kantian philosophy challenged the status quo in the theological community with its endorsement of a critical philosophy that argued "space and time are not 'out there', in the world, but rather are the subjective conditions that we necessarily apply to our sensible impressions of what is out there."[151] In addition to this shift, Kant understood human freedom as a matter of the will being governed by moral law and this comes about by first willing that one's volition would itself be brought into conformity with that law.[152] Naturally, this requires the following: (1) one can will the moral law only if he or she can hope that one's so willing will be effective, (2) this hope is only compelling if the laws of nature will allow an individual to be in harmony with the moral law, (3) said laws of nature only allow this if they are governed by a supreme cause which itself is moral, and (4) if one must will moral law, the existence of said moral supreme cause must be assumed.[153] However, this program of willing morality is thwarted by mankind's radical wickedness and utter self-centeredness.

Enter Christ, whose example of self-sacrifice for the sake of following the moral law demonstrates that it is, in fact, possible to commit oneself to the universals of morality. Not only does Christ's example suggest that moral transformation is possible, his morally exemplary life stands as a model for others to emulate. That Kant understood moral exemplars to be powerful agents for change is evident in his comment that those who witness such examples can and should possess the ability to match the model.[154]

---

151. Hector, "Christology After Kant," 315. He continues by elucidating the following tenants of Kant's philosophical agenda: "(2) that, for such perception to amount to knowledge, one must set them in a ruled relationship to one another by conceptualizing them; (3) that concepts, as a kind of judgment, must be governed by the rule of logic . . . (4) that concepts and perceptions must be one and all recognizable as one's own . . . (5) that one's perceptions, and thus the realm of sensible experience, must thus be governed by universal and necessary principles, most importantly the principle of causation . . . (6) that these laws do not necessarily govern objects 'in themselves', such that it is at least possible that the latter, supersensible realm is a realm of freedom; and (7) that the latter is indeed a realm of freedom, as evidenced by the fact that our wills can be governed by moral law to such an extent that natural forces, including especially those involving our self-interest, no longer determine our will."

152. Hector, "Christology After Kant," 316.

153. See Kant, "Critique of Practical Reason (1788)," 5:124–25. See also Kant, *Critique of Pure Reason*, 5:450, 452–53.

154. Kant, "Critique of Practical Reason (1788)," 5:156.

A Brief Historical Survey of Apocalyptic Christology Studies

Ultimately, it is in following Christ's example that the individual removes his or her own self-centered desires and takes on Christ's. This results in regeneration and righteousness.[155]

Dissatisfied with the distance Kant drew between human beings and nature (perception and reality), Schleiermacher decided to frame mankind's problem (sin) and proposed solution (Christ) differently. Schleiermacher understood mankind in tension between freedom and dependence. The only means capable of bringing these two into harmony is Christ who alone can lead an individual back into "attunement" (satisfying the tension mentioned above) within the context of a relationship with God. Christ alone is able to accomplish this because he is, according to Schleiermacher, distinguished from all other men both in kind and degree. Christ is the archetype of the final perfection of God-consciousness that is currently askew in humanity.[156] In his earthly form, "Christ is the very incarnation of God's being-in-act, because at every moment Christ perfectly apprehends and reproduces that act as his own."[157] This applies to his act of redemption and providing salvation—"the act in which God eternally subsists is redeeming love . . . it follows that Jesus incarnates God precisely by apprehending that love and reproducing it as his own."[158]

Because of this, salvation for Schleiermacher is Christ reproducing in the believer what he is in God by means of the Holy Spirit. This is what happened in the lives of his disciples. After becoming aware of God through Christ's activity on the earth, they were transformed when Christ's activity became their own.[159] As this applies to mankind's general problem of tension, God is the only one who perfectly satisfies the paradox between freedom and dependency. By extension, God provides Christ who perfectly

---

155. Hector, "Christology after Kant," 318. "It seems plausible that what one is here supposed to emulate is Christ's pure commitment to moral law (even when such commitment runs contrary to all natural incentives), and that the emulation of this commitment can itself embody such purity, since his example elicits in one a respect for the moral law that is likewise contrary to natural incentives . . . Kant claims that one thus regenerated could reasonably hope to be regarded as righteous by god, since the moral law is now his or her ground-maxim and new nature." See also Kant, "Religion with the Boundaries of Mere Reason (1793)," 6:48, 66–67.

156. A. McGrath, *Modern German Christology*, 22.

157. Hector, "Christology After Kant," 321. See also Schleiermacher, *Christian Faith*, 397.

158. Hector, "Christology After Kant," 321. See also Schleiermacher, *Christian Faith*, 166–7, 381, 272.

159. Hector, "Christology After Kant," 322–23.

The Humility and Glory of the Lamb

satisfies who God is at every moment and whose Spirit translates this to those who apprehend him and are transformed by him. More succinctly, Schleiermacher's Christology is primarily concerned about his work of attuning people to God by means of the Holy Spirit and this is archetypally realized in the person of Christ.

Falling in line with what began with Kant and continued in Schleiermacher was G. W. F. Hegel. For Hegel, there exists a "cleavage" between God and humanity inasmuch as men and women fall short of their truth, becoming, as a result, "abstractions."[160] As such, humans live in a contradictory state in relation to God and the world. Hegel believed that God overcomes this contradiction and redeems the abstractions by taking in this contradiction himself through Christ (by means of his life, death, and resurrection). In so doing, he overwhelms the cleavage between God and man.

> "The abstraction of humanity, the immediacy of subsisting singularity, is sublated, and this is brought about by death. But the death of Christ is the death of this death itself, the negation of negation. . . . It is their finitude that Christ has taken [upon himself], this finitude in all its forms, which at its furthest extreme is evil. . . . This finitude, on its own account (as against God), is evil, it is something alien to God. But he has taken it [upon himself] in order to put it to death by his death. As the monstrous unification of these absolute extremes, this shameful death is at the same time infinite love."[161]

In this christological program, Christ is a conduit by which God is able to overwhelm the contradictions and abstractions in mankind. Put differently, Christ took on the separation between God and man so that this separation would no longer exist, thereby allowing humanity to be fully at home with God and the world.

However, this transformation is not possible aside from Jesus' incarnation, which, for Hegel, is the supreme *Vorstellung* (representation) from

---

160. Hector, "Christology After Kant," 324–35. "Reconciliation is necessary, on this account, because of the cleavage that exists between us and God, inasmuch as we fail to correspond with our truth or what we ought to be, and because us and the world, inasmuch as we experience the world as a hostile, or at least indifferent, environment. Hegel terms the former cleavage 'evil', and the latter, 'misery'. This is not how things should be, however, since both sorts of cleavage indicate that we have fallen short of our truth, or have become what Hegel calls an abstraction from our actuality."

161. Hegel, *Lectures on the Philosophy of Religion*, 324–25.

A Brief Historical Survey of Apocalyptic Christology Studies

which theological and philosophical speculation begins.[162] Here, Hegel assumes that while the *Gedanke* (idea) of incarnation is common to all religions (inasmuch as all sacred programs desire to, in some way, formalize a program in which the divine interacts with human experience),[163] the Christian *Vorstellung* of this *Gedanke* is the most adequate and compelling.[164] One might say that Christianity provides the most forceful explanation of humanity's alienation from God and the most complete program of remedy by means of the most fascinating amalgamation of divinity and humanity ever purported—the incarnation of Jesus Christ.

All three of these theologians/philosophers understand Christ primarily as God's means of transforming mankind—as a moral exemplar in Kant, an attuning archetype in Schleiermacher, or an incarnated bridge in Hegel. However, inasmuch as these were fascinated most by the human transition from estrangement to righteousness, Revelation's presentation of the future implications and ultimate culmination of salvation played only a small role in their Christologies. Unfortunately, the same neglect of the Apocalypse of John is witnessed in those who responded to these post-Kantian thinkers.

Reaction to the aforementioned christological programs (especially their subjectivity) led many to pursue the historical person of Christ with renewed interest. Those like Isaak August Dorner wanted Jesus to be more than an archetype or representation of divine–human interaction.[165] Enter Ritschl, who in 1870 concluded that the starting point for Christian theology is the "moral effects of the life, passion, death, and resurrection of Christ towards the founding of the church."[166] For Ritschl, these ideas are inextricably mediated through the community of faith,[167] rendering it

---

162. A. McGrath, *Modern German Christology*, 33.

163. Hegel, *Vorlesungen uber die Philosophie*, 11.77.

164. Hegel, *Vorlesungen uber die Philosophie*, 11.77. "Although *Vorstellungen* in all religions implicitly, and with varying degrees of adequacy, bear witness to the incarnational truth of the human and divine natures, and to the reconciling action of God in the midst of human alienation, it is the Christian *Vorstellungen* which are supreme."

165. Dorner, *System der Christlichen*, 357. "It must be said that, in the present century, our dogma has again, in its exegetical, historical and dogmatic aspects, come to the fore, and been affected by more profound change than at any time since the first centuries. The most vital concern is to gain a true and living view and knowledge of the person of Christ." See also Dorner, "Die deutsche Theologie," 1–47.

166. Ritschl, *Die christliche Lehre*, 1.

167. A. McGrath, *Modern German Christology*, 56. "It is, in effect, axiomatic for Ritschl that there is no direct or immediate relationship between the believer and God,

difficult to ascertain exactly who Jesus is apart from the church. As a result, he concluded that it is improper to hold Christ's person and work as the same. In his comment on Ritschl's move, McGrath concludes the following:

> "It is difficult to avoid the conclusion that Ritschl considers Jesus to be nothing more than the historical point of departure for a self-sufficient idea. The 'divinity' of Christ is thus not truth in any objective sense of the term, as had been suggested by the theologians of Orthodoxy, but is a value-judgment evoked by, and conveyed in, the proclamation of the community of faith. Although Jesus may be viewed as a man objectively, faith recognizes him as having the religious value of God . . . The existence of the man Jesus of Nazareth is undoubted reality, adequate in itself as the basis of personal faith. The starting point of Christian faith, and hence also of Christian theology, must be with the historical Jesus with whom the believer is confronted in the gospel narratives"[168]

Inasmuch as the gospel narratives reveal the history of Jesus, a growing fascination with these works began to take shape, especially in discussing and formalizing Christology. This brand of christological investigation became a mainstay for theologians for the better part of the next one hundred years.

The bifurcation between history and dogma, especially pertaining to the person of Christ, found its champion in Adolf von Harnack, who claimed, "Dogma must be purified by history."[169] For him the origins of christological doctrine are only exposed through critical historical analysis.[170] Such analysis distinguished between the Jesus of Nazareth and the Son of God that developed, according to Harnack, within two generations of his death.[171] Jesus was added to the gospel after he was exalted as Christ and this is what is presented in Matthew, Mark, Luke, and John (for those of Harnack's ilk, the gospels are evangelistic rather than historical documents). Harnack ultimately concluded that "Jesus does not belong to the

---

in that the presence of God or Jesus Christ is always mediated through the community of faith." See also Hok, *Die Elliptische Theologie*, 6–8.

168. A. McGrath, *Modern German Christology*, 57–58. See also Herrmann, *Communion of the Christian*, 52. That Ritschl depended heavily on the Gospels for his christological program is found in his use of John 4:34 to demonstrate the identity of will, purpose, and function between Christ and God in *Rechtfertigung und Versöhnung*, 3.424–25.

169. For this quote, see Zahn-Harnack, *Adolf von Harnack*, 130–31.

170. Harnack, *History of Dogma*, 1.75.

171. Harnack, *Das Wesen des Christentums*, 97.

gospel as one of its elements, but was the personal realization and power of the gospel, and we still perceive him as such."[172]

Those following Ritschl and Harnack studied the NT in an effort to differentiate between the religious personality of Jesus and the historical Jesus. Only those NT works that helped delineate the Jesus of Nazareth, particularly the synoptic gospels, were worthy of special consideration by many as they looked for a "firmly drawn and life-like portrait which, with a few bold strokes, should bring out clearly the originality, the force, the personality of Jesus."[173] For these,

> "The firm ground of historical truth upon which Christian faith depended was not supernatural or anti-rational, but merely the personality of Jesus, a fact of history open to scientific investigation. The impression which he made upon his contemporaries could be reproduced in his followers of every age. The first century legendary embellishments to the gospel stories could thus be discarded, as could the anachronistic dogmatic formulations of a later age concerning him."[174]

As in any scientific investigation, evidences/data pools that are nearest to the subject are given highest priority. Therefore, during this quest for the historical Jesus, the Apocalypse of John was largely inconsequential. This is not to say that these and others were not interested in the *eschaton*. In fact, while the Kingdom of God was understood by the Ritschlians to reflect a moral life lived out in present society, Johannes Weiss and Albert Schweitzer drew attention to the eschatological character of Jesus' teaching that said that the Kingdom of God was an event to be brought about in the imminent future.[175] In spite of this, the eschatological interests of many during

---

172. Harnack, *Das Wesen des Christentums*, 98. See also A. McGrath, *Modern German Christology*, 62. "Although it is clear that Harnack has the highest possible estimation of Christ, he insists that the irreducible element of the gospel concerns man's relationship to God the Father. Such a faith in God the Father is linked to Jesus Christ historically, not theologically."

173. Schweitzer, *Quest*, 242.

174. A. McGrath, *Modern German Christology*, 69.

175. A. McGrath, *Modern German Christology*, 71–71. See also Issel, *Die Lehre von Reich* and Schmoller, *Die Lehre vom Reich Gottes*. Weiss, *Jesus' Proclamation*, 133. Here, Weiss states, "The interpretation of the Kingdom of God as an inner-worldly ethical idea is a vestige of a Kantian Ideal, and does not stand up before a more precise historical examination . . . the Kingdom of God, as Jesus thought of it, is never something subjective, inward or spiritual, but always the objective messianic Kingdom, which is usually portrayed as a territory into which one enters, a land in which one has a share, or a

this period were limited to what Jesus taught concerning the *parousia* in the synoptics.[176]

From Barth to Pannenberg: The Christ of Faith and the Eschaton

During this period, many believed that God was an object that could be understood by human subjects through historical critical analyses. However, when the World Wars erupted onto the scene, theological programs saw drastic changes, especially at the hands of Karl Barth and his dialectic theology. In an adverse reaction to the horrors of war and the German intellectual community's affiliation with the war policy of Kaiser Wilhem II, Barth writes, "I can no longer follow their ethics and dogmatics, or their understandings of the Bible and history, and that the theology of the nineteenth century no longer had any future for me."[177] In contrast to liberal theology's claim that man (subject) can know God (object) and Christ (the Word) historically, Barth, borrowing from Kierkegaard, reestablished the great gulf between God (subject) and man (object), and made Christ (the Word) God's sole means of reaching mankind.[178] Therefore, in order to know anything of God, one must know Christ who undergirds all theology. Christology is of first significance for Barth, for, in knowing him, one is able to understand everything else.[179]

---

treasure which comes down from heaven." It is obvious from the "portrayals" that Weiss admits to here that he is using the Kingdom of God language of passages that include but are not limited to the following: Matt. 13; Lk. 13:18ff.

176. Schweitzer, *Quest*, 222ff. In his chapters "The Eschatological Question" and "The Struggle Against Eschatology," Schweitzer surveys the use of Mark 12:35–37 and Matt 19:28 and their depiction of the eschatological/messianic "Son of Man." He also examines Matt 24–25 and Mark 13's depiction of the *parousia*.

177. Barth, *Evangelische Theologie*, 6.

178. McGrath, *Modern German Christology*, 105. See also J. Brown, *Subject and Object*, 34–82. See also Barth, *Der Römerbrief*, xiii. "If I have any system, it is restricted to bearing in mind, as much as possible, what Kierkegaard called the 'infinite qualitative distinction' between time and eternity, in its negative and positive aspects. 'God is in heaven, and you are on earth'. For me, the relation of this God and this man, the relation of this man and this God, is, in a nutshell, the theme of the Bible and the totality of philosophy. The philosophers term this crisis of human knowledge the prime cause; the Bible sees Jesus Christ at this cross-roads." (Quoted in McGrath, *Modern German Christology*, 96.)

179. A. McGrath, *Modern German Christology*, 107.

A Brief Historical Survey of Apocalyptic Christology Studies

These and other revelations are made in Barth's commentary on the Epistle to the Romans. More than historical critical investigation, Barth believed that works like the NT were inspired, and therefore worthy of theological inquiry.

> "The historical-critical method of biblical investigation has its rightful place; it is concerned with the preparation of the intelligence—and this can never be superfluous. But were I driven to choose between it and the venerable doctrine of inspiration, I should without hesitation adopt the latter, which has a broader, deeper, more important justification. The doctrine of inspiration is concerned with the labour of apprehending, without which no technical equipment, however complete, is of any use... My whole energy of interpretation has been expended in an endeavor to see through and beyond history into the Spirit of the Bible, which is the eternal Spirit."[180]

This radical statement from this former liberal suggests that the NT was more than an archaeological collection of documents: "It is a book by which men and women have lived, and in which century after century they have found renewal of their faith."[181] As such, it is compelling not just on a historical level, but on a theological level. These convictions provided an incredible service to biblical studies and to systematic theology. In an old world liberal milieu in which theology was almost entirely anthropocentric, Barth argued that God is a judge of mankind and that his word of judgment will only become a word of mercy if and when men find themselves restored in the context of a relationship with the Lord through Christ.[182] This, according to Barth, is largely a matter of faith. Inasmuch as Romans delineates how this kind of restoration occurs, Barth's christological program is largely dependent on this NT work and the peripheral theological issues appertaining thereunto.[183]

Equally passionate about the theology of the NT, equally resolute on acceptance of the gospel as a matter of faith, and equally committed to God as "wholly other" is Rudolph Bultmann. However, Bultmann employed critical analysis in his approach to the NT as he believed it was a necessary

---

180. Quote from Barth's *Epistle to the Romans* in Neill and Wright, *Interpretation of the New Testament*, 221–222.

181. Neill and Wright, *Interpretation of the New Testament*, 223.

182. Neill and Wright, *Interpretation of the New Testament*, 227.

183. These include but are not limited to the Trinity, election, and salvation.

first step in sharing the gospel message (*kerygma*) to his own context.[184] Upon critically analyzing the NT, Bultmann believed it to be a large word-picture that required de-mythologizing.[185] In other words, the NT as it exists is cast in idiomatic phrases and presentations that are unintelligible today. As a result, it is up to today's philosopher to reinterpret what the NT says in a way that both explains and speaks to the present era.

Therefore, borrowing from Heidegger's existentialist philosophy, Bultmann reinterpreted the Christian faith in the terms and categories that were found in his own socio-historical localization.[186] For him, humans are "ever in the moment of decision between the past and future."[187] In this tension, humans can either accept responsibility and live an authentic life or lose themselves to a variety of pressures. Thankfully, while humans choose the latter of these options, God has liberated humanity from their fallen and inauthentic selves so that they might live an authentic life again. This is where Christ is applied. However, to apply Jesus properly to this program, one must demythologize him as well for,

> "The concept of a Christ who pre-existed as a heavenly being, and the corresponding concept of man's own translation to a heavenly world of light, in which the self is destined to receive a celestial nature, a spiritual body, are to him not merely inapprehensible by any rational process, they are totally meaningless [according to today's standards]. For he cannot understand how it could be that salvation could take the form of the attainment of such a condition, or that in it he could reach the fulfilment of human life, and of his own authentic character as a personal being."[188]

---

184. Neill and Wright, *Interpretation of the New Testament*, 240. For an example of Bultmann's theological concern and pastoral heart see his sermon on Mark 13:31–33 in *Marburger Predigten*.

185. Neill and Wright, *Interpretation of the New Testament*, 241. See also Neill and Wright's quote from Bultmann's *Kerygma und Mythos*, 15. "The world is like a three-storeyed building. In the middle is the earth; above it is heaven, below it is the subterranean world. Heaven is the dwelling place of God and of the celestial beings, the angels; the lower world is hell, the place of torment. But the earth itself is not simply the scene of natural, everyday events, of forethought and of labour, in which it is possible to reckon with a regular and unchanging order; this earth too is the scene of the action of supernatural forces, of God and of his angels. These supernatural forces intervene in natural events, in the thoughts, in the will, in the actions of men."

186. Neill and Wright, *Interpretation of the New Testament*, 245.

187. Bultmann, *New Testament & Mythology*, 30.

188. Bultmann, *Kerygma und Mythos*, 15–16.

A Brief Historical Survey of Apocalyptic Christology Studies

So then, what can be known of Christ? In order to know anything about Christ, Bultmann distinguishes between *historisch* (things that merely happened) and *geschichtlich* (meaningful/significant history). In his program it does not matter if specific events in Christ's life, like the resurrection, literally happened (in *historisch*). Instead, what we do know is that the first disciples came to believe that these things happened and that these events proved meaningful to them on an existential level (*geschichtlich*). For these followers, Jesus was raised, thereby verifying all that he said, all that he did, and all that he is. In the same way Jesus became all of this for his disciples, he can be the same for people today on an existential level.[189]

If Bultmann found it necessary to demythologize the truth out of the straightforward accounts of the gospels, it is no wonder that John's Apocalypse is absent from Bultmann's theology in general and Christology in particular. Bultmann even claimed that the judgment of God to which the Scripture refers, "is not a cosmic event that is still to happen but is the fact that Jesus has come into the world and issued the call to faith."[190] Not only that, eschatology in Bultmann's program is not future-oriented as much as it is an ongoing existential reality in the human person.[191]

This is not true in the work of Wolfhart Pannenberg. With Barth, Pannenberg desired a high Christology but desired something more than what many believed looked like fideism. With Bultmann, Pannenberg desired to mine the Scriptures for their theological content; however, he did not want to go about this enterprise at the expense of diluting Christianity to the merely existential. Instead, Pannenberg understood God's revelation as history and therefore endorsed a historical pursuit of the God-Man.[192] For

---

189. Bultmann, *Theologie des Neuen Testaments*, 305–6. "The truth of the resurrection of Christ cannot be understood until that faith which acknowledges the Risen One as Lord has sprung up in us . . . Christ is present in the *Kerygma*, not as a great historic personage is present in his work and in its effect in history . . . What we are concerned with is the fact that an historical personage with his own personal destiny has been raised to the level of the eschatological event . . . if a man accepts the word as directed to himself, as the word which offers to him death and life by means of death, he has believed the Risen One."

190. Bultmann, *New Testament & Mythology*, 19.

191. Bultmann, *History and Eschatology*, 155. "The truth of the resurrection of Christ cannot be understood until that faith which acknowledges the Risen One as Lord has sprung up in us."

192. In *Revelation as History*, Pannenberg argues that that revelation cannot be adequately understood as the disclosure of truth about God, but must be interpreted as the self-revelation of God. "The heart of his argument is that if there is any revelation, there

The Humility and Glory of the Lamb

Pannenberg, if history's end is the goal of all that is taking place, Jesus Christ and his earthly ministry is the midpoint and climax. Additionally, the end of all events is anticipated in the fate of Jesus Christ.[193] In Jesus' earthly work (especially in the resurrection), the end is not only witnessed ahead of time, but it is experienced by means of a foretaste. Although, as already stated, the whole of history alone can demonstrate the deity of God and this only at the end of all history, the Christ event, insofar as it anticipates the end of history, is one particular event that has absolute meaning as the revelation of God.[194] In its relation to mankind, so long as mankind is heading toward the future, the Christ event is not overtaken by any later event and remains superior to all other concepts as the anticipation of the end. Also, the Christ event that culminated in the resurrection satisfies the eschatological character of history as it projects a future state yet to be experienced.[195] In other words, God's eschatological self-revelation is proleptically actualized in the realized destiny (particularly in the resurrection) of Jesus Christ.

Although one might be led to believe that Pannenberg would eagerly endorse the Apocalypse of John for his understanding of Christ (inasmuch as Christ is depicted in his concluded/cumulative form therein), robust analysis and use of Revelation is scant in Pannenberg's corpus. For instance, in *Jesus—God and Man*, Pannenberg's remarks concerning the end of time are limited to his explanation for the delay of the *parousia*.[196] That said, he does endorse Revelation to speak of Jesus' role of ushering in the *eschaton* and bringing to light totality of God's self-disclosure to the world:

> "The unveiling of the riddles of existence, of the whole cosmos and of history, will take place in the end events because they will happen in the light of the glory of God himself: the day of Judgment will 'have neither radiance nor brightness nor light but only

---

can only be a single unique revelation in which God is both the author and medium of revelation; indeed, that 'form' and 'content' are one in God, and this, mode and content are equally revelatory . . . God's full self-revelation can only be placed at the end of history, in relation to which the totality of history and all of reality is illuminated and received meaning." Stefano, "Christology after Schleiermacher," 363. See also Pannenberg, *Jesus—God and Man*, 53–65 and Von Balthasar, *Theo-Drama Volume*, 18–54.

193. Pannenberg, *Revelation as History*, 139. "The universal revelation of the deity of God is not yet realized in the history of Israel, but first in the fate of Jesus of Nazareth, insofar as the end of all events is anticipated in his fate."

194. Pannenberg, *Revelation as History*, 144.

195. Pannenberg, *Revelation as History*, 144.

196. Pannenberg, *Jesus—God and Man*, 106ff.

A Brief Historical Survey of Apocalyptic Christology Studies

the radiance of the glory of the Most High alone, by which all can see what is determined for them' (IV Ezra 7:24; cf. Rev 21:23). Thus the revelation of God brings with it the revelation of all occurrences. For apocalyptic the glorification of the righteous and the making known of God's glory especially belong together. So, too, the revelation of salvation for men may not be separated from God's revelation in Jesus. By creating eschatological salvation and by the fact that whoever he whom Jesus rejects incurs eschatological judgment, Jesus shows himself to be the executor of the end."[197]

The only time Revelation is endorsed in this important work aside from this reference is in connecting how the Apocalypse of John corresponds to what is said of Christ elsewhere.[198]

Although Pannenberg's application of the Apocalypse of John to his Christology is sparse, his gaze toward the *eschaton* has had a profoundly positive influence on many who came after him. For instance, Kevin Vanhoozer has argued "In the final analysis, the ideal of the single correct interpretation must remain an eschatological goal."[199] Anthony Hoekema adds that Revelation provides this full-orbed picture of God's revelation when he says:

> "The book of Revelation refers to both the past and the future. It builds its expectations for the future on the word Christ has done in the past. Among the many references in the book to the victory that Christ has won in the past, the following may be cited: 1:18, 5:5–7, 9–10; 12:1–5, 11. Therefore, the book of revelation pictures

---

197. Pannenberg, *Jesus—God and Man*, 193.

198. Pannenberg, *Jesus—God and Man*, 67. "Christ is raised as the first-fruits of those who have fallen asleep (1 Cor 15:20). Correspondingly, in Col. 1:18 Jesus is called the firstborn of the dead. The same expression is found in Rev 1:5, indicating that this is a traditional, widely circulated formulation." On page 272, Pannenberg cites Rom 10:7; Eph 4:8f; and Acts 2:24ff as texts that depict Jesus in Hades and having victory over death. He then mentions Rev 1:18 as a passage that adds to this idea the fact that Christ freed the dead in Hades by overcoming death for himself and for them.

199. Vanhoozer, *Is There Meaning*, 303. He continues and says that for him, "eschatology puts into question a fundamentalist (foundationalist) epistemology that aspires to absolute truths and objective certainties" of the arrogant and dogmatic type." See also his comment on page 335 in which he says "the final context, in light of which alone the proper meaning of all things will be seen, is an eschatological, theological horizon. All human knowing is thus partial until the end of history, when the final judgment will be given."

the church of Jesus Christ as saved, secure in Christ, and destined for future glory."[200]

One might conclude that Pannenberg cracked open a door of eschatological consideration that others, later in the twentieth century, have since walked through in their own pursuits to better understand Christianity as a whole and the person of Christ in particular.

However, before this survey of christological consideration progresses further, it is important to consider the reasons why Revelation was largely ignored in the first part of the twentieth century. Barth, for his part, wanted to return the discussion to the Jesus of faith as witnessed in the gospel—particularly in those places that enunciate the gospel most clearly (like Romans). Bultmann, inasmuch as he was skeptical of the miraculous and delimited eschatology to present existentialism, made little if any room for what John's Apocalypse offers. Finally, though intrigued by the *eschaton*, Pannenberg was most fascinated with what has already been realized—the resurrection of Jesus—and the hope that it brings for the future when all will be revealed. Though each of these in their own way failed to utilize Revelation in their respective programs, each of these men contributed something to the discussion that rendered the Apocalypse of John ripe for renewed christological interest. Barth reminds the liberal critic of the importance of faith, Bultmann re-establishes the present and compelling nature of Christ on an existential level, and Pannenberg returns the student's gaze toward the future in which what happened to Christ will be one day be realized for the faithful.

Conclusion

This chapter has succeeded in demonstrating that Revelation has, on a historical level, been largely neglected for its christological offerings, especially as it pertains to John's use of Lamb. Though the book of Revelation proved to be, in part, a sophisticated and multifaceted christological presentation at the end of the first century, eventually other concerns, distractions, and agendas began to steal focus away from what John produced. As a result, only an incomplete appreciation for the person of Christ has been enjoyed. In the period between Revelation's publication and the council of Chalcedon, radical fringe groups like the Montanists gave Revelation a

---

200. Hoekema, *Bible and the Future*, 69.

A Brief Historical Survey of Apocalyptic Christology Studies

bad name and debates concerning the nature of Christ found little use for the Apocalypse. Mediaeval Christology was largely fascinated with Christ's incarnation, especially as witnessed at the cross, to the neglect of Jesus' realized glorification. Reformation leaders did not embrace Revelation generally, let alone the presentation of Christ therein. Post-Kantian Christology understood Christ as God's way of reconnecting humans with the Divine (albeit in different and largely subjective ways). However, critical reaction to such subjectivism took hold that was primarily concerned with dissecting the gospels in an effort to piece together the historical Jesus. Although, Barth, Bultmann, and Pannenberg reintroduced faith, experience, and the *eschaton* back into the discussion, Barth focused on soteriology to the neglect of eschatology, Bultmann lost the future by delimiting the end to the existential and present, and Pannenberg was more concerned about what the resurrection said about the end than what John presented in his prophetic apocalypse.

3

Contemporary Johannine Christology with Special Attention to the Apocalyptic Lamb

Now that a historical investigation of apocalyptic Christology has been provided, it follows next that a review be given for what is currently underway in the christological discussion in general and lamb Christology in particular. This chapter will demonstrate that while many have revisited the Apocalypse of John in an effort to understand what it says about Christ, much work still needs to be done in order to more fully understand why John has chosen to primarily frame the Son of God as the Lamb in Revelation. To this end, the present discussion will seek to explicate the current christological research, primarily in Johannine literature. Thereafter, a brief review of what many are saying about the Lamb will be given. Finally, a critical analysis will be provided on a more recent and exhaustive work that is exclusively focused on the Lamb Christology of Revelation.

Currents in Johannine Christology

Running alongside what was taking place theologically in Barth, Bultmann, and Pannenberg was the recognition and acceptance of the NT by a new slew of historical critical scholars. Following the quests for the historical Jesus and a myriad of investigations into the sources that were used to create the NT, some, like Bart Ehrman, have suggested that what is currently found in the twenty-seven books of the NT Canon is supposed to be there. One quote in particular helps encapsulate what more and more scholars like Ehrman are concluding after rigorous study.

> "What, in conclusion can we say about the utility of the manuscript tradition of the NT for the scholar of Christian antiquity? Textual scholars have enjoyed reasonable success at establishing, to the best of their abilities, the original text of the NT. Indeed, barring extraordinary new discoveries or phenomenal alterations in method, it is virtually inconceivable that the character of our Greek NTs will ever change significantly."[1]

One might say that while Pannenberg gave theologians the clearance to look to the end to understand the present and past (especially as it pertains to the person of Christ), Bart Ehrman's conclusion opens all NT works to exploration and use.

These trends birthed a biblical Christology renaissance that is still being witnessed today (particularly as it concerns Johannine literature in general and Revelation in particular). James F. McGrath makes this observation when he says, "In recent times an area which has attracted a great deal of scholarly attention is the development of Christian doctrine, and, in particular, Christology."[2] One way this is accomplished is by concentrating on a specific writer and his presentation of Jesus. After such analysis, John Knox discovered what he believed to be different christological emphases among NT writers.[3] The first emphasis, indicated in the Petrine speeches, the synoptic accounts of the baptism of Jesus, and in Paul's letters, ascribes divine qualities to Jesus.[4] The second, as found in the writings of Paul and Hebrews, accentuates Jesus' preexistence and a kenotic view of

---

1. Ehrman, "Text as Window," 825. He continues by saying, "Critics have been less assiduous in pursuing the history of the text's subsequent transmission. At the same time, scholars have already used some of the available data to unpack some aspects of Christian social history: the nature of the early theological controversies, the polemical relations between Christians with both Jews and pagans; the oppression of women in the church, the social history of scribes, the use of magic and fortune telling among ordinary Christians, the extent and character of the early Christian mission, the use of Christian scripture in public worship and private devotion. Much more, however, is left to be done, both on these issues and on others, as we move beyond a narrow concern for the autographs to an interest in the history of their transmission, a history that can serve as a window into the social world of early Christianity."

2. J. McGrath, *John's Apologetic Christology*, 3.

3. J. Knox, *Humanity and Divinity*, 25–31.

4. See Acts 2:22; 3:13, 19ff; 5:31; 10:38f; Rom 1:4.

his person (i.e., that he emptied himself in order to become a man).⁵ The third christological flavor Knox identifies is localized in John's gospel and first letter. Therein, John makes much of the incarnation of Christ in which divinity and humanity come together.⁶ Though various studies have been conducted to further delineate particular Christologies of individual authors, Raymond Brown acknowledges that Paul and John often receive the greatest attention "because the 'high' Christology come to the fore there."⁷ Thankfully, this tendency is in keeping with the scope of this work.

In fact, numerous works have been written more recently that deal specifically with John's presentation of Christ both in his gospel account and in his Apocalypse. One of the many includes McGrath's work on *John's Apologetic Christology*. Therein McGrath argues that John's presentation of Christ as found in his gospel is apologetically framed for the benefit of a predominately Jewish community in a recently Hellenized world from which the Christian movement sprang.⁸ To this end, John applies contemporary concepts like the "logos" to Christ in an effort to articulate something of Jesus' nature in a way that made sense to his unique audience.⁹ Additionally, Jesus' proximity to and statements made while attending the

---

5. See Phil. 2.

6. Pollard, *Johannine Christology*, 5.

7. R. Brown, *Introduction*, 196. Brown also points out that "one way of studying NT Christology is to concentrate on the Christology of each writer."

8. R. Brown, *Introduction*, 3ff.

9. Pollard, *Johannine Christology*, 12. That such a concept would have proven compelling to a Jewish audience is affirmed by what has been learned about the Qumran community and its own Jewish milieu. There exists a remarkable parallel between John 1:3 and *The Manual of Discipline* 11:11—a text that reads, "All things come to pass by His (God's) knowledge; He establishes all things by his design and without him nothing is done." William Brownlee concludes that this Qumranic text comparable to the "Logos" of John 1 in "Comparison of the Covenanters," 71ff. Oscar Cullmann says that here, "the divine though appears as mediator of creation in "Significance of the Qumran Texts," 216. Also, B. I. Reicke says that "what the Qumran text call 'the knowledge' or 'the thought' of God is actually his creative intellect or very much the same as what the Fourth Gospel calls the Logos of God" in "Traces of Gnosticism," 140. These similarities help build the case that John is utilizing an existing concept to defend something about Christ in what has been called an apologetic Christology.

Contemporary Johannine Christology

festivals,[10] the many "I am" statements,[11] and the structure of the gospel itself[12] betray John's apologetic agenda.

However, not only do recent studies of John's works reveal that Jesus is cast as the Logos through which the entire world was conceived and is maintained, they also show how Jesus is portrayed by means of certain characteristics that are consistently held in tension. For instance, Jesus is identified both as the subordinate Son of the Father[13] and the co-equal member of the Trinity who has been sent as God's agent for a special mission.[14] He is also called the immaterial "Word" made flesh.[15] Such presentations establish a paradoxical precedent to John's greater christological scheme. Still other more comprehensive presentations of Johannine theology and Christology identify the many offices that are ascribed to Jesus in the apostle's body of work.[16] These include, but are not limited to, the Lamb of God, teacher and prophet, Messiah/Christ, and Son of Man.

Concerning these titles that John endorses, the phrase "Son of Man" surfaces some thirteen times in John's gospel, predominantly in the sayings of Jesus. The apostle utilizes this particular label to highlight the incarnational language of descent into death (as this particular title is related to other occurrences in the synoptics)[17] and subsequent ascent into glory (as portrayed in Daniel).[18] As for John's presentation of Jesus as "Christ," the "beloved" apostle is the only NT writer to transliterate "messiah" as Μεσσίας followed by its translation χριστός.[19] That this christological title

---

10. All of the Passovers that took place in Jesus' ministry are found only in John's gospel (see John 2–3; 5; 6; 13ff). Also, Jesus' activity during the feast of tabernacles and the Feast of Dedication is found in John 7 and 10, respectively.

11. See John 6:35, 41, 48; 8:12; 10:7, 11, 14; 11:25; 14:6; 15:1.

12. See the introduction of John's argument in John 1:1–14ff and the climax in John 20:31. "But these are written that you may believe that Jesus is the Christ."

13. See John 1:18; 3:36; 5:19; 6:45–47; 8:55; 14:13; 15:15; 16:15; 20:31.

14. Bauckham, *Gospel of Glory*, 193. "John's 'agency Christology' combines the idea that Jesus is the Son of his Father with the idea that he has come into the world as his Father's agent, commissioned and sent by the Father to represent the Father and to accomplish his Father's work."

15. See John 1:1; 14.

16. See Rainbow, *Johannine Theology*.

17. See Mark 8:31; 9:9, 12, 31; 10:33, 45; 14:21, 41; Matt 12:40; Luke 11:30; John 3:14; 6:27, 53; 8:28; 12:23, 34; 13:31.

18. See "Son of Man" in Daniel 7:13–14. See also Ashton, "Johannine Son of Man," 508–29.

19. See John 1:41; 4:25.

The Humility and Glory of the Lamb

is significant is confirmed by the "summary verse" of John—"these things are written so that you may believe that Jesus is the Christ, the Son of God."[20] This special label refers to the eschatological King of Israel—the last and greatest from the line of David. In his epistles and in the Apocalypse "Christ" becomes a standard title, often coupled with "Jesus" and "the Son of God."[21] Concerning "Teacher" and "Prophet," John uses these far more than his synoptic colleagues, thereby uniquely accentuating Jesus' ability to speak on God's behalf.[22]

Of special consideration to this current project is any work done on the title/office of the Lamb. However, in what has been dubbed the "only English-language textbook on John's theology that aims to be both critical and comprehensive,"[23] analysis of this pervasive apocalyptic title is only awarded a cursory glance. In Paul Rainbow's comprehensive volume, interpretation of John's Lamb in delimited to "an image of atoning sacrifice."[24] Though Rainbow claims that this Lamb receives glory, is awarded worship, conquers beasts, marries the bride, and rules forever, little analysis is provided that would explain why the choice of Lamb is a fitting symbol that satisfies/reinforces all of these activities/offices.

Perhaps demanding a complete analysis of the Lamb is too much to ask of a work that has chosen to analyze Johannine theology in general. As Lamb (that is, ἀρνίον) occurs only once in John's gospel and twenty-nine times in Revelation, it stands to reason that recent theological/christological studies that have chosen to narrow their scope to the Apocalypse itself provide a better chance of a full delineation of this unique title. After all, according to Peter Carrell, Revelation is fertile ground for christological analyses.

> "the majority of scholars have had no difficulty in affirming the 'high Christology' for the Apocalypse . . . for example . . . John believes that 'the glory of God has been seen in the face of Jesus Christ' (cf. 2 Cor. 4.6). Consequently, Christ bears 'all the attributes of deity' in his initial portrayal (Apc. 1.12–16), is marked by the

---

20. John 20:31.

21. Rainbow, *Johannine Theology*, 186. See 1 John 1:3; 2:1, 22; 3:23; 4:2, 15; 5:1, 6, 20; 2 John 3, 7 9; Rev 1:1, 2; 11:15; 12:10; 20:4, 6; 22:21.

22. Rainbow, *Johannine Theology*, 184. See also Cho, *Jesus as Prophet*.

23. Rainbow, *Johannine Theology*, 9. In speaking of his own book Rainbow writes "As far as I am aware, this volume is the only English-language textbook on John's theology that aims to be both critical and comprehensive."

24. Rainbow, *Johannine Theology*, 183.

titles of God (e.g. 22.13), and, as the Lamb, has his name coupled together with the name of God (e.g. 22.1, 3). In short, 'God, once hidden from human sight, [is] now revealed in the known person of his Son'. A similar conclusion is reached by Schillebeeckx who argues that the secret name in Apocalypse 19.12 signifies that 'Revelation explicitly maintains the mystery of the eschatological identity of the person of Jesus . . . The author evidently means to suggest that the nature of Christ is intrinsically bound up with that of God himself'. Most recently Bauckham has argued that the pattern of 'I am' self-declarations by God (1.8, 21.6) and Christ (1.17, 22.13) reveals 'the remarkable extent to which Revelation identifies Jesus Christ with God'. In particular, Apocalypse 22.13 (Where Christ is 'the Alpha and the Omega, the first and the last, the beginning and the end') reveals 'unambiguously that Jesus Christ belongs to the fullness of the eternal being of God.'"[25]

Though one might assume that a thorough investigation of John's favorite word for Christ in Revelation would grow in the christologically charged soil of Revelation, this is unfortunately not always the case.

For instance, in a collection of essays totally devoted to *Imagery in the Book of Revelation*, the Lamb is barely mentioned.[26] In fact, the most prolific word applied to Christ in the Apocalypse of John is given very little if any analysis. Instead, in this and other works, different discussions steal focus.[27] One example is Carrell's own *Jesus and the Angels: Angelology and the Christology of the Apocalypse of John*. Though these works and the analyses therein are to be commended for their fruitful scholarship, it is at least curious and at most negligent that very little is mentioned or sought by way of an understanding of John's most prolific symbol for Christ in current theological scholarship.

Thankfully, this trend is not true of all theological investigations into the Apocalypse of John. In his discussion on the theology of Revelation, Bauckham argues along with deSilva that one of the Apocalypse's major

---

25. Carrell, *Jesus and the Angels*, 2. See also Schillebeeckx, *Christ: The Christian*, 432–62, and Bauckham, *New Testament Theology*, 54–5.

26. Labahn and Lehtipun, *Imagery in the Book of Revelation*.

27. Labahn and Lehtipun, *Imagery in the Book of Revelation*. These include but are not limited to the following: "Idol Meat and Satanic Synagogues," "Utopia and Apocalypsis," "Roman Imperial Imagery in Revelation," "Apocalyptic Motifs in the Early Christian Literature and Art," "Merchants and Commerce in the Book of Revelation," and others. See also deSilva, *Seeing Things John's Way*.

The Humility and Glory of the Lamb

symbolic themes is that of "eschatological exodus."[28] Accordingly (for Bauckham), one image that John endorses is that of Jesus as the Passover Lamb. This is Bauckham's general interpretation of ἀρνίον. Evidence in favor of such an interpretation includes similarities between Revelation 5:9–10 and Exodus 19:5–6 and other parallels that the apocalypse shares with the Moses' OT narratives.[29] That said, even Bauckham concedes that "when Revelation treats the blood of the Lamb as the price of redemption, this really goes beyond the role which the blood of the Passover Lamb played in the exodus."[30] He adds the possibility that John may also have Isaiah 53 in mind as he uses Lamb inasmuch as the Suffering Servant is portrayed as a sacrificial lamb.[31] However, after floating the idea that an interpretation of John's apocalyptic Lamb may involve more than one referent, he quickly concludes that "it is the central role which the death of Jesus played in the Christian understanding of redemption which accounts for the centrality of the Lamb to Revelation's use of the new exodus motif."[32]

Devoting an entire chapter to the Christology of Revelation in his own work, titled *Interpreting Revelation*, Merrill Tenney argues that the christological character of the Apocalypse is closely related to four main visions that each contain a portrait of Christ.[33] The second of these visions

---

28. Bauckham, *Theology*, 70. "Since the exodus was the keep salvation event of the history of Israel, in which God liberated his people from oppression in Egypt, destroyed their oppressors, make them his own people and led them to theocratic independence in a land of their own, it was naturally the model for prophetic and apocalyptic hopes of another great salvation event in the future." See also deSilva, *Seeing Things John's Way*, 162ff.

29. Bauckham, *Theology*, 70–71. Both passages suggest that by the Lamb's blood he "ransomed" a people and made them a kingdom/distinct people. Also, both Exodus and Revelation endorse the use of plagues, corrupt word leaders (Pharoah and the Beast from the sea), miracles, salvation for a people in tribulation, and the promise of a new land/kingdom.

30. Bauckham, *Theology*, 70–71. He further adds, "Moreover, the Passover lamb played no role in Jewish expectation of a new Exodus."

31. Bauckham, *Theology*, 70–71. See also Isa 53:7.

32. Bauckham, *Theology*, 70–71. See also p. 64, "he is present as the Lamb who conquers by suffering. Christ's suffering witness and sacrificial death are, in fact . . . the key event in God's conquest of evil and establishment of his kingdom on earth." See also Bauckham, *Climax of Prophecy*, 184. "Doubtless the Lamb is intended to suggest primarily the Passover lamb, for throughout the Apocalypse, and in a passage as close as 5:10, John represents the victory of the Lamb as a new Exodus, the victory which delivers the new Israel."

33. Tenney, *Interpreting Revelation*, 117. These visions include the "Lord of the Church" in Rev 1:12–17, the "Lamb on the throne" (5:1–14), the "Word of God"

is found in 5:1–14, in which Christ is portrayed as the Lamb. For Tenney, the sacrificial character of the Lamb is stressed by the phrase "standing as if slain." However, this sacrificial character is not where the Lamb's significance ends. "The reason for His worthiness is not ascribed to His regal appointment as Lion of the Tribe of Judah nor to His lineal descent from David, but rather to His redemptive death on behalf of men."[34] Also, as Tenney states, "because He has redeemed the world, He has the right to judge it and to cleanse it for His use."[35]

This brief survey of current christological studies, particularly of Johannine literature, does not strive to be exhaustive, but comprehensive. Generally speaking, theological studies into Johannine literature in general tend to pay only superficial attention (if any) to the Lamb motif in Revelation. More specific studies of the theology/Christology of Revelation tend to delimit John's Lamb in Revelation to either the Passover or sacrificial Lamb. That said, all fall short of explaining how they arrive at their interpretations of this integral apocalyptic image. While there is at least one who has provided an exhaustive analysis of his interpretation of John's Apocalyptic Lamb, his work is the exception, not the rule, and therefore deserving of special attention later.

Currents in Lamb Christology

As mentioned earlier in this study, the word ἀρνίον occurs thirty times in the NT: once in John 21:15[36] and twenty-nine times in the book of Revelation.[37] These occurrences in John's apocalypse are not limited to one

---

(19:11–16), and "a Roman general . . . [in] triumph" (19:11–16). Tenney claims "this Christology emphasis is one of the most important keys to Revelation."

34. Tenney, *Interpreting Revelation*, 128–29.

35. Tenney, *Interpreting Revelation*, 129.

36. "So when they had finished breakfast, Jesus said to Simon Peter, 'Simon, *son* of John, do you love Me more than these?' He said to Him, 'Yes, Lord; You know that I love You.' He said to him, "Tend My lambs."' Here, it is obvious that "lambs" (ἀρνία) is being used not of Jesus but of his disciples/followers. This means that John is the only NT writer and Revelation is the only NT book that uses the singular form ἀρνίον for "lamb" for anyone/anything, let alone Christ.

37. Whale, "Lamb of John," 290. Whale is quick to correct the assumption that John reserves ἀρνίον exclusively for Revelation and points out that John does, in fact, use it once in his gospel. However, this is a moot point for John uses the term exclusively in Revelation while endorses multiple words for the same in his gospel. This suggests that John is trying to say something deliberate and distinct about Christ.

context or series of passages but pervade the entire book. In fact, the Lamb (ἀρνίον) is by far the most prolific title given to Christ in John's latest work as it appears more than twice as often as any other christological label—even overwhelming other more expected designations like "Messiah" or "Christ." However, as pervasive as the Lamb is in Revelation, this book is the only work in the NT that applies this specific word to Christ. Also, although John uses ἀρνίον liberally in Revelation, he is the only biblical writer who uses this particular term for Jesus in all of the Canon.[38] This raises two questions that must be answered before connections between ἀρνίον in Revelation and other lambs in the Bible can be drawn: "Why, in light of the vision John is given, is ἀρνίον used most often to speak of Christ?" and "Why does John use ἀρνίον for the 'Lamb' instead of other more common/expected terms?"

The latter of these questions will be dealt with first. It is not as though using Lamb for Jesus is unique in biblical literature. However, ἀρνίον is a peculiar choice for Lamb, especially as a reference for Christ, given what is used elsewhere. For instance, John could have adopted what Paul does in 1 Corinthians 5:7 when he refers to Jesus as the πάσχα (Paschal/Passover Lamb).[39] Such a choice would have immediately transfixed the literal image of a lamb to its salvific, historically rooted, and figurative antitype. However, perhaps an even more obvious choice would have been ἀμνὸς, which is what John the Baptist uses when he introduces Jesus as "the Lamb of God who takes away the sin of the world" (quoting the LXX).[40] Ἀμνὸς is also used for Jesus in Acts 8:32 when Philip quotes Isaiah 53:7-8 (again from the LXX) saying, "a sheep [πρόβατον] is brought to the slaughterhouse, and as a lamb [ἀμνὸς] before its shearer is silent, thus he did not open his mouth." First Peter 1:18-19 makes use of the same word when it says, "by means of the valuable blood of Christ, like that of a lamb (ἀμνὸς) without defect or blemish." All three of these references in their own context say something about the atonement of sin accomplished by a sacrificial lamb. A third choice for lamb was also available to John in the word ἀρήν,[41] a

---

38. For more discussion on John's unique use of ἀρνίον in Revelation see Johns, *Lamb Christology*, 22-25.

39. "Clean out the old leaven so that you may be a new lump, just as you are *in fact* unleavened. For Christ our Passover [πάσχα] also has been sacrificed."

40. John 1:29. John, the apostle, even repeats this title himself in John 1:36.

41. See Lk. 10:3, "Go; behold, I send you out as lambs [ἀρνά, plural of ἀρήν] in the midst of wolves." Although technically, ἀρήν is the noun of which ἀρνίον is the diminutive, these forms had lost their diminutive force by the time the NT was written. Johns,

Contemporary Johannine Christology

term used in Luke 10:3. Any of these choices (πάσχα, ἀμνὸς, or even ἀρήν) would have been more obvious and more literarily consistent with the existing biblical literature that was already being circulated by the end of the first century. One might also argue that these choices would have been better suited to connect the person of Jesus in the *eschaton* to a specific and previously developed christological label.[42]

Therefore, from where does John retrieve ἀρνίον? To be sure, the apostle did not make up this term nor is he the only one who uses it. However, examination of biblical and extra-biblical literature has unfortunately yielded a multiplicity of potential meanings for this word—not a specific definition. For instance, although Louw and Nida's *Greek-English Lexicon of the NT Based on Semantic Domains* claims that ἀρνίον can refer to either a sheep of any age, a lamb, or a ram,[43] Loren Johns points out that "all occurrences of the word ἀρνίον in biblical and classical Greek refer to a young sheep or lamb. Nowhere does it refer to an adult ram in literature that predates the Apocalypse."[44] Johns's analysis of ἀρνίον referring to young lambs, thereby highlighting their vulnerability, seems to be confirmed by rabbinic literature that defines this term (albeit two centuries later) more precisely as pertaining to a sheep that is not more than one year old.[45] This suggests that it was the youth of these lambs that rendered them qualified to be used in sacrifices. In fact, in both the Mishnah and the Talmud, sheep that were between one year and thirteen months were known by an entirely different word that is analogous to πάλλάξ, meaning "adolescent" (before the age of 18).[46] These were not able to be used as sacrifices.

Robert M. Mounce believes that John's use of Lamb in Revelation is derived from the literature of Jewish apocalyptic. With R. H. Charles, Mounce believes that John is merging the two ideas of the Lamb as victim

---

Lamb Christology, 26.

42. For instance, πάσχα would have immediately connected Jesus to his christological function of appeasing God's wrath, ἀμνὸς would have highlighted his christological ministry of atoning sacrifice, and ἀρήν would have identified him with his people and as one who suffers alongside his fellow lambs.

43. Louw and Nida, *Greek-English Lexicon*, s. v. ἀρνίον.

44. Johns, *Lamb Christology*, 22.

45. See Mishnah Para 1:3, "Lambs (ἀρνίον) must be no more than one year old." This is given in the context of types of sacrifices offered.

46. Mishnah Para 1:3, "what is thirteen months old is not valid whether as a ram or as a lamb. " See also Danby, *Mishnah*, 698n4. Steinsaltz, *Talmud*, 245.

and the Lamb as leader.⁴⁷ Evidence for this interpretation of John's Lamb can be found in 1 Enoch 90 in which the Maccabees are described as "horned lambs" (similar to what is envisioned in Revelation 5). Also, in the Testament of Joseph, a lamb destroys the enemies of Israel.⁴⁸ David MacLeod believes that, in part, John uses the "unusual Lamb" in Revelation to suggest that like these other apocalyptic works, Jesus is the "warrior Lamb."⁴⁹ However, though John may have had this in mind, he would have served this interpretation better if he had used ἀμνὸς instead of ἀρνίον as these other apocalyptic sources do.

In light of all of the data presented thus far, it is clear that Revelation's use of ἀρνίον is something of an anomaly. John's unique and yet popular designation for Christ as the ἀρνίον is distinct from how other NT writers connect the image of a lamb to Jesus in the following ways: (1) there is little to no connection between John's gospel and his apocalyptic prophecy in terms of the lamb images used (as the former does not use the term for Christ at all while the second uses the term for Christ no less than twenty-nine times), (2) the NT makes significant use of ἀμνὸς, betraying a dependency on the LXX and emphasizing the atonement of sin, and (3) references to Christ in Revelation as ἀρνίον do not depend on the LXX and instead seem to emphasize the youth and vulnerability of the Lamb ready for slaughter.⁵⁰

Perhaps what is meant by ἀρνίον might be ascertained by looking at the potential predicates and/or types John had in mind (in his NT subject/antitype) that are found in the Hebrew Bible—a work Revelation widely endorses. Careful scrutiny will be given to each of the following possibilities: (1) the lambs used for atonement of sins,⁵¹ (2) the Passover Lamb of the Exodus, (3) Daniel's vision of a ram and a goat, (4) the suffering ser-

---

47. Mounce, "Christology of the Apocalypse," 43. Charles, *Revelation*, exii–vi.

48. Testament of Joseph 19:3, "And I saw that from Judah a virgin was born, wearing a linen garment; and from her a lamb without spot came forth, and on its left side it was as a lion; and all the beasts rushed against it, and the lamb overcame them and destroyed them to be trodden."

49. MacLeod, "Lion Who Is a Lamb," 337.

50. More support of this conclusion will be provided when Loren Johns's work is critically analyzed. His interpretation of the Lamb is largely dependent on ἀρνίον's use in the LXX. However, as will soon be discovered, this term is only used five times (Ps 113:4, 6; Song 8:23; Jer 11:19; 27:45), and even then not all of these betray the concept of vulnerability.

51. See especially Exodus and Leviticus.

vant song of Isa 53: 7, (5) the lamb of Aqedah,[52] (6) the eschatologically victorious lamb of Micah, and (7) the lamb as a symbol of vulnerability in visions of eschatological peace.[53]

Arguments in favor of John's Lamb predominantly endorsing connotations surrounding the lambs of the sacrificial system abound. First, lambs were used for both daily sacrifices and special sacrifices throughout the Hebrew Bible. That John's Lamb is emblematic of a sacrificial lamb is sympathetic to how Jesus is described in Revelation 5:6—"a Lamb standing, as if slain." Also, this type-antitype connection seems to work well with the hymn that immediately follows the introduction of the Lamb. In this praise ballad, the death of the Lamb is shown to be one reason for his worthiness.[54] These considerations, taken alongside the pervasive connections between ἀρνίον and "with the blood," the verb ἀγοράζω (purchase or redeem), and prolific Hebrew ritualistic language,[55] support what Johns and Isbon T. Beckwith have concluded—that "the figure is clearly that of the Lamb as an atoning sacrifice."[56] However, this is not the only option.

It is possible that John's use of ἀρνίον might instead focus more on Christ as the Passover Lamb, especially given the early Christian traditions that suggest such a connection.[57] In fact, the apostle's own references to the Passover (particularly in John 19:18:33, 36) are said by many to support John's introduction of Jesus as the "Lamb of God" in John 1:29, 36 as associated with the Passover Lamb.[58] Additionally, numerous other connections to the Exodus narrative in the book of Revelation seem to make it possible that John is most concerned about highlighting Jesus' connection to the greatest ever Passover that saves people from the wrath of God essentially at present and existentially in the end.[59]

---

52. See Gen 22.

53. This list of potentialities is elucidated by Johns, *Lamb Christology*, 128ff.

54. See Rev 5:12, "Worthy is the Lamb that was slain to receive power and riches and wisdom and might and honor and glory and blessing."

55. That is, the presence of the altar before the throne (Rev 6:9; 8:3, 5; 9:13; 11:1; 14:18; 16:7) and of bowls of incense (Rev 5:8; 8:3, 4).

56. Beckwith, *Apocalypse*, 315. See also Johns, *Lamb Christology*, 128–129.

57. See 1 Cor. 5:7; 1 Pet. 1:18–19, and the copious allusions to the Passover in the passion narratives in all four gospels.

58. Those who say ἀρνίον in Revelation most nearly speaks of Jesus as the greatest Passover Lamb include the following: Baukham, *Climax of Prophecy*, 184; Roloff, *Revelation of John*, 78–79; and Aune, "Revelation," 1310.

59. Connections between Revelation and Exodus include the Seals, Trumpets, and

The Humility and Glory of the Lamb

However, another viable option suggests that the suffering servant song in Isaiah 52–53 played an essential role in the early Christian development of Christology and that John is using this OT passage to inform the christological presentation in his final treatise.[60] Verse 7 of this song reads as follows:

> "He was oppressed and He was afflicted, yet He did not open His mouth; like a lamb that is led to slaughter, and like a sheep that is silent before its shearers, so He did not open His mouth."

Biblical precedent for a connection between these lyrics and Christ is found in Acts 8:32–33[61] and 1 Peter 1:18–19[62] where these same words are applied to Jesus. Perhaps John is making a similar connection to Jesus' redemptive ministry in his pervasive use of ἀρνίον in Revelation.

An even better case can be made for John's endorsement of another OT book altogether—Daniel. Few deny Revelation's heavy use of Daniel as both endorse similar apocalyptic language. Daniel 8 in particular parallels how John might be making use of Daniel not only to foretell the future, but also to highlight something of Jesus' Christology (as Daniel 8 is one of the few OT passages in which animals symbolize humans).[63] Daniel's imagery bears a striking resemblance to how Revelation utilizes animal imagery for certain eschatological personalities.[64]

Another possible source for the lamb Christology in Revelation is found in Genesis 22's drama of Abraham's near-sacrifice of Isaac. After retrieving the supplies necessary for a trip up the mountain to make a sacrifice, Isaac inquires, ". . . 'Where is the lamb for the burnt offering?' Abraham said, 'God will provide for Himself the lamb for the burnt offering,

---

bowls looking a lot like the plagues that were enacted on Egypt. This leads Eugene Boring to say, "as Israel once stood on the banks of the Red Sea and celebrated God's liberating act of the exodus, the church will stand on the shore of the heavenly sea and sing the ode of Moses and the Lamb." Boring, *Revelation*.

60. Johns, *Lamb Christology*, 133ff.

61. Isa 53:7, "He was led as a sheep to slaughter; and as a lamb before its shearer is silent, so He does not open His mouth."

62. "Knowing that you were not redeemed with perishable things like silver or gold from your futile way of life inherited from your forefathers, but with precious blood, as of a lamb unblemished and spotless, *the blood* of Christ."

63. Dan 8:3, "I looked up and saw a ram," 4, "I saw a ram butting westward . . . and no other beasts could stand before him . . ."

64. That is, beasts, dragons, horses, and so on.

my son.'"[65] When they arrived at the mountaintop, Abraham proceeded to prepare Isaac for the sacrifice and nearly completed the act when an angel stopped him from harming his son. "Then Abraham raised his eyes and looked, and behold, behind *him* a ram caught in the thicket by his horns; and Abraham went and took the ram and offered him up for a burnt offering in the place of his son."[66] Though the traditions that were yielded by this episode in Jewish history are wide and varied,[67] some believe it is possible that the Lamb of Revelation is patterned after this lamb turned ram in Genesis 22.[68]

One lesser known archetype John could have had in mind is found in Micah 5, particularly in verses 7–8 when it says,

> "Then the remnant of Jacob will be among many peoples like dew from the Lord, like showers on vegetation which do not wait for man or delay for the sons of men. The remnant of Jacob will be among the nations, among many peoples like a lion among the beasts of the forest, like a young lion among flocks of sheep, which, if he passes through, tramples down and tears, and there is none to rescue."

Many connections can be made between this passage and what is found in the Apocalypse of John—a Jewish remnant is in view,[69] the context involves the "days to come,"[70] and conflict with and "among the nations" is an included theme. However, perhaps the most compelling connection is that this is the only example, outside of Revelation, in which lambs and lions are juxtaposed while representing the same figure.[71]

One final candidate to consider is the lamb of eschatological peace. Loren Johns reveals that lambs play a central role in several passages that

---

65. Gen 22:7–8.

66. Gen 22:13.

67. To trace a complete interpretive history of this episode, see Caspi and Cohen, "The Binding," and Swetnam, *Jesus and Isaac*, 23–85.

68. See the horned Lamb in Rev 5 for further support for this view.

69. See Rev 12.

70. See Mic 4:1 and Rev 4:1.

71. Johns, *Lamb Christology*, 141. See Rev 5:5–6, "and one of the elders said to me, "Stop weeping; behold, the Lion that is from the tribe of Judah, the Root of David, has overcome so as to open the book and its seven seals. And I saw between the throne (with the four living creatures) and the elders a Lamb standing, as if slain, having seven horns and seven eyes, which are the seven Spirits of God, sent out into all the earth."

The Humility and Glory of the Lamb

look forward to eschatological peace in the Hebrew Bible.[72] One among them is Isaiah 11:6–7,

> "The wolf will live with the lamb, the leopard will lie down with the goat, the calf and the lion and the yearling together; and a little child will lead them. The cow will feed with the bear, their young will lie down together, and the lion will eat straw like the ox."[73]

Inasmuch as God's disciples are being sent out "like lambs into the midst of wolves" to bring the peace of God to the world and, as prophesied in Revelation, the Lamb of God will ultimately bring about lasting peace, there is good reason to include these passages on the ballot for consideration in John's writing. Not only that, but because Johns's scholarship on this particular subject represents one of the only exhaustive studies of John's favorite christological term (ἀρνίον), his analysis and resulting conclusions are worthy of special consideration.

Special Case Study: Loren Johns's Lamb Christology

Summary

In *The Lamb Christology of the Apocalypse of John*, Loren Johns provides a rigorous linguistic–historical–rhetorical–critical analysis of the most pervasive term for Christ in the book of Revelation. Interestingly, Johns's work betrays a commitment to historical criticism alongside a commitment to responsible Christology. However, analysis of his project will demonstrate that while Johns proves exemplary at delineating the historical backgrounds necessary for understanding the apostle's context, he is deficient in the kind of canonical and contextual analysis that provides an accurate understanding of the Lamb as it exists and is used in Revelation.

From the beginning, Johns reveals his bias toward historical criticism and, by proxy, a pseudo-community-response approach to the text (sympathetic to Stanley Fish) when he claims, "like any text, the Apocalypse has no inherent 'Meaning' within itself, even if 'Meaning,' especially in regard to the Apocalypse has been slippery all along."[74] Johns claims this for

---

72. Johns, *Lamb Christology*, 143.

73. See also Isa 65:25, "'The wolf and the lamb will graze together, and the lion will eat straw like the ox; and dust will be the serpent's food. They will do no evil or harm in all My holy mountain,' says the Lord."

74. Johns, *Lamb Christology*, 15. Fish, *Is There a Text*, 171–72.

two reasons: to strike a sympathetic chord with his intended audience (a primarily liberal audience of like-minded colleagues), and to open the door for a creative interpretation that is not strictly tethered to authorial intent. His fascination with the likes of Tina Pippin demonstrates a desire to "play with the polyvalence of the symbols"[75] in an effort to uncover "as accurately as can be captured from this distance the origins and force of John's Lamb Christology within the author's cultural, political, and religious milieu."[76] This admission reveals Johns's preference to know how the apostle's *Gestalt* defines the Christology of Revelation over how the apostle himself understands and presents the God-Man.[77]

After admitting these presuppositions, Johns defines his thesis as follows: "the Lamb Christology of the Apocalypse has an ethical force: the Seer sees in the death and resurrection of Jesus Christ both the decisive victory over evil in history and the pattern for Christians' nonviolent resistance to evil."[78] According to Johns, this is witnessed most succinctly in the apostle's pervasive use of Lamb which indissolubly connects the apocalypse to its theology and Christology. In making this case, Johns is interested in what the following aides have to offer in support of this thesis (and this in this order): the various terms used for Lamb and the linguistic implications thereof, possible historical referents, Jewish backgrounds, Hebrew OT backgrounds, and finally, the book of Revelation itself. This descending list of priorities suggests that the design of Johns's study is largely deductive.

That said, Johns begins his argument by revealing that the term in question (ἀρνίον) is seldom used outside the book of Revelation. In fact, as already revealed, it is only used one other time in the NT,[79] only a handful of times in the LXX,[80] and is rarer still in extra-biblical literature.[81] Inasmuch as Johns champions linguistic and historical elements and their supervening influence on the meaning of ἀρνίον in the Apocalypse of John

---

75. Pippin, *Death and Desire*, 16.

76. Johns, *Lamb Christology*, 18

77. Johns, *Lamb Christology*, 20. In fact, in opposition to G. B. Caird, who says, "John has told us what he means by it" (in speaking of the symbol of the Lamb), Johns claims, "I cannot agree with this statement. If we are to understand what John does with this symbol, we must first understand what associations or traditions it may have evoked in the mind of his readers." See Caird, *Revelation of St. John*, 74.

78. Johns, *Lamb Christology*, 20.

79. John 21:15.

80. Jer 11:19, 50:45; Ps. 114:4, 6; Isa 40:11; Song 8:23.

81. Josephus uses ἀρνίον two or three times.

The Humility and Glory of the Lamb

(over and above authorial intent), he leans most heavily on its use in the OT to make his case. He argues (almost a priori and with very little exegetical analysis) that "the few times ἀρνίον occurs in the LXX it has the symbolic value of expressing vulnerability. This makes a prima facie case that in the Apocalypse its symbolic value communicates vulnerability in some way."[82] However, even Johns admits that this prima facie argument is potentially precarious and must be supported by the unique historical localization and symbolic *Gestalt* of John's day.

This is why Johns spends the next portion of his argument delineating the animal symbolism present in Egyptian and Greek mythology and the potential influence this may have had on the origin and function of the Lamb as it appears in the Apocalypse. Although Johns proves adept at perusing the contours of Egyptian beliefs, Aesopic fable traditions, Homeric epics, and sacrificial practices leading up to the first century, ultimately, there is very little that these traditions offer by way of connection and/or help in understanding the Apocalypse and what it has to say about Christ. However, after admitting that this historical analysis was largely unprofitable for this study[83] Johns seems to pad his argument by saying, "What emerges most significantly in relation to the Apocalypse is that lambs in the Greco-Roman world were often associated with . . . [among other things] . . . vulnerability."[84]

The same pattern is followed when Johns examines the Jewish literature that may or may not have influenced the apostle's work. In contrast to the conclusions reached by C. H. Dodd and Friedrich Spitta in this arena,[85] Johns assumes a vulnerable Lamb and then sets out to reinterpret passages like 1 Enoch 90, Psalms of Solomon 8, and Mishnah Para 1:3, accordingly. He even says of the Mishnah, "In a few instances, lambs prove victorious over their more powerful traditional enemies. Although not immediately obvious, this is properly to be seen as part of the category of vulnerability."[86]

---

82. Johns, *Lamb Christology*, 39.

83. Johns, *Lamb Christology*, 75.

84. Johns, *Lamb Christology*, 75.

85. Friedrich Spitta claims that the Apocalypse possesses a unique convergence of not one but two separate lamb traditions that each stem from Jewish traditions: (1) the lamb as sacrificial victim, and (2) the powerful ram. Spitta, *Streitfragen der Geschichte Jesu*, 172–224. Dodd associates both power and violence with the lamb of Revelation and argues that this paradoxical relationship is supported in Jewish apocalyptic tradition. Dodd, *Interpretation of the Fourth Gospel*, 231ff.

86. Johns, *Lamb Christology*, 101.

While Johns is happy to welcome this tenuous connection into his interpretative apparatus, he is quick to deny that a more recognizable redeemer-like lamb figure is evidenced in the apocalyptic traditions.[87]

Next, prior to his investigation of the OT and the Apocalypse, Johns contradicts his earlier insistence on a linguistic–historical approach by conceding the kinds of categories advocated by Vanhoozer in *Is There Meaning in This Text?*[88] Though Johns never compares the "steno" symbol and "tensive" symbol[89] to "locution" and "illocution," these terms seem to be used synonymously. Johns even states that if "tensive" symbols abound, so too does the author's vested interests and "greater-than-referential meaning."[90] In spite of this discussion, Johns immediately disregards this phenomenon saying, "these observations suggest that while the distinction between steno and tensive symbols has some heuristic value, how and where one makes the distinction may—and usually does—say as much about the reader as it does the text or the author."[91] Because the reader's interpretation of a text is equated with the author's intent, Johns believes he is well within his hermeneutical rights to advance his linguistic-historical-critical approach accordingly and entertain any number of interpretations of the Lamb.

In so doing, much as was demonstrated above, Johns offers several hermeneutical options for the use of ἀρνίον in the context of Revelation.[92] First, the Lamb could be a reference to the sacrificial system (after all, the Lamb is depicted as slain, his death has some expiatory force, and the phrases "in the blood" and "redeem" elicit this association). However, the apocalyptic vocabulary is not sacrificial and the OT primarily uses ἀμνὸς for these atoning lambs. Second, Revelation's Lamb could be understood as the Paschal Lamb of the Exodus (inasmuch as Passover Christology existed in the early first century, there is widespread critical support for this interpretation, and literary similarities between Revelation and the Exodus

---

87. Johns, *Lamb Christology*, 106. "There is no evidence at this point to establish the existence of anything like a recognizable redeemer-lamb figure in the apocalyptic traditions of Early Judaism. Connection with haggadic legend is possible, though this tends to give credence to the view that the lamb imagery has more to do with the symbolism of vulnerability than to an apocalyptic redeemer figure."

88. Vanhoozer, *Is There Meaning*.

89. These categories were made popular by Philip Wheelwright in his *Burning Fountain*.

90. Johns, *Lamb Christology*, 113.

91. Johns, *Lamb Christology*, 113.

92. Johns, *Lamb Christology*, 113. These options are delineated in chapter 4.

The Humility and Glory of the Lamb

abound). However, πάσχα, not ἀρνίον, would have made for a more distinct connection between Revelation and Exodus and the Passover victim was not always a lamb. Third, the Lamb of the Apocalypse may serve as the antitype for Isaiah 53:7 (as both contexts include the image of the slaughter). However, ἀμνὸς, not ἀρνίον, is used in Isaiah and the suffering servant motif at work in Isaiah is absent in Revelation. Fourth, Daniel's vision of a ram and a goat in Daniel 8 might provide a potential background for the apostle's Christology (as this passage is one of the only OT passages in which humans are symbolized as animals, both have apocalyptic undertones, and both contexts cry out for justice). However, Daniel reveals that the two horns of the ram and the male goat is not Christ.[93] Fifth, the Lamb could be understood in comparison with the *Aqedah* of Genesis 22 (the tradition of the story believed that the ram had been prepared before the foundations of the world and, according to Johns, both contexts involve vulnerability). However, no explicit appeal is made to the Abraham episode in the Apocalypse and the traditions surrounding the Abrahamic story could have been later than the writing of Revelation. Both the lambs of Micah 5:6 and the eschatological lamb of peace are two additional options that Johns explores as potential backgrounds for the apocalypse. However, each of these falls short as well.[94]

This leaves Johns with only one other option—the vulnerable lamb of the LXX. Johns believes that every time ἀρνίον is used in the LXX, vulnerability and innocence is suggested. Therefore, when the apostle chose this particular term for his apocalypse and employed it every time he refers to Christ as the Lamb, especially given the linguistic-historical-critical case he has made, the Apocalypse is adopting the same sentiments. Though vulnerability, as Johns admits, might prove to be an unnatural association with the victorious eschatological Christ, he reassures his readers by saying, "if vulnerability is in view, it can only be a gutsy, costly, and effective kind of vulnerability and an apocalyptic challenge to the usual meaning and value

---

93. Dan. 8:21 states, "The shaggy goat *represents* the kingdom of Greece, and the large horn that is between his eyes is the first king."

94. For Johns's discussion on all of these potential options, see *Lamb Christology*, 128–145. There he argues that although in both Revelation 5 and in Micah 6 a lamb is juxtaposed alongside a lion, both contexts are eschatological, and both contexts deal with the conflict of Israel, some believe that the presence of the lamb in Micah was added much later. As it pertains to the eschatological lamb of peace, while Isaiah 11:6 and 62:25 depict the lamb as feeding alongside and living with the wolf, Johns believes that the vision of the Apocalypse is anything but peaceful and unlike the lamb of Isaiah, the lamb of the Apocalypse is slaughtered.

of these nouns and adjectives."[95] Furthermore, Johns argues that if Christ is the vulnerable and yet conquering lamb as witnessed in Revelation, then Christ's followers ought to adopt the same posture of nonviolent resistance to forces of evil and in that, find victory—"The hearing/reading community is empowered to engage in such resistance because the Lamb has already won the victory."[96]

Critical Analysis

Though Johns is to be commended for his rigorous linguistic and historical data-collecting and should be admired for his call for Christians to lead a holy life after Jesus' example, there are several issues with his argument that undermine the interpretation he provides for ἀρνίον in Revelation. First, the greater part of John's interpretation of ἀρνίον is dependent on its use in the LXX. He concludes that most if not all of these OT occurrences communicate the vulnerability of the lamb, either in the presence of a potential enemy or as a symbol of eschatological peace. However, upon closer inspection, the verses upon which Johns's leans so heavily (Jer 11:19; 50:45; Ps 114:4, 6; Isa 40:11) do not necessarily nor explicitly convey a vulnerable subject nor do they even apply to God's people. For instance, Jeremiah 50:45 uses the term in reference to the Babylonians. Not only that, but Isaiah 40:11 states "like a shepherd He will tend His flock, in His arm He will gather the lambs and carry them in His bosom; He will gently lead the nursing ewes." To read vulnerability in this text would be to discredit the protective power of the shepherd who in this context is God. This leaves only three passages (Jer 11:19; Ps 114:4, 6) that lend themselves to the conclusions that Johns reaches. Such evidences are hardly a strong foundation upon which to build an interpretation of Revelation's principal character, especially when the context of Revelation is exceedingly unique and, in many ways, distinct from Jeremiah and the Psalms.

In spite of this, Johns assumes that vulnerability is nearly always associated with ἀρνίον and even endorses this meaning in the very few places it is found in extra-biblical literature. In so doing, Johns proves guilty of

---

95. Johns, *Lamb Christology*, 149.

96. Johns, *Lamb Christology*, 205. Johns's conclusion is sympathetic to the findings of Richard Bauckham when he says, "While rejecting the apocalyptic militancy that called for literal holy war against Rome, John's message is not, 'Do not resist!' it is 'Resist!—but by witness and martyrdom, not by violence.'" Bauckham, *Theology*, 92.

what D. A. Carson calls a "false assumption of technical meaning"—"In this fallacy, an interpreter falsely assumes that a word always or nearly always has a certain technical meaning—a meaning usually derived from either a subset of the evidence or from the interpreter's personal systematic theology."[97] Not only is Johns guilty of this fallacy, but one might also argue that Johns is guilty of "semantic obsolescence." This infraction is defined as follows: "Here the interpreter assigns to a word in his text a meaning that the word in question used to have in earlier times, but that is no longer found within the live, semantic range of the word. That meaning, in other words, is semantically obsolete."[98] Johns commits this when he assumes that the vulnerability associated with ἀρνίον remains consistent in the ever-fluid and evolving literary world (especially as one considers the time difference between the completion of the LXX and the writing of Revelation). Could not the connotation of ἀρνίον have changed between the writing of the LXX and the writing of the Apocalypse of John? A third hermeneutical strike against Johns's program is his endorsement of "an appeal to unknown or unlikely meanings."[99] Johns commits this when he assumes that in Revelation—in which Jesus is clearly depicted as a conquering, victorious, powerful warrior king—ἀρνίον must continue to convey something about vulnerability. However, vulnerability as a theme in Revelation does not seem tenable, especially as it pertains to how Christ is delineated.

As these trends surface throughout Johns's work, it becomes clear that he is inevitably reading his own theology into the text.[100] Johns betrays his liberal tendencies by insisting on a vulnerable ἀρνίον in the book of Revelation to prop up a program of nonviolent resistance.[101] While the latter is taught elsewhere in the NT and vulnerability may highlight one aspect of Christ and his work in Revelation, Johns's argument that vulnerability is the primary or most significant characteristic of the apocalyptic Lamb is less than satisfactory.[102] Instead, a more canonically based study would prove

97. Carson, *Exegetical Fallacies*, 45f.

98. Carson, *Exegetical Fallacies*, 35.

99. Carson, *Exegetical Fallacies*, 37ff.

100. Carson, *Exegetical Fallacies*, 128. This is what Carson refers to as "fallacies arising from omission of distancation in the interpretative process."

101. Johns, *Lamb Christology*, 203. "The theology of the Apocalypse can even be characterized as a theology of peace if peace is defined not as absence of conflict, but as an ethic of nonviolent resistance to evil."

102. Similar sentiments are shared by John Howard Yoder in his work *The War of the Lamb*.

that considerations of Christo-centric eschatological victory—messy, total, and immanent—alongside his docile visage (as a Lamb) suggest that this figure is far more complicated and multivalent.

Ultimately, the flaws with Johns's understanding of the lamb Christology in the Apocalypse stem from the general design of his approach. His interpretation follows the following process: linguistic analysis—possible origins—Jewish background—OT backgrounds—Revelation (in that order). However, this deductive approach succeeds only in discoloring the connotation of the word in question (ἀρνίον) prior to its reconfiguration into the context in question (Revelation). Matthew Streett calls Johns's heavily linguistic approach even more into question when he concludes: "While the particular word John uses does mean Lamb, the term he uses may not match any LXX occurrence of that word, and so there is no clear or easy link between ἀρνίον in the LXX and ἀρνίον in Revelation."[103] A better approach (a more inductive and canonically contoured approach) would reverse John's program, allowing for the authorial intent to guide the meaning within the context of the Apocalypse itself first. After an understanding of its use in Revelation is reached, then appeals to the Canon and then to historical–linguistic studies can be perused in an effort to fine-tune what has been yielded.

Conclusion

Johannine literature in general and Revelation in particular has only more recently been cultivated for its christological content. Even there, the delineation of Revelation's Christology is weak and any elucidation of John's favorite christological label—the Lamb—has only just begun to receive adequate attention. Even when this Lamb is studied, most, if not all who identify his special character choose to delimit their interpretation of this figure in any number of univocal ways. Also, while there is much to be gleaned from Johns's work by way of linguistic analysis and historical insight, the conclusions reached by means of his exercises are incomplete and tenuous. Not only is his work guilty of several hermeneutical fallacies, it inevitably reveals that Johns's interpretation of the Lamb is more in keeping with his own presuppositions and the reader's interpretation[104] than it is with what is actually present in Revelation. This only means that as it

---

103. Streett, *Here Comes the Judge*, 172.
104. See notes on Pippin and Fish above.

The Humility and Glory of the Lamb

pertains to any robust understanding of the Lamb of the Apocalypse, there is still much work to be done. Such work must take on a different design and plant a more fitting tree in the christologically rich clearing that has been discovered in current Revelation studies. It is to this work that this argument will now turn.

4

The Humble and Glorious Lamb of Revelation

BECAUSE THE LAMB OF Revelation has failed to elicit the kind of attention historically and more contemporary analyses of this figure have failed to yield a complete interpretation, it follows next that this project provide what, thus far, has been lacking—a more robust understanding of Christ in general, apocalyptic Christology in particular, and apocalyptic Lamb Christology especially. To this end, few passages are more contextually significant, literarily meaningful, and vividly presented in the Apocalypse of John than Revelation 5:6–10.[1] In fact, even Caird has referred to these verses as some of the most important in the Book of Revelation.[2] In this passage, the apostle's protagonist is introduced (that is, in the prophetic section of Revelation) and sets in motion the judgment that envelopes the better part of the book. It is also in this passage that ἀρνίον is used for the first time and the only time this term is employed without the definite article. Although every other use of ἀρνίον is *arthrous* (containing the definite

---

1. Guthrie, "The Lamb in the Structure," 64. "Indeed it is part of the intention of the whole scene in chapters 4 and 5 to set the stage for the dramatic introduction of the Lamb to the readers." Here, Guthrie also points out that Revelation 4–5 is the first worship passage of the Apocalypse.

2. Caird, *Revelation of St. John*, 73. On these verses William Hendrickson writes, "They relate Jewish Messianic hopes to the distinctively Christian good news of the advent of the Messiah in the person of Jesus of Nazareth, but a Messiah of a character so wholly unexpected by the Jews that they rejected him." Hendrickson, *More Than Conquerors*, 109.

article), in Revelation 5:6 the term is *anarthrous* (absent a definite article), thereby indicating that at least potentially, every subsequent use refers back in some way to the first occurrence connotatively and/or hermeneutically.[3]

However, many in an effort to explicate the prophetic elements of these verses fail to appreciate the theological and christological message that is being presented by the author, particularly as it applies to this passage's presentation of the Lamb. The present hermeneutical analysis will remedy this by means of a thoroughly contextual–grammatical–canonical–historical interpretation of Revelation 5:1–10 in general and its use of Lamb in particular and ultimately reveal the following christological message: Jesus is the only one worthy to set in motion the end of the world in part because he is the most humble[4] and, by proxy, the most gloriously worthy candidate to do so.

In many ways, the design of what follows will invert the hermeneutical program witnessed in Loren Johns's project and strive for a more contextually and canonically based understanding of the Lamb that begins with the text of Revelation itself. The following analysis of Revelation 5 and the interpretation of ἀρνίον will serve as a foundation upon which a more complete understanding of the apocalyptic Lamb will be constructed in chapter 5 of this book. For the purposes of this argument, it will be assumed that John the Apostle is the author of Revelation and that this book was penned

---

3. Possible functions of the definite articles attached to the "lamb" as it is found elsewhere in the Book of Revelation include the following: anaphoric (denoting previous reference—a reference that is typically anarthrous because in its original or first occurrence it is being introduced), par excellence (pointing out that the Apocalyptic Lamb is in a class by itself as introduced in Revelation 5:6–10), monadic (indicating that, as in Revelation 5, the Lamb is one-of-a-kind). Although a case might be made for each of these in the various contexts in which ἀρνίον is found, these possibilities in general and the anaphoric function in particular indicate that the first anarthrous use of Lamb is of special interpretative significance, especially as it pertains to the arthrous examples that follow. For discussion on these possible functions, see Wallace, *Greek Grammar*, 217ff.

4. Humility as opposed to "vulnerability," as Loren Johns suggests. Humility as a quality does not necessarily denote vulnerability and or potential danger. This is witnessed in Jesus' foreshadowing of his death (the greatest spectacle of humiliation) in John 10:17–18, "For this reason the Father loves Me, because I lay down My life so that I may take it again. No one has taken it away from me, but I lay it down on My own initiative, I have authority to lay it down." According to these verses, it was not Jesus' vulnerability, but Jesus' humility that led to his sacrifice. In order for Jesus to have been truly vulnerable, the active voice of these verses would have to be replaced with passive voice and he would have had to give up his "authority to lay [his life] down."

around 90 AD. These choices are supported in a more thorough discussion on pertinent background issues found in appendix A.

Contextual Analysis

Concerning the Genre of Revelation

If, as Aune suggests, "a literary genre consists of a group of texts that exhibit a coherent and recurring pattern of features constituted by the interrelated elements of form, content and function,"[5] then identifying Revelation's form is exceedingly difficult as there are few if any texts that can compare to its awesome variety, sophisticated form, and figurative prowess. This is why reaching any broad consensus on the genre of the book of Revelation has proven difficult.[6]

First, a small contingency of scholars affirm that Revelation is primarily an epistle because of its named authorship and clearly defined addressees in chapters 1–3.[7] Aune also recalls that the Canon Muratori 57–59 recognizes the epistolary character of Revelation. This reveals that this particular genre was associated with this work (at least superficially) in the ancient church world.[8] However, even Aune admits that recognizing Revelation as epistolary was "accorded little or no interpretive significance."[9] As a result, very few if any NT scholars today redact their understanding of Revelation's genre down to a mere epistle.

Others, in keeping with what Revelation says about itself in verse 1 ("Ἀποκάλυψις Ἰησοῦ Χριστοῦ"), consider the book as primarily apocalyptic. Supporters of this view cite the unveiling nature of Revelation along with its symbolism, angelic mediums, episodes of cosmic catastrophe, showdown between good and evil, and figurative nature as evidences in favor of this position.[10] Stephen Smalley adds that Revelation's use of vivid

5. Aune, *Revelation 1–5*, lxxi. See also Hellholm, "Problem of Apocalyptic Genre," 13–64.

6. J. Blevins, "Genre of Revelation," 396.

7. Lucke, *Die Offenbarung Des Johannes* and Karrer, *Die Johannesoffenbarung als Brief*.

8. Aune, *Revelation 1–5*, lxxii. See also Dionysius of Corinth as quoted in Eusebius *Hist eccl*, 7.25.9–10.

9. Aune, *Revelation 1–5*, lxxii.

10. See discussion of the apocalyptic genre in Lea and Black, *New Testament*, 583 and Harris, "Apocalyptic Genre," 241ff. For proponents of Revelation as apocalyptic, see

metaphors, numerals, dualism, pessimism toward contemporary society, and determinism render it apocalyptic in style.[11] To be sure, Revelation shares these characteristics with other works that have been identified as apocalyptic by scholars.[12] Such scholars believe that John adopted these traits and borrowed from previously existing works in an effort to fit this unique genre. After all, most, if not all other apocalyptic works were written prior to Revelation (sometime between 200 BC and 100 AD). In fact, although John's Apocalypse is one of the latest installments in the apocalyptic corpus, Stephen Cook believes it is the most "intricate and sophisticated."[13]

However, there are at least three arguments against delimiting the genre of Revelation to mere apocalypticism. First, apocalyptic works were pseudonymous.[14] By contrast, John names himself no less than four times throughout the work. Second, apocalyptic writings tend to accompany their visions with lengthy interpretations.[15] John does not spend much time explaining what he reports to see in his visions. Instead, while John's visions play a central role in his dramatic presentation, the author rarely stops to ask for or provide an interpretation of these phenomena.[16] Also, in most apocalyptic works, ultimate victory is understood as a primarily future act of God. However, in John's apocalypse, the past sacrifice of Jesus joins this future picture as an existential and historical reality.[17]

Rowland, *Open Heaven*, 14, 21, 356–57; Tenney, *Interpreting Revelation*, 26; and Witherington, *Revelation*, 32ff.

11. Smalley, *Revelation of John*, 7.

12. Apocalyptic works include but are not limited to the following: portions of Ezekiel, Daniel 7–12, 1 Enoch, 2 Enoch, 2 Baruch, 3 Baruch, 4 Ezra, The Shepherd of Hermas, The Apocalypse of Abraham, The Testament of Abraham. K. I. Nitzsch coined the term "apocalypse" on the basis of Rev 1:1 and has since been used as a generic category. See Schmidt, *Die judische Apokalyptik*, 98–99. For identification of apocalyptic works see Collins, *The Apocalyptic Imagination*; Carey, *Ultimate Things*; and Cook, *The Apocalyptic Literature*.

13. Cook, *Apocalyptic Literature*, 192.

14. Smalley, *Revelation of John*, 7.

15. Smalley, *Revelation of John*, 7. Here, Smalley identifies the following formula that most apocalyptic works apply: a mystery determining the future destiny of humanity is concealed in heaven, and an angelic figure appears to explain it. For examples of this pattern, see Dan 7:15–27, 4 Ezra 10:29–59, and 1 Enoch 27:1–5.

16. Smalley, *Revelation of John*, 7. "The exceptions are 17:13–17 and 17:7–18 . . . but even there the author seems to be using a literary technique to gain the attention of his audience, rather than offering through the angel a clear explanation of the imagery involved."

17. Osborne, *Revelation*, 14. See also Rev 5:5; 7:14; 12:11.

The Humble and Glorious Lamb of Revelation

Those who are hesitant to juxtapose Revelation to apocalyptic works like the *Shepherd of Hermas* opt for a second generic option and argue that John's Apocalypse is primarily prophetic (see Rev 1:3—"Μακάριος ὁ ἀναγινώσκων καὶ οἱ ἀκούοντες τοὺς λόγους τῆς προφητεία"). Evidences that support this position include the similarities this work shares with Daniel and other OT prophets.[18] While proponents of this view concede that Revelation resembles apocalyptic works, these believe that apocalypticism is really a subset or extension of the prophetic genre.[19] As Revelation seems to contain and accomplish more than what is found in or accomplished by other apocalyptic works, some ask, why delimit the genre of this book to this narrower classification?

Like other prophetic works, the author appears to write in his own name and declares that he has divine knowledge to report to his audience. Additionally, the exhortations given to the seven churches in Revelation 2–3 seem consistent with previous prophetic works—both are oracular, include commands, communicate encouragements, and promise judgment.[20] Not only that, but Smalley argues that John is deliberate in his attempt to fall in line with the OT prophets. For instance, passages like Revelation 1:1 and 10:8–11 appear to echo Isaiah 1:1 and Jeremiah 1:10, respectively.[21]

However, the three positions concerning the genre of Revelation presented thus far are viewed by many to be incomplete and, as a result, unsatisfactory. Perhaps this is why a growing number of contemporary scholars promote a broader and more inclusive delineation of Revelation's genre. For example, Everett Harrison concludes that Revelation "is apocalypse with respect to its contents, a prophecy in its essential spirit and message, and an epistle in its form."[22] Robert L. Thomas agrees with Eugene Boring when he says that a view that leaves "no room for an apocalyptic document such as Revelation to be considered also as a genuinely prophetic document directly concerned with the realities of political history" is tenuous.[23] Therefore, the conclusion Carson and Moo reach—that "elements of proph-

---

18. Hellholm, "Problem of Apocalyptic Genre," 164–65.

19. Ladd, "Why Not Prophetic-Apocalyptic?," 192–200, Bauckham, *Theology*. Therein, Bauckham calls Revelation "apocalyptic prophecy." See also Osborne, *Revelation*, 13.

20. Smalley, *Revelation of John*, 7–8.

21. Smalley, *Revelation of John*, 8. See the similarities between Rev 1:1 and Amos 1:1; 3:7 also.

22. Harrison, *Introduction*, 458.

23. Thomas, *Revelation*, 29 and Boring, "Theology of Revelation," 261.

ecy, apocalypse, and letter are combined in a way that has no close parallel in other literature"—not only seems to be the current representative view endorsed by most critical scholars, but the most robust understanding of the text's form.[24] Even Smalley agrees saying,

> "Such diversity, prophetic and apocalyptic, combines the discrete audience of Hebrew prophecy . . . with the universal appeal inherent in the literature of the apocalyptists . . . Revelation may be identified . . . as apocalyptic deepened by prophetic insight, and also as prophecy intensified by apocalyptic vision. John is not simply a seer, but a prophet-seer."[25]

Ultimately, the similarities Revelation shares with epistles, apocalyptic works, and prophecies advance the view that John's last treatise is a multifaceted work that cannot be so easily redacted to one particular form/genre.

As it pertains to the scope and direction of this argument, it serves the reader well to understand that the genre of John's Apocalypse is highly unique and sophisticated. Therefore, it might stand to reason (at least potentially) that major themes and repeated symbols, like the genre in which they are found, are not as one-dimensional as one might initially concede.

Concerning the Theme and Organization of Revelation

Both Revelation and the Gospel of John share at least one common motif: God is revealing himself through Jesus Christ as Savior of the World. In John's gospel, Jesus is shown to be the incarnate Logos that ushered in the church age. In Revelation, Jesus is depicted as the victorious ruling Savior who upon purging a sinful world and vanquishing enemies, ushers in an eternal heaven. Also, in both works the author goes to great lengths to highlight Jesus' divinity. Therefore, a good statement of Revelation's theme, especially as it applies to Jesus, might read: the one who saved us from sin (through his death, burial, and resurrection) is the one who is coming to finally eradicate sin and bring about perfect peace (through his programmatic return, judgment, and re-creation).

---

24. Carson and Moo, *Introduction*, 716. See also Baukham, *Theology*, 1–17; Michaels, *Interpreting the Book of Revelation*, 29–33; Jurgen Roloff, *Revelation of John*, 5–8; Beale, *Book of Revelation*, 37–43.

25. Smalley, *Revelation of John*, 8.

The Humble and Glorious Lamb of Revelation

John paints this thematic portrait upon a canvas that is stretched across a very sophisticated framework. In fact, so sophisticated is John's organization that outlining Revelation has proven to be something of a conundrum to many (as evidenced by the variety of analyses produced).[26] However, after considering a myriad of potential chronological, thematic, and organizational options, one appropriate outline of the major units of Revelation might read as follows:

1. The Introduction of the Prophet: 1
2. The Message Concerning Today's World: 2–3
3. The Prophecy Concerning the Eschaton: 4–22:5
    A. The Opening of the Seven-Sealed Scroll: 4:1–8:1
    B. The Sounding of the Seven Trumpets: 8:2–11:19
    C. The Pouring of the Seven Bowls: 12:1–18:24
    D. The Last Things: 19:1–22:5
4. The Conclusion and Charge: 22:6–21

Concerning the Remote Context: Revelation 4–22:5

The largest section of Revelation (and the remote context pertinent to this particular study) involves the recording of John's prophetic vision that spans from Revelation 4 to Revelation 22:5. One thing that these verses share is that they are eschatological in perspective. While elements of the preface (chapter 1) and the message to the seven churches (chapters 2–3) are historically situated, most of Revelation 4–22:5 is painted in predictive hues. Therefore, it is appropriate to consider this large portion of the book as its own section. Textual support for this division is also present. In verse 1 of chapter 4, the writer begins with an emphatic transition, "after these things I looked" (Μετὰ ταῦτα εἶδον), suggesting both a topical and temporal shift

---

26. Smalley, *Revelation*, iiiff. Stephen Smalley organizes Revelation into two acts (creation and salvation through judgment [1:9–11:19], and salvation through judgment, and new creation [12:1–22:17]). Osborne, *Revelation*, 30–31. Osborne cashes Revelation out into six major divisions (Prologue [1:1–8], churches addressed [1:9–3:22], God in majesty and judgment [4:1–16:21], final judgment at the arrival of the *eschaton* [17:1–20:15], new heaven and new earth [21:1–22:5], and the epilogue [22:6–21]). Thomas, *Revelation*, 43ff. Thomas divides Revelation into only three categories: the preparation of the prophet (1:1–20), the preparation of the people (2:1–3:22), and the publication of the prophecy (4:1–22:21).

The Humility and Glory of the Lamb

from what was presently witnessed in the world of John's day to what will be witnessed by the world at another time.[27] That this large section ends at 22:5 is supported by the beginning of 22:6, which says, "and he said to me, 'these words are faithful and true'" (Καὶ εἶπέν μοι οὗτοι οἱ λόγοι πιστοὶ καὶ ἀληθινοί). To what words is John referring? The answer is the many words of prophecy previous disclosed in Revelation 4:1–22:5.

With broader literary domain firmly in view, it is important to acknowledge that the remote context of Revelation 5:6–10 can be loosely divided according to the programs of judgments that are predicted for the world during the tribulation. However, this is not absolute, for, as is evident in the text itself, there are significant pauses that break up an otherwise neat and chronological/logical order.[28] Also, chapters 4–5 act as a kind of overture that precludes the major prophetic events. That said, in spite of these literary idiosyncrasies, the easiest way to follow the program of this major section of Revelation is to track the seals, trumpets, and bowls as these betray the most obvious organizational key offered in the text.[29] Everything else can be understood by means of its relationship to these judgments/plagues.

What is clear about 4–22:5 is that the distress witnessed and the acuity of the wrath poured out increases as the text progresses. The book reads like a piece of music that includes one large crescendo toward a climactic fortissimo. Here, the fortissimo is the victory of the Lamb in 17–21 and the implications thereof (Babylon's fall [18:1–24], and the celebratory worship

---

27. Although Rev 7:1, 15:5, and 18:1 all employ the same phrase to mark another markedly important transition of their own, 4:1 is the first occurrence of Μετὰ ταῦτα εἶδον. Not only that, but 4:1 bifurcates between the epistlatory section of Revelation and the apocalyptic/prophetic vision that John witnesses (transporting the audience from the world as it existed in the first century to the heavenly realm). These context clues imbue this particular example of Μετὰ ταῦτα εἶδον with special literary significance.

28. These breaks include the interlude of Revelation 7, the interruption of chapters 10–11 between the sixth and seventh seal, and the presentation of characters immediately following the seventh seal in chapters 13–14.

29. Bauckham, *Climax of Prophecy*, 7, "The section of chapters 6–16 is the most structurally complex part of the book, but precisely for that reason John has made his structural markers prominent and emphatic. It is therefore important to base our understanding of the structure on these emphatic markers. Most obvious are the three series of sevens: the seven seal-openings, the seven trumpets, the seven bowls." See also Percer, "War in Heaven," 55–56. Percer adds, "the septets are linked by a technique of overlapping or interweaving in which the seventh item introduces the next set of judgments. . . . The point here is that John uses repetition to tie these judgments together and to aid in the progression of the story."

of Christ [19:1ff], etc.). As in a beautiful piece of music when a dissonant chord resolves, chapters 4–22 turns up the tension, only to have the Lamb of God resolve this tension in a way that elicits peace and hope. Within this remote context, Revelation 4–5 acts as a literary catalyst—a powerful downbeat—that galvanizes the events that are vividly described in chapters 6–22:5.[30]

Concerning the Immediate Context: Revelation 4–5

In the verses leading up to 5:6–10, there is a great deal of potential literary energy that when released successfully instigates the judgments that are unleashed upon the earth through the seals, trumpets, and bowls. Again, "after these things" (Μετὰ ταῦτα) in verse 1 of chapter 4 successfully divides chapters 1–3 and the next major unit (chapters 4–22). Not only does the temporal change marked in 4:1 suggest a degree of literary separation, but phrases like "in the Spirit" and a pervasive use of "like" followed by vivid descriptions of places (4:2), people (4:4), phenomena (4:5), and creatures (4:8) successfully imbue the text with a worshipful and other-worldly connotation that is absent from the previous chapters. This worship reaches a climax in verse 8 of chapter 4 when a doxology rings out over the halls of a heavenly scene—"Holy, Holy, Holy, is the Lord God, the Almighty, who was and who is and who is to come." This worshipful verse is then, in many ways, mirrored by three stanzas of praise that are offered in the remainder of chapter 4 and into chapter 5.[31] However, the worship that is expressed by the heavenly inhabitants of these two chapters is temporarily interrupted by a scene that breaks out in the beginning of chapter 5.

---

30. That Rev 4–5 is able to stand as its own unit is confirmed by J. Charles in "An Apocalyptic Tribute," 461–62 when he says, "Chapters 4 and 5 of this apocalyptic drama mark the introduction of the Lamb. The audience is transferred in John's vision from the seven churches to the courts of the heavenly throne room to observe, in a liturgical context, the pivotal event of human history along with its ramifications."

31. 4:11, "Worthy are You, our Lord and our God, to receive glory and honor and power; for You created all things, and because of Your will they existed, and were created." 5:9–10, "Worthy are You to take the book and to break its seals; for You were slain, and purchased for God with Your blood men from every tribe and tongue and people and nation. You have made them to be a kingdom and priests to our God; and they will reign upon the earth. 5:12, "Worthy is the Lamb that was slain to receive power and riches and wisdom and might and honor and glory."

The Humility and Glory of the Lamb

The interruption is introduced by a phrase indicating a new observation—"I saw in the right hand" (5:1).[32] Here, John witnesses a seven-sealed book and hears "a strong angel proclaiming with a loud voice . . . 'Who is worthy to open the book and to break its seals?'" (5:2). Although the reader might assume that the one who was holding the book (the one who "sat on the throne") could break this volume open, John learns that no one yet present in the scene can, by all appearances, expose the contents of this mysterious scroll. Fearing that no one can open the book, break its seals, and thereby implement the things that are revealed therein, John weeps.[33] John's weeping ceases when he is told that "the Lion that is from the tribe of Judah, the Root of David, has overcome so as to open the book and its seven seals" (5:5). In other words, a hero exists that has provided salvation and as a direct result is qualified to provide salvation for John's present distress (opening the seven-sealed scroll and paving the way for the eschatological judgment and salvation to be disclosed in the remainder of the Apocalypse).[34] The description attributed to this hero is two-fold. First, he is described as the "Lion of the tribe of Judah," indicating a "kingly might and boldness" that is similar to what is portrayed in Genesis 49:9 and Proverbs 28:1.[35] Second, he is depicted as the "root of David," a title that John will eventually use again in 22:16. In Isaiah 11:1, 10, this label identifies the Lion as the head of the Davidic kingdom that was prophesied in the OT. Taken together, these messianic labels indicate that it is by virtue of this hero's unique membership in David's family that he is called the greatest of the tribe of Judah and a branch from the root of this regal line.[36]

---

32. See the major division suggested in 4:1 by "After these things I looked, and behold."

33. John had been promised in 4:1 that he would be shown "what must take place after these things." Therefore, this closed book, for John, represents a barrier keeping him from seeing/experiencing what God is going to do. John is therefore weeping over the apparent indefinite postponement of God's final and decisive action. See Thomas, *Revelation*, 386.

34. MacLeod, "Lion Who Is a Lamb," 328–29. "The breaking of the seals is preparatory to God's people entering the promised inheritance."

35. Thomas, *Revelation*, 387. Gen. 49:9, "Judah is a lion's whelp; from the prey, my son, you have gone up. He couches, he lies down as a lion, and as a lion, who dares rouse him up?" Prov. 28:1, "The wicked flee when no one is pursuing, but the righteous are bold as a lion."

36. Robertson, *Word Pictures*, 6:333–34.

The Humble and Glorious Lamb of Revelation

Concerning the Internal Context: Revelation 5:6–10

However, the figure that appears after this introduction does not match the title and description he is given in verse 5. When John turns to look at the regal hero, not a lion, but a "Lamb" (ἀρνίον) emerges onto the scene, "standing as it slain, having seven horns and seven eyes, which are the seven Spirits of God, sent out into all the earth" (5:6). This Lamb takes the scroll from the hand of the one who sits on the throne, thereby eliciting the worship and praise of those present in verses 9–10. It is obvious by this description that no longer is John limiting himself to the prophetic nuances of verse 5. Instead, he allows himself the literary freedoms that the apocalyptic genre affords and the metaphorical elements therein to describe this central character.

While praise was limited to the one who occupied the throne in chapter 4, worship is extended to this Lamb in verses 9–10 and then again in verse 12 in response to his ability to take the scroll and set into motion what John and the world have been waiting for—the *eschaton* complete with its judgment and final victory. Therefore, the immediate context might be understood most appropriately as an apocalyptic prophecy—prophetic in its content (as it references OT types like "Lion" and "line of Judah" that serve as a foundation for an eschatological antitype), and apocalyptic in its metaphorical description of the central character and its ability to unveil the process of judgment that will one day be unleashed.

Grammatical Analysis of Revelation 5:6–10

In an effort to understand how the immediate context of Revelation 5:6–10 is put together on a grammatical level, a diagrammatical analysis of this passage is provided in appendix B. The visual analysis offered there reveals that in 5:6 the interpretation of the direct object of the main independent clause (ἀρνίον) is dependent on the two complex dependent participial phrases that are used by John to describe him ("standing as if slain, having seven horns and seven eyes"). Also, as mentioned earlier, it is worth reiterating that ἀρνίον in verse 6 is anarthrous, indicating that it is without previous reference in the Apocalypse and thereby requiring special interpretative care.[37] The relative temporal phrase in verse 8—"when he had

---

37. Possible functions of the definite articles attached to the "Lamb" as it is found elsewhere in the Book of Revelation include the following: anaphoric (denoting previous

The Humility and Glory of the Lamb

taken the book"—betrays why the Lamb was worshipped. This "worthiness" is further evidenced in verses 9–10 by means of the explanatory ὅτι clauses that are attached to the phrase "worthy are you."[38] The horned and slain Lamb is described as worthy not only because of what he is presently doing (taking the book), but because of what he has already accomplished—". . . purchased for God with Your blood men from every tribe and tongue and people and nation. You have made them to be a kingdom and priests to our God" (5:9–10).

Toward an Interpretation of Revelation 5:6–10

Before a complete interpretation of this passage can be achieved, special attention needs to be given to what the diagrammatical analysis demonstrates. First, much of what this passage has to say is contingent on one's understanding of ἀρνίον. It is worth noting that verse 6 of chapter 5 contains the first time that John employs this term. Additionally, and as mentioned earlier, ἀρνίον is by far the most frequent designation for Christ in Revelation. In fact, it appears more than twice as frequently as any other label for Jesus in the Apocalypse. For John, this is especially telling, for, as witnessed in his gospel, John often uses different synonyms for the same concept.[39] Therefore, the special use of ἀρνίον for Christ in Revelation might indicate that John is deliberately conveying something of theological significance. However, understanding what this significance is requires that the reader pay close attention to how John juxtaposes the "Lamb" of verse 6 with the "Lion" in verse 5.

John appears to be intentionally highlighting the antithetical nature of these two images—Lion and Lamb—and their connection to one figure

---

reference—a reference that is typically anarthrous because in its original or first occurrence it is being introduced), par excellence (pointing out that the Apocalyptic Lamb is in a class by itself as introduced in Rev 5:6–10), monadic (indicating that, as in Revelation 5, the Lamb is one of a kind). Although a case might be made for each of these in the various contexts in which ἀρνίον is found, these possibilities in general and the anaphoric function in particular indicate that the first anarthrous use of Lamb is of special interpretative significance, especially as it pertains to the arthrous examples that follow. For discussion on these possible functions, see Wallace, *Greek Grammar*, 217ff.

38. "Worthy are You to take the book and to break its seals; for You were slain, and purchased for God with Your blood *men* from every tribe and tongue and people and nation. You have made them *to be* a kingdom and priests to our God; and they will reign upon the earth."

39. See John's use of ἀγαπάω and φιλέω in John 21 as an example.

The Humble and Glorious Lamb of Revelation

who embodies the connotations of both. As has already been determined, "Lion" is a direct reference to the powerful and royal line of Judah and David. Its use appears to present Christ as the prophesied Davidic King.[40] This particular title refers back centuries to the days of Jacob who, while on his deathbed, blessed his sons and prophesied over them saying, "Judah is a lion's whelp from the prey, my son, you have gone up. He crouches, he lies down as a lion, and as a lion, who dares rouse him up?"[41] As Judah is perpetually connected to Christ (as Jesus emerges from his family line), this eschatological connection helps demonstrate Christ's place as the long-awaited champion of the Jews. Employing this figure of the lion, 2 Esdras 12:31 says, "this is the Messiah"[42] and appreciates him for his glory, strength, and worthiness to judge the wicked. The description of this Lion does not cease with this reference to Judah. Instead, John also calls the Lion the "Root of David."[43] Alluding to Isaiah 11:10, this title describes the Lion as that descendent of David who will restore the long-awaited Davidic kingdom.[44] These references imbue the figure in question with connotations of victory, power, and prestige.

However, when John turns to view this "Lion," he beholds something unexpected—a "Lamb." "Lamb" hardly conveys the same prestigious connotations as "Lion of the tribe of Judah" (and "Root of David"). The former is one of the humblest creatures while the latter regal, powerful, and glorious. The theme of humility in connection with ἀρνίον (distinct from other words for Lamb in the remainder of Scripture) is consistent with how this word is used in the LXX. Jeremiah 11:19 employs ἀρνίον alongside the qualifier "gentle" and "led to the slaughter," demonstrating the humble ways in which a lamb was both viewed and used in connection with sacrifice for sin. Not only that, but Isaiah 40:11 states, "like a shepherd He will tend His

---

40. Köstenberger, Kellum, and Quarels, *Lion and the Lamb*, 387.

41. Gen 49:9. See also MacLeod, "Lion Who Is a Lamb," 332.

42. The full quote of 2 Esdras 12:31–33 reads "And as for the lion whom you saw rousing up out of the forest and roaring and speaking to the eagle and reproving him for his unrighteousness, and as for all his words that you have heard, this is the Messiah whom the Most High has kept until the end of days, who will arise from the offspring of David, and will come and speak with them. He will denounce them for their ungodliness and for their wickedness, and will display before them their contemptuous dealings. For first he will bring them alive before his judgment seat, and when he has reproved them, then he will destroy them."

43. Rev 5:5.

44 Caird, *Revelation of St. John*, 74, Mounce, *Book of Revelation*, 131; Aune, *Revelation 1–5*, 350–51. Osborne, *Revelation*, 254.

The Humility and Glory of the Lamb

flock, in His arm He will gather the lambs and carry them in His bosom; He will gently lead the nursing ewes." This demonstrates that the humility of a lamb is so severe that its survival depends on the care and protection of a shepherd.

Therefore, while πάσχα and ἀμνὸς are employed elsewhere in the NT for Lamb (to more specifically draw from the Passover tradition and the pervasive sacrifices of the OT respectively), John chooses a more connotatively neutral and altogether unique term in an effort to highlight something different—humility (especially when juxtaposed alongside the use of "Lion" in verse 5)—and applies this to Revelation's most important character.

This interpretation is supported by the participial phrases attached to this term in verse 6, "standing as it slain, having seven horns and seven eyes, which are the seven spirits of God." The only way for a lamb to be more humiliated than it already is to have it slain. Here, the obvious reference is to the death of Christ, who, even though slain, is erect and alive in this heavenly scene.[45] In other words, while the marks of death are visible, they are not debilitating.[46] This provocative image, along with the descriptions that follow of the Lamb, help demonstrate that while John may be capitalizing on the humility of the Lamb, there is more at work in this term and the connotations it is capable of eliciting.

This becomes clearer as the next participial phrase is uttered "having seven horns and seven eyes, which are the seven spirits of God" (5:6). In one breath, John depicts the Lamb as slain and in the next he assigns images of dominion and rule to this humble figure. Inasmuch as the OT uses the horn as a symbol of strength and power,[47] seven of them together in this context indicate the fullness of power that rests on this all-powerful, warrior-like Lamb.[48] Something similar may be said about the seven eyes,

---

45. Thomas, *Revelation*, 391.

46. Alford, *Greek Testament*, 4:607; Swete, *Apocalypse of St. John*, 78; Beckwith, *Apocalypse of John*, 510.

47. See Num 23:22; Deut 33:17. See also 1 Sam 2:1; 2 Sam 22:3; 1 Kgs 22:11; Ps 75:4; 132:17; Dan 7:20–21; 8:5. Thomas also points out that later books in the OT it "symbolizes dynastic force or kingly dignity and is thus used in Apocalypse several times (Rev 12:3; 13:1; 17:3, 12)." *Revelation*, 392.

48. W. Kelly, *Revelation*, 90. Ladd, *Revelation of John*, 87. "Here, we must guard against the temptation to visualize the Lamb . . . the symbols of Revelation are intended to communicate truth, not to serve as photographic reproductions." Mounce, "Christology of Apocalypse," 44. See also Swete, *Apocalypse*, 78–79.

The Humble and Glorious Lamb of Revelation

which indicate the inescapable view by which the Lamb discerns the world and all that happens within it. Some have connected this set of eyes to Zechariah 3:9 and 4:10, believing that they indicate the Lord's ability to remove iniquity from the land of Israel.[49] However, the explanatory relative clause that closes verse 6 ("which are the seven spirits of God sent into all the earth") seems to support what Thomas and others have concluded concerning the Lamb's eyes—that "not only is he omnipotent, as indicated by his seven horns, he is also omniscient."[50]

If one takes these two participial phrases together, he might argue that a cause–effect relationship exists between them. Some might conclude that the great humility of the Lamb as witnessed in his slaying affords him the power and omniscience indicated by the horns and eyes it possesses. There is, in other words, a greatness enveloped within the humility of this Lamb, the kind of greatness that a humble form only accentuates.

The greatness of the Lamb is further illustrated in his being "worthy . . . to take the book and break its seals" (5:9–10). In fact, this is why the Lamb is worshipped in the same manner that the occupier of the throne was worshipped in 4:8. "Worthy" (ἄξιος) was applied to the enthroned figure first in 4:11. This same worthiness is applied to the Lamb in verses 9–10 of chapter 5 and then again in 5:12. John connects the worship of the Lamb to the worship of the Father in an effort to demonstrate their shared divinity (as only God is an appropriate recipient of worship in John's writings). As MacLeod rightly concludes, "His worthiness to open the scroll and inherit the kingdom is based on the victory he won as the Lamb on the cross"[51]—Jesus' greatest *and* most humble act.

A tentative interpretation of this passage and its most central term, especially given the context in which it is found, involves Jesus' unique ability to set in motion the *eschaton* and thereby the ultimate salvation

---

49. Zech 3:9, "For behold, the stone that I have set before Joshua; on one stone are seven eyes. Behold, I will engrave an inscription on it,' declares the Lord of hosts, 'and I will remove the iniquity of that land in one day.'" Zech 4:10, "For who has despised the day of small things? But these seven will be glad when they see the plumb line in the hand of Zerubbabel—these are the eyes of the Lord which range to and fro throughout the earth."

50. Thomas, *Revelation*, 392. Thomas believes that those who believe the "eyes" are connected to Zechariach 3:9 and 4:10 are pressing the meaning of the OT source of the words too far. See also Mounce, "Christology of Apocalypse," 44; Swete, *Apocalypse*, 78–79; R. H. Charles, *Revelation*, 141; Robertson, *Word Pictures*, 6:334–35; Caird, *Revelation*, 75.

51. MacLeod, "Lion Who Is a Lamb," 335.

The Humility and Glory of the Lamb

(glorification) of his people. This ability is afforded him because he (the Lion of the Tribe of Judah) humiliated himself to the point of death (a Lamb standing as if slain)[52] and as a result has been given all power (seven horns) and perception (seven eyes) to continue to perform God's will. Because of this, he is worthy of worship. The christological statement made here (accentuated by the image of the ἀρνίον) successfully portrays Jesus in his humblest and therefore most glorious light (His passion).[53] This symbol affords Christ equal status with God and the praise of all present in this heavenly spectacle and it is this image in which John decides to cast Jesus throughout the remainder of Revelation.

Canonical and Historical Analysis

In order to test this tentative interpretation, this study must ask and answer whether or not there is canonical and historical precedence for this view. Therefore, beginning with what is more contextually significant (Johannine literature, the NT, and the OT) and continuing to what is more contextually remote (extra-biblical literature), the remainder of this chapter will investigate whether or not the interpretation already given requires any alteration.

First, is there Johannine precedent for humility equaling greatness inasmuch as it is juxtaposed alongside what is exceptional/glorious? The answer is a resounding "yes!" For example, Paul Rainbow acknowledges that in the beginning of John's gospel, Jesus is described as the "Word made flesh" (λόγος made σάρξ).[54] According to his view, "the evangelist wants us to read the entire book as the story of the Logos-become-flesh who laid down his life as God's lamb."[55] Immediately after this claim, Rainbow draws parallels between "Word made flesh" and "Lamb as if slain." John uses the former ("Word made flesh") in his gospel to highlight the divinity of the

---

52. MacLeod, "Lion Who Is a Lamb," 334. "John was assured that the Lion 'has overcome,' which, as noted earlier, refers to His defeat of Satan, sin, and death at the cross." Osborne calls this "a great Christian paradox—Jesus has 'conquered' primarily not through military might, though that is to come, but through his sacrificial death (5:6, 9, 12) . . . As the Royal Messiah, Jesus wages a messianic war against evil, and the major weapon that defeats the enemies of God is the cross. This cosmic victory enables him 'to open' the scroll." Osborne, *Revelation*, 254.

53. "The crucified Christ is central to the Book of Revelation." McDonald, "Lion as Slain Lamb," 31.

54. John 1:14.

55. Rainbow, *Johannine Theology*, 183.

The Humble and Glorious Lamb of Revelation

Son by emphasizing his incarnation while John uses the latter ("Lamb as if slain") in his apocalypse to demonstrate the glory of the Son by accentuating his humility.[56]

That Jesus is depicted as gloriously humble in Johannine literature is evident in passages like John 4:34 in which Jesus says, "My food is to do the will of Him who sent me and to accomplish His work." Such a statement renders Christ a uniquely modest deity. This sentiment is repeated just one chapter later when Jesus says, "I can do nothing on My own initiative. As I hear, I judge; and My judgment is just because I do not seek My own will, but the will of Him who sent Me."[57] However, perhaps one of the most humble descriptions of Jesus is made in John 10:11ff when in another pastoral passage Jesus speaks about his unique authority alongside his utter humiliation saying, "I am the good shepherd; the good shepherd lays down his life for the sheep." Here, goodness/greatness is juxtaposed alongside a willingness to humble oneself—particularly, as it pertains to Jesus' humblest act on the cross.

However, the theme of humble greatness is not limited to Christ's passion. While in the upper room, John describes how Jesus "began to wash the disciples' feet and to wipe them with the towel with which He was girded."[58] Though this is a foreshadowing of an even greater act of service that he would soon accomplish,[59] the lesson is explained by Jesus as follows: "If I then, the Lord and the Teacher, washed your feet, you also ought to wash one another's feet. For I gave you an example that you also should do as I did to you."[60] The acuity of Jesus' humiliation in this act is highlighted by Peter's revulsion at the idea that Jesus, his teacher and Lord, would stoop to wash his feet—an act reserved for the humblest of servants.[61] However, this is exactly Jesus' point: the greatest is not the one who would never wash feet, but the one who will choose to humble himself even to the point of performing such an activity.

---

56. Rainbow, *Johannine Theology*, 183. Rainbow draws special attention to the Lamb's humility as witnessed in Christ's atoning sacrifice.

57. John 5:30.

58. John 13:5.

59. Carson, *Gospel According to John*, 463. "Peter and the others will understand later . . . [that] this does not refer to the footwashing, but to the passion to which the footwashing points."

60. John 13:14–15.

61. Köstenberger, *John*, 405.

These findings are consistent with what is found elsewhere in the NT. In Matthew 23:11–12 Jesus says, "but the greatest among you shall be your servant. Whoever exalts himself shall be humbled; and whoever humbles himself shall be exalted."[62] Applied to the interpretation already given of Revelation 5:6–10, the one who humbled himself the most as the slain Lamb is the same one who is exalted high enough to be able to break open the seven-sealed book.

The dispute concerning greatness among the disciples in Luke 22:23ff echoes these principles. In response to their quarrel Jesus states,

> "The kings of the Gentiles lord it over them; and those who have authority over them are called 'Benefactor.' But it is not this way with you, but the one who is the greatest among you must become like the youngest, and the leader like the servant. For who is greater, the one who reclines at the table or the one who serves? Is it the one who reclines at the table? But I am among you as the one who serves."[63]

To silence the argument the disciples were endorsing, Jesus turns greatness on its head and introduces his followers to the paradox of humility affording that which is praiseworthy—pointing to himself as the example par excellence of this phenomenon.

However, this phenomenon is not limited to Jesus ("who although He existed in the form of God, did not regard equality with God a thing to be grasped, but emptied Himself, taking the form of a bondservant").[64] In fact, Jesus, in reference to his cousin states, "I say to you, among those born of women there is no one greater than John."[65] What earns John this special place in Jesus' mind? Aside from his forerunner status and faithful ministry, the Baptist in John 3:30 proved humble when he recognized Jesus' growing ministry and the shrinking of his own saying, "He must increase, but I must decrease."

All of these NT passages support the claim that humility is regarded by God and Christ as great, praise-worthy, and glorious. Some passages even go further and bestow exalted status on the humble. This appears consistent with the interpretation already given of Revelation 5:6–10 in which the Lamb is cast as the humblest of creatures and yet capable of the greatest

---

62. See also Luke 14:11; 18:14.
63. Luke 22:25–27.
64 Phil 2:6–7.
65 Luke 7:28.

The Humble and Glorious Lamb of Revelation

responsibility (the taking of the scroll) and is subsequently awarded with special exalted status.

These concepts are also found in the OT. Therein, God makes a habit of choosing the humblest people to do the most extraordinary things. Throughout the OT, the barren,[66] youngest,[67] fearful,[68] hesitant,[69] sorrowful,[70] and cowardly[71] were used by a mighty God to do what was praiseworthy and glorious. Not only that, but the people of God were in a perpetual state of humility (i.e., slavery or exile) and yet remained the Lord's promised ones. In many ways, the OT is full of ἀρνίους—the humblest of creatures—who are used for glorious purposes.

That ἀρνίον conveys humility and subsequent glory is supported not only by the few OT passages in which this word is used,[72] but also by the extra-biblical usage of this term. Although the Louw and Nida's *Greek-English Lexicon of the New Testament Based on Semantic Domains* claims that this term can refer to either a sheep of any age, a lamb, or a ram,[73] as was mentioned earlier, Loren Johns reveals that "all occurrences of the word ἀρνίον in biblical and classical Greek refer to a young sheep or lamb. Nowhere does it refer to an adult ram in literature that predates the Apocalypse."[74] This is confirmed later by passages in the Mishnah which state, "Lambs must be no more than one year old" in the context of types of sacrifices offered.[75] These humble creatures, made even more humble by their youth, were especially qualified for sacrificial use. Therefore, the sematic range of ἀρνίον as witnessed in extra-biblical literature suggests that humility of a very special kind is at least potentially integral to the connotation of this term.

---

66. See Sarah in Gen 11:27ff, Rachel in Gen 29:29ff, and Hannah in 1 Sam 1:1–2.

67. See David in 1 Sam 17:14.

68. See Moses in Exod 3–4 and Elijah in 1 Kgs 19.

69. See Jonah in Jonah 1–2.

70. See Ruth and Naomi in Ruth 1–4.

71. See Gideon in Judg 6.

72. Jer 11:19; Jer 50:45; Ps 114:4, 6; Isa 40:11; Song 8:23.

73. Louw and Nida, *Greek-English Lexicon*, s. v. ἀρνίον.

74. Johns, *Lamb Christology*, 22.

75. Mishnah Para 1:3. This passage defines "lamb" (ἀρνίον) more precisely as not more than one year old. Though this occurrence is two centuries removed from the writing of John's Apocalypse, it demonstrates that at least on a historical level, there are uses of the term that appear to imbue ἀρνίον with some level of meaning that renders the humility of the creature in question especially humble.

The Humility and Glory of the Lamb

The image of humble sheep also emerges in 1 Enoch 89. Although God's people were described as bulls early in the chapter, Isaac's son Jacob is a depicted as a sheep as is Jacob's twelve sons and Moses after him. One might say that bulls become sheep upon the emergence of Israel (Jacob). These sheep spawn other sheep who are then led by a series of "seventy shepherds" (alluding perhaps to Jeremiah's prediction that Israel's exile will last for seventy years).[76] Once strong bulls, these apocalyptic sheep demonstrate the humble place that God's people occupied on the world's stage, especially in times of tribulation and exile. At times this apocalyptic tribulation is self-induced, as witnessed in Zechariah 11:4–17. Here, the shepherd-sheep imagery takes on a new flavor when the prophet is depicted as a "shepherd of the flock doomed to slaughter."[77] Having disobeyed their natural shepherd, Yahweh, the sheep are handed over by God to other shepherds to be disciplined[78] for a time.

The word ἀρνίον itself along with the preexistent themes of humility and greatness seem to work together on both a linguistic, historical, and thematic level outside of and within the Canon to support the interpretation given for Revelation 5:6–10—namely that Jesus' unique status as witnessed in his ability to take the scroll and set in motion the end times, is confirmed in his matchless glory which is wondrously encased in the humblest of forms—"the Lamb standing as if slain." Because none could humble themselves greater than Jesus did, no one is as gloriously capable of doing what he will accomplish in the *eschaton*.

Conclusion

In Revelation 5:6–10—which might be likened to the downbeat that begins the major eschatological movement of Revelation—Jesus is cast as a brilliant paradox that accentuates not only his matchless glory but his uncompromising humility. The words used (particularly ἀρνίον), descriptions offered (seven horns and seven eyes), worship witnessed, precedent given

---

76. Frederick Murphy, *Apocalypticism in the Bible*, 90. See also 1 Enoch 89:59. Others hold that the number seventy corresponds to Daniel's seventy weeks of years and the common division of history into seventy generations. See Jeremiah 25. J. Collins, *Apocalyptic Imagination*, 68ff.

77. Zech 11:4.

78. Carey, *Ultimate Things*, 59. Petersen, *Zechariah 9–14 and Malachi*, 90. "Yahweh cedes power to malevolent human rulers."

The Humble and Glorious Lamb of Revelation

(in both the Old and NTs), and even the extra-biblical usage of the same term support these claims. The unique genre of the context in which this is provided—equal parts apocalyptic and prophetic—allows John the literary freedom to accomplish his goal of describing a humble and therefore glorious Christ that he calls to mind no less than 28 additional times throughout the remainder of this letter to the Church by means of the term ἀρνίον.

The interpretation of the Lamb of Revelation 5 articulated in this chapter is contextually informed, grammatically sound, canonically tested, and extra-biblically sufficient. As a result, this approach tells us what the original author intended and is not as susceptible to endorsing superimposed and ill-fitting connotations onto this important term (as Johns's approach was shown to do in chapter 3). The result of this analysis suggests that the apostle uses ἀρνίον in Revelation 5, especially in connection with the Lion, to expose Jesus as the humblest and therefore most glorious eschatological figure. Augustine reached a similar interpretation of this term as connected to this passage when he said,

> "Who is this, both Lamb and lion? He endured death as a lamb; he devoured it as a lion. Who is this, both lamb and lion? Gentle and strong, lovable and terrifying, innocent and mighty silent when he was being judged, roaring when he comes to judge."[79]

Given this interpretation, John's use of ἀρνίον allows for a more sophisticated and multifaceted understanding of who Christ is and, by proxy, what he is capable of accomplishing along with the christological implications thereof—something that other more narrowly defined terms are not able to achieve.[80] As will be revealed in the next chapter, this paradoxical interpretation of the Lamb in Revelation 5 will be supported by surveying its use in the remainder of this last canonical book.

---

79. Augustine, "Sermon 375."
80. See discussion on πάσχα and ἀρνίον above.

5

John's Christological Use of Lamb in Revelation

JOHN'S USE OF THE Lamb in Revelation 5:6–10 is only one branch of many in Revelation's Lamb Christology tree. Therefore, a brief survey of the copious other passages that use ἀρνίον must be provided along with a brief analysis of how each contributes to John's christological program. Not only do the passages that will be surveyed in the present chapter relate to what has already been concluded in the previous chapter by means of their shared use of ἀρνίον, but the contexts that employ this term are also parallel to the context of Revelation 5 by means of shared images, activities, characters, and connotations. Such connections, along with the presence of the definite article in every occurrence of Lamb following 5:6, suggest that what was concluded about ἀρνίον in its initial context might inform what is observed as it is used elsewhere in Revelation. Given what was concluded in the previous chapter, the present discussion will argue that the continuum existing between the two related but opposite poles of humility and glory implicit in John's use of ἀρνίον in Revelation 5:6 allows the author the creative license required for this term to be endorsed in a variety of different contexts throughout the remainder of his Apocalypse. As this presentation is given, the connotative range implicit within the term ἀρνίον will also prove to highlight different christological themes that can be applied to John's most central eschatological character.

John's Christological Use of Lamb in Revelation

The Lamb of Worship

There are many worshipful scenes throughout John's presentation,[1] a myriad of reasons present for why worship is offered,[2] differentiating ways in which worship is expressed,[3] and several recipients of worship explicit in the book of Revelation.[4] Therefore, it should come as no surprise, especially given the frequency with which John uses ἀρνίον and how often he incorporates praise throughout his work, that such literary phenomena would find themselves in the same context on more than one occasion. The first occurrence of this phenomenon is discovered within the passage discussed earlier (5:6–10) and what immediately follows.

At this pivotal juncture of John's presentation, the prophet has a vision that prompts a worshipful response.[5] This worship is motivated in large part because of what is learned about the Lamb as he emerges. After being made aware of the paradox of God's plan to redeem creation (that is, equal parts humble and glorious) upon the entrance of the Lion/Lamb, John reveals that this figure is especially worthy of adoration.[6] In fact, the surrounding context of this passage (Revelation 4–5) demonstrates that the Lamb is just as worthy of worship as God himself. What began as exaltation of God the

---

1. See Rev 4; 5; 7:9, 12; 8:3–4; 11:15–19; 15:2–4; 16:5–7; 19:1–8; 22:1–5.

2. Nakhro, "Manner of Worship," 165–80. These reasons include but are not limited to the following: worship for God's creative works (4:11; 14:7), worship for Christ's redemptive activity (5:9–10; 7:14–15), worship for God's realized design (11:15–18; 19:6), worship for righteous judgment (14:7; 15:4; 16:5; 19:2), and worship for consummated union (19:7–9).

3. Nakhro, "Manner of Worship," 165–80. Nakhro includes the following modes of worship in her delineation of apocalyptic worship: the offering of praise (4:6–11, 5:1–10, 11–14), the offering of thanks (11:17–18), the singing of songs (4:8, 11; 5:9–12; 7:10, 12; 11:15, 17; 12:10–12; 14:7; 15:3–5; 16:5–7; 19:2–3), the offering of prayers (5:8; 8:3–5; 16:5–7; 19:2), the offering of gifts (4:10; 21:24, 26), response to God' revelation (5:1–5, 8–14; 6:1, 3, 5, 7; 10:1–11; 19:13), anticipatory silence for God's intervention (8:1) and festive celebrations of God's goodness (7:9–10; 12:12; 18:20; 19:7).

4. God the Father, Jesus (the Lamb), Satan (see 2:9, 13–14; 3:9; 9:20), and the Beast (see chapter 13). For more on the worship of the beast see Peterson's *Engaging with God*, 266ff and Beale, *We Become What We Worship*, 241ff.

5. Witherington, *We Have Seen His Glory*, 21. Here, Witherington discusses how the pattern of worship following prophecy that found in Revelation 4–5 is not unlike what is witnessed in Isaiah 6 and Ezekiel 1. For an extended discussion on special considerations involving the context in which this passage is found, see Stuckenbruck, "Revelation 4–5," 235–248.

6. Kraybill, *Apocalypse and Allegiance*, 98. "From this moment onward, John is privy to the paradox of God's plan to redeem creation."

The Humility and Glory of the Lamb

Father in response to the theophany present in Revelation 4 transitions to worship of the Lamb in response to the christophany present in Revelation 5. In both passages a heavenly court of creatures and elders with instruments in hand lies prostrate before these figures in total praise. While God is called "worthy" because of his creative acts,[7] the Lamb is called "worthy" because of his completed redemptive work.[8] Even this completed work is depicted in the same paradoxical hues as the Lion/Lamb's entrance earlier (5:5–8). His "worthy"-ness to "take the book" (the same worthiness that is extended to God the Father in chapter 4) is dependent on his humble death ("for you were slain").[9] Because of this worthiness, the song of praise that was directed toward God in Revelation 4 ends with the inclusion of the Lamb in chapter 5 in a "new song" and new worshippers—"angels" (5:11) and "every created thing" (5:13).[10]

So evocative are the images of the worshipped Lamb that they have proven to be the inspiration behind more modern sacred works. The best known of these is the penultimate chorus of Handel's *Messiah*.[11] Drawing from Revelation 5:9, 12–13 Handel penned the following:

> "Worthy is the Lamb that was slain, and hath redeemed us to God by his blood, to receive power, and riches, and wisdom, and strength, and honor, and glory, and blessing. Blessing and honor, glory and power, be unto Him that sitteth upon the throne, and unto the Lamb, forever and ever. Amen."

---

7. Rev 4:11, "Worthy are You, our Lord and our God, to receive glory and honor and power; for You created all things, and because of Your will they existed, and were created."

8. Rev 5:9, "Worthy are You to take the book and to break its seals; for You were slain, and purchased for God with Your blood men from every tribe and tongue and people and nation."

9. Rev 5:9.

10. Kraybill, *Apocalypse and Allegiance*, 98ff. "The Lamb is worthy of praise, not just by the heavenly court, but also by all of creation. . . . In Jewish tradition, a new song is what the people of God offer in worship at a time of victory or deliverance. Most famously, Moses and the Israelites composed a hymn of praise at the Red Sea after their escape from the Egyptians (Exod 15:11–13) . . . [the Lamb's] authority issues from the fact that he, like Moses, has ransomed a people." See also Bauckham, "Creation's Praise of God," 61. "This news starts the expanding circle of worship that begins again with the living creatures and the elders (5:8–10) and then widens, as we have seen, to involve the whole creation. This new circle of worship is initially worship of the Lamb, though when all creatures worship their praise is for both God and the Lamb (5:13). Thus the worship of God in chapter 4 and the worship of the Lamb in chapter 5 finally come together."

11. Gorman, *Reading Revelation Responsibly*.

Echoes of the worthiness of the Lamb can also be heard in Matthew Bridges's nineteenth-century work "Crown Him with Many Crowns," which reads:

> "Crown him with many crowns, the Lamb upon his throne. Hark, how the heavenly anthem drowns all music but its own! Awake, my soul, and sing of Him who died for thee. And hail Him as thy matchless king through all eternity."[12]

All of these later celebrations of Revelation 5 capitalize on the worthiness of the Lamb who was acutely humbled in death and subsequently exalted to the highest heights of glory and worship.

However, worship of the Lamb is not limited to Revelation 5. In 7:9–12 John reveals the following:

> "After these things I looked, and behold, a great multitude which no one could count, from every nation and all tribes and peoples and tongues, standing before the throne and before the Lamb, clothed in white robes, and palm branches were in their hands; and they cry out with a loud voice saying, 'Salvation to our God who sits on the throne, and to the Lamb.' And all the angels were standing around the throne and around the elders and the four living creatures; and they fell on their faces, before the throne and worshiped God, saying, 'Amen, blessing and glory and wisdom and thanksgiving and honor and power and might, be to out God forever and ever. Amen.'"

Here, the same characters present in Revelation 5 (the multitude, angels, elders, creatures) resurface to offer their praise. In both contexts, worship of the Lamb is juxtaposed alongside the worship of God and specific reasons are offered for why the Lamb is worshipped. In Revelation 7, the "Palm branches" serve as a euphemism for what was celebrated earlier—that Christ was "slain, and purchased for God . . . men from every tribe."[13] As far as Revelation 5 and 7 are concerned, John's presentation of Christ's worthiness is consistent, especially given the way in which the Lamb is portrayed when he is worshipped in each. The Lamb's humility in death renders him uniquely glorious and worthy, and this worthiness testifies to his equality with God.

---

12. See also Edward Perronet's eighteenth-century hymn, "All Hail the Power of Jesus' Name," which reads, in part, "All hail the power of Jesus' name, let angel's prostrate fall."

13. See Rev 5:6; 9–10.

The Humility and Glory of the Lamb

Worship of the Lamb resurfaces in Revelation 13:8 following a description of the beast from the sea. In yet another striking contrast, John distinguishes between two different kinds of people—those of the beast and those of the Lamb. In this context, John reveals the following about those who follow the former: "All who dwell on the earth will worship him, everyone whose name has not been written from the foundation of the world in the book of life of the Lamb who has been slain."[14] Even here (as in Revelation 5), the Lamb, who is the keeper of the book of life, is portrayed as the one who has been killed. Inasmuch as God alone can give life and this power is said to be attributed to a slain sheep, this particular occurrence of the Lamb is a paradoxical demonstration of an incredibly high Christology. John's argument here is that the once-humiliated Lamb now gloriously supervenes over the book of life[15] and as such is an appropriate recipient of worship.

The final passage in which explicit worship and the Lamb intersect is Revelation 15:3-4. Like Revelation 5:6-14 and 7:9-12, Revelation 15:3-4 involves a praise and worship service set in the heavenly realm in which angels are present. Also, as in Revelation 13, Revelation 15 places the superiority of the Lamb alongside the inferiority of the beast. However, in Revelation 15, the song offered to the Lamb follows another hymn—the "song of Moses." In keeping with his theme of humility and glory and its connection to or association with the Lamb, John introduces the song of the glorious Lamb only after he describes Moses as a "bond-servant" and connects the two together by saying "and they sang the song of Moses, the bondservant of God, and the song of the Lamb."[16] Therefore, the song of Moses referenced here only forwards the theme of humility and glory further as Revelation 15 is a celebration of the Lord's strength and power that was realized when he saved a weak and vulnerable people.[17]

In all of these examples it is the glory of the Lamb (informed by his willingness to humble himself in death) that provides the reason for the worship he receives. Whether this theme is alluded to in the Lamb's comparison to other works (like the song of the bond-servant Moses),[18] the

---

14. Rev 13:8.

15. This he does in much the same way that he was capable of taking and opening the scroll in Rev 5.

16. Rev 15:3.

17. Exod 15:1ff.

18. Rev 15:3-4.

John's Christological Use of Lamb in Revelation

Lamb's authority over life (though slain),[19] or the reasons expressed for his worship (particularly as it concerns his sacrifice),[20] the paradoxical interpretation of the Lamb yielded earlier[21] and the christological implications thereof are supported, at least in part, every time Christ is worshipped in John's Apocalypse.

Lamb of Judgment

Not only is the uniquely humble and glorious Lamb introduced in 5:6 worthy of worship, "he is [also] the only one worthy to set in motion the events contained in the scroll."[22] The Lamb accomplishes this by taking the seven-sealed scroll and breaking its seals, thereby unleashing the judgment of God upon the earth. This process unfolds in chapters 6–19 of Revelation. Osborne concludes that "in one sense, the opening of the six seals flows naturally out of chapters 4–5, concluding with the worthiness of the Lamb to open the seals.[23] Although the worthiness of the Lamb to judge is initially mentioned in chapter 5,[24] it is not until Revelation 6 that one witnesses the execution of God's judgment.

Here, the apostle goes to great lengths to accentuate the Lamb's role as executor of God's judgment by both explicitly and implicitly acknowledging that he is the opener of each one of the seals. In 6:1, John reveals "then I saw when the Lamb broke one of the seven seals." In other words, the revelation of God's judgment is portrayed as dependent on the Lamb's choosing to break the seals according to his prerogative.[25] The Lamb's divine activity and supervening will is reiterated again and again as the formulaic pattern

---

19. Rev 13:8.
20. Rev 5:9; 7:9–12.
21. See discussion in chapter 4.
22. Thomas, *Revelation*, 415. See also Mounce, *Revelation*, 140. "He alone is worthy to set into motion those events that will bring about the culmination of human history." See also Tenney, *Interpreting Revelation*, 129, "Because he has redeemed the world, He has the right to judge it and to cleanse it for His use."
23. Osborne, *Revelation*, 269. See also Smalley, *Revelation of John*, 146. There, Smalley says "The Lamb opens all seven of the scroll's seals (cf. 5.1); for he alone is qualified to do so (cf. 5.5, 9), and thus to set in train events which will ultimately bring about the consummation of human history."
24. Rev 5:9.
25. Streett, *Here Comes the Judge*, 177.

of the seals unfolds in the remainder of chapter 6.[26] What is exclaimed by the recipients of this judgment in 6:16 emphasizes that the Lamb owns this program of wrath as he carries out the punishment of God.

> " and they said to the mountains and to the rocks, 'Fall on us and hide us from the presence of Him who sits on the throne, and from the wrath of the Lamb; for the great day of their wrath has come, and who is able to stand?'"

Here, the genitive case of Lamb (connected grammatically to "wrath") either indicates that the Lamb owns this wrath (possessive genitive), is the subject executing this wrath (subjective genitive), or is the agent responsible for the presence of the wrath experienced (genitive of agency).[27] These interpretative options both individually and collectively portray the Lamb as serving a prominent role in God's program of judgment upon the world.

The authority of the Lamb witnessed in his execution of judgment was foreshadowed in the first description given of this central character in 5:5–6. Although at first the Lamb appeared to be slaughtered, calling to mind his nonviolent death and great humility, he was also described as covered with horns—"a lamb with a ram's distinguishing characteristics of strength and power."[28] Inasmuch as horns are often used in the OT as symbols of strength, power, and violence,[29] it should come as no surprise that the horned Lamb of the Apocalypse would execute God's judgment in the remainder of Revelation with similar qualities. That said, John's wrathful and judging Lamb is unique as nowhere in the OT are lambs associated with wrath. In his own understanding of the anomaly that is this judging Lamb, Streett writes,

> "The symbol seems to work against itself, since John's meek lamb possesses fearful wrath. Yet this is precisely the point. The ἀρνίον is a multivalent symbol. Although he is a lamb, and a slain one at that, he possesses ramlike characteristics of strength and ferocity.

---

26. See repetition of relative temporal particle "ὅτε" in the phrase "ὅτε ἤνοιξεν τὴν σφραγῖδα" ("when he/the Lamb broke the . . . seal") in 6:3, 5, 7, 9, 12, and 8:1. These relative phrases indicate that what follows is dependent on the timing of the breaking of each seal as determined by the subject—the Lamb. See also Smalley, *Revelation of John*, 146–47.

27. For more discussion on these genetic case categories, see Wallace, *Greek Grammar*, 72ff and Young, *Intermediate NT Greek*, 23ff.

28. Streett, *Here Comes the Judge*, 177.

29. See Deut 33:17; 1 Kgs 22:11; 2 Chr 18:10; Ps. 22:21.

John's Christological Use of Lamb in Revelation

He has a role in judgment. Although the idea of the Messiah's role as judge also appears in other literature, John complicates the idea of Messiah as judge by making people afraid here not of the horseman (19:11–16) or of the glorious and intimidating figure that had initially appeared to John (1:9–20) but of the most innocuous and helpless symbol in Revelation."[30]

Streett acknowledges that while some commentators like Caird have tried to discredit the more violent and judgmental connotations of the Lamb,[31] the context of the Apocalypse of John clearly demonstrates that "Christ opens the seals, he instigates their cataclysm and thus fulfils a Messiah's role as judge."[32] On the judging Lamb's presence in Revelation 6–8, Streett concludes, "A lion was expected for a Messiah, yet a Lamb came; still, this Lamb is also a lion because of his terrible wrath."[33] In Revelation 14:10, John solidifies the Lamb's association with the wrath of God when he describes the doom of the worshipers of the beast. There he says,

> ". . . he also will drink of the wine of the wrath of God, which is mixed in full strength in the cup of his anger; and he will be tormented with fire and brimstone in the presence of the holy angels and in the presence of the Lamb."[34]

This commentary on the Lamb as it appears in Revelation 6–8 and in 14 is sympathetic to what was learned from the Lamb's initial entrance in Revelation 5. The fierceness of the wrath described, power and authority to judge, and ability to open the seals in Revelation 6–8 are consistent with the juxtaposition of the Lion and the Lamb in Revelation 5:5, the power and authority symbolized in the horns in 5:6, and the reason for the worship revealed in 5:9, respectively. Not only that, but that a humble Lamb is granted the authority to judge so completely in the first place is consistent with the

---

30. Streett, *Here Comes the Judge*, 178. For other passages on the Messiah as judge, see 4 Ezra 13:8–11, 37–38; 12:32–33; 1 Enoch 46:4–6; 49:4; 52:9; 55:4; 69:27; Pss Sol 17:21–25, 35.

31. See Caird, *Revelation of St. John*, 92, "There is no need to find a place in John's theology for any concept of the wrath of the Lamb, since it is not a phrase which he uses *propria persona*, but one which he puts on the lips of the terrified inhabitants of earth. It has its source not in the true nature of Christ, but in the tragic and paranoiac delusion to which they have surrendered themselves."

32. Streett, *Here Comes the Judge*, 179.

33. Ibid. See also Swete, *Apocalypse of St. John*, 93.

34. Rev 14:10. See Thomas, *Revelation 8–22*, 211, "The holy environment of the holy angels and the Lamb enhances the misery of punishment for the wicked."

general thematic juxtaposition of humility and glory that is delineated in chapter 4 of this argument.

Lamb of Leadership

The Shepherd

Not only does the Lamb lead the judgment unleashed upon the world's stage, he is described as leading his people. This presentation begins in chapter 7 as one of John's interludes breaks up the plot of the unfolding apocalyptic prophecy.[35] Therein, John reveals a remnant of 144,000 saved Jews and a numberless multitude clad in white robes that, much as they do in chapter 5, worship the Lamb in 7:9–12.[36] Thereafter, the robed multitude is identified as "the ones who come out of the great tribulation, and they have washed their robes and made them white in the blood of the Lamb."[37] Because the bleaching power of the blood of the Lamb (a paradox all its own) has been applied to this multitude, they "serve Him day and night" and "the Lamb in the center of the throne will be their shepherd, and will guide them to springs of the water of life; and God will wipe every tear from their eyes."[38] Just as the Lamb possesses the right to judge the world because of his sacrifice in chapter 5, the reappearance of "blood" in 7:14 demonstrates that he also possesses the right to lead his followers away from judgment because this same sacrifice has been applied to their sin.

In this context the Lamb is cast in a divine leadership role—a shepherd. This leadership role is further emphasized by the placement of the Lamb "in the center of the throne."[39] Much as he did in Revelation 5, the Lamb occupies the same throne space as the Father and is worshipped. This demonstrates the Lamb's equality with God and subsequently, a distinctly high Christology. However, the symbol of the shepherd adds even more to this christological presentation as in the OT God himself is called the "Shepherd of Israel,"[40] and is depicted as going before his flock (Ps 68:7), guiding

---

35. For other examples of such interruptions, see the following passages: Rev 7:1–17; 10:1–14; 12:1–14:20 and how they break up the apocalyptic narrative in Revelation.
36. See discussion above.
37. Rev 7:14.
38. Rev 7:15–16.
39. Rev 7:17.
40. Gen 48:15; 49:24; Ps 80:1.

John's Christological Use of Lamb in Revelation

his sheep (Ps 23:3), leading them to pasture (Jer 50:19) and springs of water (Ps 23:2; Isa 40:11), protecting them with his staff (Ps 23:4), gathering the dispersed (Zech 10:8; Isa 56:8), and carrying them in his bosom (Isa 40:11). Therefore, by applying the OT image of a shepherd to the apocalyptic Lamb, John is affirming that Jesus will be the same aid and savior of God's people in the *eschaton* that Yahweh was proved to be in the OT.[41]

However, a lamb is hardly the kind of image one would expect to be so closely associated with the leadership of God. The shepherding Lamb of Revelation employs a contrast of metaphors that is as striking as it is profound—"A Lamb is a submissive figure who is usually shepherded, yet this lamb shepherds others."[42] So radical is this conflation of symbols that Osborne even compares it with the Lion and the Lamb of chapter 5.[43] The shepherding Lamb of Revelation 7 is yet another example of humility and glory coming together to say something about how Christ is depicted in the Apocalypse of John.

That the Lamb would serve in this capacity in the end is not without precedent. In John 10:3, Jesus says that he calls his own sheep by name and leads them out. In John 10:11, he reveals, "I am the good shepherd; the good shepherd lays down His life for the sheep." These Johannine parallels demonstrate that it is precisely because the Lamb was willing to humble himself in laying down his life that he is uniquely qualified to lead his sheep into glory as their exalted shepherd. The Lamb's shepherding leadership, introduced first in Revelation 7, is reiterated in Revelation 14. There, in another Johannine interlude, the Lamb is leading those introduced in chapter 7 (the 144,000)—"these are the ones who follow the Lamb wherever He goes."[44] Revelation 14's inclusion of a throne room worship service, complete with thunderous noises, the four living creatures, and the elders, is also comparable to Revelation 4–5 and the introduction of the Lamb therein.[45]

---

41. Roloff, *Revelation of John*, 98.
42. Streett, *Here Comes the Judge*, 179.
43. Osborne, *Revelation*, 331.
44. Rev 14:4.
45. Rev 14:1–4. "Then I looked, and behold, the Lamb was standing on Mount Zion, and with Him one hundred and forty-four thousand, having His name and the name of His Father written on their foreheads. And I heard a voice from heaven, like the sound of many waters and like the sound of loud thunder, and the voice which I heard was like the sound of harpists playing on their harps. And they sang a new song before the throne and before the four living creatures and the elders; and no one could learn the song except

The Humility and Glory of the Lamb

The General

In addition to leading as a shepherd, the Lamb leads as an overcoming general. In another heavenly scene found in Revelation 12, John provides an account of a victory that the followers of the Lamb enjoy over the dragon. Part of his account reads as follows: "and they overcame him because of the blood of the Lamb and because of the word of their testimony, and they did not love their life even when faced with death."[46] Here, another paradox is witnessed as sympathizers of the Lamb are said to be successful in battle against formidable powers of evil—that is, the dragon and his angels.[47] Also, life and victory are placed alongside death and expected defeat in the phrase "they did not love their life even when faced with death." Such a comparison, though unexpected, fits the theme of victory in humiliation—a theme that is referenced by the phrase "blood of the Lamb" in 12:11. Though spilled blood is most often associated with the losers of war, here, the blood of the Lamb (spilled at his first advent) covers believers and marks their eschatological victory.[48] In other words, the bloody death of the Lamb in the past assures that his followers will enjoy a glorious conquest in the future.

Nowhere is the Lamb so closely associated with martyrdom in the context of John's Apocalypse than here in Revelation 12. Given the unique genre of this work—that it is apocalyptic as well as prophecy—it should come as no surprise that John would educate his audience (particularly those in the seven churches of Romans 2–3) in how they should live when the events predicted in this book come to pass.[49] Given the unique his-

---

the one hundred and forty-four thousand who had been purchased from the earth. These are the one who have not been defiled with women, for they have kept themselves chaste. These are the ones who follow the Lamb wherever He goes. These have been purchased from among men as first fruits to God and to the Lamb."

46. Rev 12:11.

47. In Rev 12:3–4 the dragon is described as follows: "Then another sign appeared in heaven: and behold, a great red dragon having seven heads and ten horns, and on his heads were seven diadems. And his tail swept a third of the stars of heaven and threw them to the earth..."

48. Mounce, *Revelation*, 239. "The great redemptive act that freed them from their sins (1:5) and established their right to reign (5:9) is the basis for their victory."

49. See Carey, *Ultimate Things*, 14: "Like other Jewish and Christian texts, apocalyptic literature aims to persuade its audiences to adopt certain dispositions, believe particular things, and behave in specific ways...many apocalyptic texts inspire resistance against the dominant imperial or internal powers of their day." See also Cook, *The Apocalyptic*

torical localization in which this work was written, some of the church's population were already facing martyrdom.[50] Therefore, "John links the Lamb with Christian martyrdom because the Lamb is the blueprint for martyrdom."[51] Because the Lamb suffered death though was not defeated, so too can those who follow him overcome by his blood and the word of their testimony.

Interestingly, as in many of the preceding contexts (particularly Revelation 5), after the Lamb is mentioned in connection with what is discussed, praise and adoration is demanded—"for this reason, rejoice oh heavens and you who dwell in them."[52] Similar praise is extended to the militaristic Lamb upon his victory over another set of imposing forces in Revelation 17.[53] After describing the beast and his followers and explaining how they will grow "drunk with the blood of the saints, and with the blood of the witnesses of Jesus,"[54] John continues in Revelation 17:14 by saying,

> "These will wage war against the Lamb and the Lamb will overcome them, because He is Lord of lords and king of kings, and those who are with Him are the called and chosen and faithful."

Both here and in Revelation 12, the Lamb is introduced in a context of "overcoming" an enemy of God's people as blood is being spilled and testimony is being offered.[55] Additionally, the Lamb is mentioned in the midst of a shocking contrast between a far more intimidating figure. In Revelation 12, the followers of the Lamb appear humble as they stand up to the

---

Literature, 195. "Revelation claims, however, that unconventional methods are key to reader's successful engagement with the world. They key player in Revelation is an immolated lamb, who conquers the forces of evil and death through humility, selflessness, and sacrifice (Rev 5:5–6, 9–10). Following the example of this lamb (Christ), readers are to effect tangible social change through faith, endurance, and willed suffering (Rev 12:11). What a paradox, that such means constitute effective, aggressive forces that upend the whole world." This comment comes as Cook delineates the apocalypticism inherent within Revelation itself.

50. See discussion of date in Appendix A.
51. Streett, *Here Comes the Judge*, 180.
52. Rev 12:12.
53. See Rev 17:1–13.
54. Rev 17:6.
55. Compare "and they will overcome" (12:11) to "and the Lamb will overcome" (17:14). Both passages use the verb "νικάω" and describe similar victories by a most unusual leader. Also compare "because of the blood of the Lamb and because of the word of their testimony" (12:11) to "with the blood of the saints, and with the blood of the witnesses of Jesus" (17:6).

The Humility and Glory of the Lamb

dragon.[56] In Revelation 17, the Lamb appears vulnerable against a beast.[57] However, this humility and vulnerability is turned on its head as in both passages the Lamb leads his followers in glorious victory over these foes.

The Host

The Lamb's leadership role in the Apocalypse of John evolves from a shepherd to a general and then to a host of a grand wedding feast in Revelation 19.

> ". . . Let us rejoice and be glad and give the glory to Him, for the marriage of the Lamb has come and His bride has made herself ready.' It was given to her to clothe herself in fine linen, bright and clean; for the fine linen is the righteous acts of the saints. Then he said to me, 'Write, "Blessed are those who are invited to the marriage supper of the Lamb."'"[58]

Inasmuch as the marriage and supper mentioned is framed by the genitive phrase "of the Lamb," it is clear that this figure presides over the festivities in some authoritative way. The Lamb's glorious authority is reiterated by his relationship to the bride who has at this point "made herself ready" for the marriage feast. In the OT, God's people are often described as a bride[59] and the idea of an eschatological wedding seemed to have broad circulation in early Christianity.[60] If, as John appears to insinuate, the Lamb is the bridegroom in Revelation 19,[61] then even here, he assumes a leadership role in the *eschaton* that is comparable to God's relationship with his people in the OT.

Like Revelation 4–5, Revelation 19 is a worshipful context. In 19:1–6 the same twenty-four elders and four living creatures that were first

---

56. See Rev 12:3–4, 13.

57. See Rev 17:8ff.

58. Rev 19:7–9.

59. Hos 2:19–20; Jer 3:20; Ezek 16:8–14; Isa 49:18; 50:1; 54:1–6.

60. Matt 9:15; 25:1–13; Mark 2:20; Luke 5:35; 2 Cor 11:2; Eph 5:25–32. See also Streett, *Here Comes the Judge*, 184.

61. This is supported by prediction made in Revelation 18:23 that says, "and the light of a lamp will not shine in you any longer; and the voice of the bridegroom and bride will not be heard in you any longer." Though the Lamb is not mentioned here, that he resurfaces in chapter 19 in connection with the bride seems to demonstrate, by something akin to the transition property, that the Lamb is, in fact, the bridegroom.

John's Christological Use of Lamb in Revelation

witnessed in Revelation 4 emerge for the last time to sing a final song immediately before John's favorite image for Christ emerges yet again. This works to connect the completed work of the eschatological Lamb in Revelation 19 to the emergence of this same figure in Revelation 5. The same Lamb that was humbled and slain at his first coming is that same Lamb who is imbued with unprecedented glory and authority in his second coming. This glory allows him to receive worship, judge the world, lead his people, vanquish enemies, and host a culminating celebration. This latest juxtaposition of humility and glory is perfectly comfortable among the many other comparisons and paradoxes present in the context of Revelation 19.[62]

Lamb of Heaven

The worshipped Lamb, following his program of judgment and leadership of his people, is also present in John's description of the final state in Revelation 21–22. Therein, following the final judgment, a new heaven and new earth take shape. As this new realm is introduced as follows:

> "Then one of the seven angels who had the seven bowls full of the seven last plagues came and spoke with me, saying, 'Come here, I will show you the bride, the wife of the Lamb.'"[63]

Following this introduction, many of the characteristics of the Lamb that were present earlier in John's work coalesce as the eternal state is described. His humility as inherent from his emergence (as witnessed in the term ἀρνίον),[64] his judgment (seen in the reference to the seven bowls and plagues),[65] and his final victory (as seen in the reference to his wife) is all referenced in Revelation 21:9.[66]

---

62. Roloff draws attention to the contrast between the beast (Rev 13:1–10; 19:20) and the Lamb and how the Lamb's bride contrasts with the evil harlot (Rev 17:1ff; 19:2) in *Revelation*, 212. See also Streett, *Here Comes the Judge*, 183–84. Smalley also identifies how the images of celebration and joy among God's people in 19:7–10 contrast sharply with the total annihilation of God's enemies in 19:17–21 in which an angel invites birds to feast on those who have been vanquished. *The Revelation to John*, 485.

63. Rev 21:9.

64. See conclusions reached in chapter 4.

65. See discussion above on the "Lamb as Judge."

66. The reference to "wife" immediately calls to mind the marriage supper celebrated in Revelation 19:7ff and the victory that followed. For more, see discussion above on "The Host."

The Humility and Glory of the Lamb

It is possible that at the end of Revelation, John is seeking to celebrate the work and ministry of his most central character *en toto* by describing the blessings and wonders of heaven. For instance, as the description of the New Jerusalem is given, the wall of the city is said to have "twelve foundation stones, and on them were the twelve names of the twelve apostles of the Lamb."[67] This description is one of the only direct historical references to the ministry of Jesus of Nazareth in the book of Revelation (aside from the possible allusions to his death, resurrection, and exaltation).[68]

Alongside these references to NT phenomena are allusions to OT institutions that Christ originally came to retrofit and fulfill. One example of this is witnessed as John's description of the New Jerusalem continues. As he tours heaven, he notices not only what is there, but what is missing—a temple, sun, and moon.

> "I saw no temple in it, for the Lord God the Almighty and the Lamb are its temple. And the City has no need of the sun or of the moon to shine on it, for the glory of God has illumined it, and its lamp is the Lamb."[69]

In this description John gives equal status to God and the Lamb as both are shown to illuminate the new city and serve as the center of corporate worship.[70] Unlike the OT institution of the temple and the space that was established between Christ and man following his ascension, in Revelation 21, God's presence is near, real, and palpable, requiring no mediation and no accommodating structures.[71] Also unlike the OT temple, "all whose

---

67. Rev 21:14.
68. Aune, *Revelation 17–22*, 1156–8. See also Streett, *Here Comes the Judge*, 184.
69. Rev 21:22–23.
70. For an OT reference in which God/Yahweh is depicted as a worship space, see Isa 8:14, which states "Then He shall become a sanctuary." For passages on God's illuminating power, see John 1:4, "In Him was life, and the life was the Light of men. The Light shines in the darkness, and the darkness did not comprehend it," and John 8:12, "Then Jesus again spoke to them, saying, 'I am the Light of the world; He who follows Me will not walk in the darkness, but will have the Light of life.'"
71. Roloff, *Revelation*, 245. Streett, *Here Comes the Judge*, 184, "God's presence is actual and direct, and the perfected salvation community no longer requires mediation but is itself the place in which God's presence dwells." See also Tenney, *Interpreting Revelation*, 133, "No structure nor ritual will be necessary and longer, for symbolism will be replaced by reality, and buildings will be superseded by the eternal presence of Christ."

John's Christological Use of Lamb in Revelation

names are written in the Lamb's book of life" will be allowed to enjoy these glorious blessings.[72]

The flood of OT imagery continues as John rounds the corner in the final chapter of his Apocalypse. In 22:1 he witnesses "a river of the water of life, clear as crystal coming from the throne of God and of the Lamb."[73] Streett believes that this might be a "christological interpretation of Psalm 110:1," which states, "The Lord says to my Lord: 'Sit at My right hand until I make your enemies a footstool for Your feet.'"[74] Here, as referenced in Revelation 3:21[75] and witnessed in Revelation 5:6–10,[76] the Lamb shares the throne and the sovereignty of God.[77] The image of the Lamb, one of the lowliest creatures imagined, occupying a place of such power, sovereignty, and authority is yet another endorsement of the same paradox of Christ's humility and glory that was originally established in Revelation 5 and has been traced throughout John's Apocalypse. The Lamb's authority is solidified in the final state once again in Revelation 22:3 when, as in 5:6, the Lamb is shown with God on the throne for the last time, surrounded by his servants.

The Lamb of heaven in Revelation 22 is, in many ways, like the Lamb who is worshipped in Revelation 5. In chapter 5, the Lamb occupies the throne and is worshipped for what he did in his first coming that renders him capable of setting into motion the things that are to transpire in the *eschaton* (judgment and victory). In chapter 22, the Lamb occupies the throne and is served for what he did in his second coming that validates his sovereignty over a new heaven and new earth.

---

72. Rev 21:27. See also Rev 13:8.

73. The river is frequently a symbol of life-sustaining power in the OT and in the ancient near east. For instance, Ezek 47:1–12 mentions a river flowing from the Temple. Zechariah 14:8 prophesizes a day when living waters will flow out from Jerusalem. Joel 4:18 predicts a day when a fountain shall come forth from the house of the Lord. Streett, *Here Comes the Judge*, 184.

74. Streett, *Here Comes the Judge*, 184.

75. Rev 3:21, "He who overcomes, I will grant to him to sit down with Me on My throne, as I also overcame and sat down with My father on His throne."

76. Rev 5:6–10, "And I saw between the throne (with the four living creatures) and the elders a Lamb standing, as if slain."

77. Aune, *Revelation 17–22*, 1176–7.

The Humility and Glory of the Lamb

Conclusion

This survey of John's use of Lamb in Revelation betrays a lush and flowering apocalyptic Christology. Ἀρνίον, a term that is not so heavily associated with any one particular referent or tradition, allows John the literary freedom required to ascribe multiple christological superlatives to Christ. In other words, according to John's apocalyptic prophecy, Christ is more than merely a sacrifice, Passover antitype, or vulnerable advocate for nonviolent resistance, and so on. He is all of these things and more because he has proven himself to be the most humble and therefore most glorious character in history. In perfectly satisfying the paradox of humility and glory witnessed first in Revelation 5, Christ is shown in the remainder of Revelation to be uniquely qualified to receive worship, serve as judge, lead his people, and establish himself as the illuminating "center of the new creation."[78]

---

78. Tenney, *Interpreting Revelation*, 117.

6

Conclusion

THIS CURRENT STUDY HAS successfully drawn attention to a conspicuous clearing in the christological forest in chapters 2–3, provided a robust interpretation of John's apocalyptic Lamb in chapter 4 (to replace the few and incomplete interpretations of this eschatological figure already in play), and given a nuanced delineation of how John employs ἀρνίον in Revelation for christological purposes in chapter 5. Such christological cultivation has yielded a better and more complete understanding of the apocalyptic Lamb and, by proxy, the apocalyptic Christ. With all of this complete, this final chapter will present the following: (1) a summary of what has been concluded from this study, (2) a brief analysis of some of the important theological implications that follow from this project's findings, and (3) an explanation of how this venture impacts Revelation studies and ought to instigate further areas of christological investigation.

The Humility and Glory of the Lamb

Revelation's central character is far more sophisticated than many have previously concluded. The apocalyptic Lamb serves as more than merely an antitype for the Passover lamb (πάσχα),[1] OT sacrifices (ἀμνός),[2] the suf-

---

1. See Bauckham, *Theology of the Book*, 70; deSilva, *Seeing Things John's Way*, 162ff; Roloff, *Revelation of John*, 78–79. See also similarities between Rev 5:9–19 and Exod 19:5–6.

2. See Tenney, *Interpreting Revelation*, 117; Beckwith, *Apocalypse of John*, 315; Carson

The Humility and Glory of the Lamb

fering servant,[3] Daniel's horned ram,[4] the substitutionary ram upon Mount Moriah,[5] or the "vulnerable lamb" of the LXX.[6] Although John's ἀρνίον may suffer similarities with each of these interpretative options to some degree, to delimit one's understanding of the leonine Lamb of Revelation to any one of these would be to settle for less than John intended. In fact, some of these interpretations (especially Loren Johns's vulnerable Lamb), were shown to be misguided as they are yielded by means of deductive approaches that prioritize the reader over the author.[7]

A better interpretation understands John's apocalyptic Lamb as the epitome of humility and glory. This is evidenced in the contextual–grammatical–canonical–historical analysis that was articulated in chapter 4. In this presentation, John's ability to juxtapose competing images (like that of the Lion and the Lamb) was highlighted along with their corresponding theological implications (glory and humility). Such an interpretation is sympathetic to what Robert M. Mounce concluded upon surveying the apocalyptic literature that John may be merging two ideas (the Lamb as victim and the Lamb as leader) when he employs the term ἀρνίον.[8] If this is true, John's use would be similar to what is found in 1 Enoch 90. There, the Maccabees are described as "horned lambs." Not only that, but in the Testament of Joseph, a lamb destroys the enemies of Israel. In concert with Mounce and Charles, David MacLeod believes that John uses the "unusual Lamb" in Revelation to suggest that like these other apocalyptic works, Jesus is the "warrior Lamb."[9]

---

and Moo, *Introduction*, 721.

3. See similarities between Isa 53 and the Lamb's description in Rev 5.

4. This is evidenced by the language shared between Revelation and Daniel, particularly, Daniel 8—8:3, "I looked up and saw a ram . . . I saw a ram charging westward . . . all beasts were" (8:3–4).

5. See Caspi and Cohen, "Binding [Aqedah]," 23–85.

6. Johns, *Lamb Christology*, 145ff.

7. For another example of this phenomenon applied to an interpretation of Lamb in Revelation, see Ewing's *Power of the Lamb*.

8. Mounce, "Christology of the Apocalypse," 43. Charles, *A Critical and Exegetical Commentary*, cxii–vi.

9. MacLeod, "Lion Who Is a Lamb," 337. See also Paul Middleton's *The Violence of the Lamb*. Therein, Middleton argues that the both martyrdom and violence are integral components to the worldview espoused by Revelation. The Lamb and his followers, according to Middleton, are certainly martyrs but also victorious in that martyrdom as their sacrifice is followed by resurrection, glory, and the judgment of God's enemies.

Conclusion

However, even the "warring/leading Lamb" interpretation of Mounce, Charles, and MacLeod is not complete. John's presentation of the Lamb in Revelation 5:6–10 and his application of this figure thereafter suggests that precisely because the ἀρνίον is the most humble and, by proxy, most glorious character imaginable, he is worthy of worship,[10] qualified to judge,[11] effective in leadership (as shepherd, general, and host),[12] and capable of illuminating heaven.[13] Therefore, it is reasonable to conclude that John does not appear to settle for an established typology to describe the protagonist of his vision. Instead, he establishes a new type/motif of his own in Revelation 5:6–10 and then endorses it in various ways as he records the vision of Christ he was provided.[14]

This new motif, because it uses a common symbol (a lamb), was familiar enough to John's audience to be intelligible (as this common pastoral animal probably called to mind any number of OT images). However, because John endorses a relatively unique term (ἀρνίον), it is malleable enough to be imbued with more general connotations (humility and glory). Because of its unique semantic range, ἀρνίον is employable in a wide variety of eschatological contexts and capable of eliciting many christological considerations.[15] If "one fruitful approach to the imagery of the Apocalypse is to concentrate on major distinct images,"[16] then the present study of the Lamb and the implications thereof are not without merit. Also, if, as Richard Bauckham admits, "the juxtaposition of more than one image with a single referent is characteristic of John's visions,"[17] then it is possible, if not, expected that John would infuse a single term with multiple associations.

This conclusion successfully cultivates an often-neglected christological theme in John's Apocalypse. Few, if any, compelling analyses of the eschatological Lamb have been offered. However, some have at least articulated the many ways in which the Lamb of Revelation is employed in

---

10. See Rev 5:8, 12; 7:10; 13:8; 15:3.

11. See Rev 6:1; 7, 9, 16; 14:10.

12. See Rev 7:14, 17; 12:11; 14:1, 4; 17:14; 19:7, 9.

13. See Rev 21:14, 23, 27; 22:2–3.

14. Carson and Moo, *Introduction*, 721. "John has restricted the typical Jewish apocalyptic perspective with his christological focus."

15. These include but are not limited to the following: Christ is worthy of worship, Christ is the perfect and coming judge, Christ is the eschatological victorious warrior King, and Christ is the glory of heaven.

16. Bauckham, *Climax of Prophecy*, 177.

17. Bauckham, *Climax of Prophecy*, 179.

The Humility and Glory of the Lamb

John's final canonical work. One example is found in *The Lamb of God: Expositions in the Writings of St. John*. Therein, W. Roberston Nicoll portrays the Lamb as the following: the holy, harmless, and undefiled Lamb, the sin-bearing Lamb, the Lamb in the midst of the throne, the Lamb opening the sealed book, the warrior Lamb, the marriage of the Lamb, and the wrath of the Lamb.[18] Although these findings are not exactly congruent with the categories provided in the previous chapter, they are consistent with this argument's insistence on John's ability to employ this term in many ways and in varying contexts.

Similarly, in *Interpreting Revelation*, Merrill Tenney betrays an appreciation for John's diverse use of Lamb in Revelation. For Tenney, although the sacrificial character of the Lamb appears to be stressed by the phrase "standing as if slain," this trait is also "the reason for His worthiness."[19] Tenney also stresses this Lamb's unique office as Judge when he says, "because He has redeemed the world, He has the right to judge it and to cleanse it for His use."[20] Even further, Tenney also reflects on the Lamb's victory and the culminating marriage supper of the Lamb that he hosts in Revelation 19.[21] As with Nicoll, these conclusions betray an affinity with what has been yielded in this present work (particularly in chapter 5). Even Carson and Moo reveal something of Revelation's complicated Christology when they say, "while Revelation focuses on Christ's glory, power, and role in judgment, the cross is never out of sight."[22]

However, what all of these works (and others) lack is the kind of interpretation of ἀρνίον that explains why this label can be used in the way that it is in Revelation. Such an interpretation has been provided in this present work. In seeking to describe the many christological presentations/activities he witnesses in his apocalyptic vision, John employs a unique and connotatively neutral term[23] in Revelation 5:6 upon Christ's grand entrance that he then ornaments with the paradoxical motif of acute humility alongside supreme glory. In so doing, he allows himself the use of a title that he can then implement throughout the remainder of his work to present vari-

---

18. Nicoll, *Lamb of God*, 73–74.
19. Tenney, *Interpreting Revelation*, 128–29.
20. Tenney, *Interpreting Revelation*, 129.
21. Tenney, *Interpreting Revelation*, 130.
22. Carson and Moo, *Introduction*, 721.
23. That ἀρνίον is connotatively neutral in Revelation 5:6–10 is also supported by the fact that it is anarthrous in this context.

Conclusion

ous christological truths that are grounded in a consistent and theologically meaningful theme.[24] What are these truths and how might we use them to further cultivate the clearing in the christological forest identified earlier?

Theological Implications

Christological Implications

Though many christological implications of John's Lamb are worth considering, three are worthy of special attention as they figure prominently in what John conveys in his apocalyptic presentation. First, in choosing the Lamb as his primary symbol for Christ, John reminds the reader that the Christ of the *eschaton* is the same Christ that the Baptist identified when he said, "Behold, the Lamb of God who takes away the sins of the world!"[25] This reference also connects Christ to the many sacrificial lambs used in the OT as payment for sins. Preeminent among these OT sacrifices was the Paschal lamb slain at the first ever Passover.[26] This lamb was killed so that God's people would be spared from his holy wrath.

Though John's description of the Lamb "standing as if slain" and Revelation's use of themes borrowed from the exodus narrative support these familiar images and corresponding theological considerations, the apostle's juxtaposition of the Lamb against the image of the Lion and the unique word employed suggest that he wants to say something more about what he saw—something that is not limited to any previously established christological image/type. Although John desires continuity between the Christ of Revelation and the Christ of his gospel and the OT, the apostle also wants to suggest that the Lamb of his vision is far greater and more complex than any previous iteration/presentation could possibly articulate.

Therefore, the apocalyptic Lamb is John's unique attempt at demonstrating the highest Christology he can in response to what he witnessed in his vision. In other words, although Christ is the same as before (the sacrifice and satisfaction for wrath), he is also far greater than previously illustrated. Like multiplying several integers to reach an enormous number,

---

24. Again, the contextual parallelisms indicated in chapter 5 and the addition of the article in every use of ἀρνίον save Revelation 5:6 suggest that what is celebrated/articulated about Christ later in the Apocalypse is semantically/hermeneutically connected to what was presented upon the Lamb's first emergence.

25. John 1:29.

26. See Exod 12.

The Humility and Glory of the Lamb

John takes familiar christological symbols (like the Lion and the Lamb) and multiplies them together to yield something far more sophisticated. That said, the Christ of Revelation is consistent and, in fact, the same Christ that has always been. In Revelation, he is simply awarded the kind of description that best fits his unmatched humility and unsurpassed glory.

The image of the Lamb also implies that Christ, even in the Apocalypse, is an incarnational agent for change. The vision that John observed describes Christ as an earthly pastoral figure—a Lamb—not an otherworldly/celestial chimera beyond description. This suggests that Christ ought to be understood in light of and appreciated for the work that he accomplished while on the earth. This idea is reinforced by the marks of death the Lamb bears in the throne room. These marks call the attention of anyone who looks upon them to the completed work of redemption that the bearer accomplished upon his first advent.

Although the redemptive activity characteristic of Christ's incarnation appears to highlight his humility (as does a slain lamb interrupting an otherwise glorious spectacle in the heavenly throne room), such humiliation leads to unparalleled glory in the worship that is directed to him in Revelation 5[27] and the authority that is implied in his ability to break the seals in Revelation 6.[28] Humility leading to glory is consistent with Paul's ruminations on the incarnation found in Philippians 2:5–11,

> "Have this attitude in yourselves which was also in Christ Jesus, who, although He existed in the form of God, did not regard equality with God a thing to be grasped, but emptied Himself, taking the form of a bond-servant, and being made in the likeness of men. Being found in appearance as a man, He humbled Himself by becoming obedient to the point of death, even death on a cross. For this reason also, God highly exalted Him, and bestowed on Him the name which is above every name, so that at the name of Jesus every knee will bow, of those who are in heaven and on earth and under the earth, and that every tongue will confess that Jesus Christ is Lord, to the glory of God the Father."

---

27. Rev 5:9, "Worthy are You to take the book and to break its seals; for You were slain, and purchased for God with Your blood men from every tribe and tongue and people and nation"; Rev 5:12, "Worthy is the Lamb that was slain to receive power and riches and wisdom and might and honor and glory and blessing"; Rev 5:13, "To Him who sits on the throne, and to the Lamb, be blessing and honor and glory and dominion forever and ever."

28. See Rev 6ff.

Conclusion

By referencing the incarnation itself (along with its many christological consequences), via the image of the slain Lamb, John draws the reader's attention to the humility and glory that is integral to any responsible Christology.

However, there is a proleptic element involved in Jesus' work that is satisfied in a second incarnation found in Revelation 19. After the Lamb enjoys a marriage feast, he enters into the worldly realm again, only this time he does so as a victorious warrior king. This glorious warrior successfully overwhelms his enemies (the beast, false prophet, and Satan) and ushers in a period of peace. Therefore, the same Christ who was an agent of creation[29] entered that creation as a humble agent of redemption (the sacrificial Lamb) and will one day reenter creation as a glorious agent of eschatological victory (the warring ἀρνίον).[30] Christologically speaking, the Lamb of the Apocalypse affords John the ability to connect what Christ has done throughout redemptive history to who he will prove to be in the end. The Lamb also helps define Christ as the incarnational agent of God (who enters and reenters the world on behalf of God's people) and the ultimate victor over evil.

Ecclesiological Implications

Such conclusions work together to inspire the ecclesiological implications of John's apocalyptic Christology. Inasmuch as John addresses his prophetic apocalypse as a letter to the seven churches and as the contents of the apostle's work appear to communicate a message of some relevance to the people of God in any socio-historical localization, it is important to identify how John's Lamb Christology is applied ecclesiologically. First, as the Lamb serves as the epitome of humility and glory, it is incumbent upon the followers of the Lamb to model the same traits as they persevere on the world's stage. Loren Johns concludes as much when he says of the apostle that,

> ". . . he represents Christ as lamb in order to represent the vulnerability that inevitably accompanies a faithful witness. Such a faithful and vulnerable witness is what enables the believers to share in

---

29. See John 1; Rev 1:8.

30. Nicoll, *Lamb of God*, 73–74, "He is the Lamb, the very ideal of innocence and gentleness, and yet He is the Judge, the enemy, the warrior. And here we have Him figured as the great antagonist of the beast, whom He is ultimately to subdue."

The Humility and Glory of the Lamb

Christ's victory (3:21). Such vulnerability is no weakness; instead, it proves triumphant over the power of evil."[31]

Though vulnerability in Johns's work might be more appropriately understood as humility (as this current work has argued), the sentiment is much the same. Humility, especially as it concerns a godly witness, not only "proves triumphant" as Johns suggests, it is in keeping with the character of the most humble and most glorious figure—the Lamb.

The persecution that is depicted in John's prophecy and the existential threat many in his immediate audience faced makes walking humbly a difficult task. Thankfully, the apostle offers the Lamb and the unusually high Christology associated with him to the church in an effort to encourage faith in the midst of struggle and galvanize steadfastness in the midst of pain. Though the Lamb is described as slain, he is "standing" nonetheless.[32] Not only that, but this same Lamb is ultimately shown to be victorious over the enemies of God's people, the judge of a fallen world, and the founder of a new and glorious kingdom. Therefore, one might say that John's christological program in general and the Lamb Christology in particular provides the church with a proper point of reference upon which to fix its gaze as it endures a brave new world (that is, within the first century context or within any context thereafter). Against the blinding light of the Lamb's glory, John hopes that the things of this world and any subsequent tribulation associated would grow strangely dim.

Another ecclesiological implication the apocalyptic Lamb affords the church is a christo-centric theology. Although this may have been inferred by the scope and focus of this study, it is worth demonstrating how John chooses to employ the Lamb throughout Revelation to this end. First, John awards the Lamb a prominent focal point at the peak of a literary crescendo that begins at the beginning of chapter 4. As mentioned earlier, the crisis introduced in the throne-room scene[33] is satisfied when the leonine Lamb emerges for the first time and successfully opens the seven-sealed scroll, thereby setting in motion the events of the *eschaton*. In many ways, John's description of the vision provided suggests that the Lamb is the hinge upon which the present age closes and the coming age opens. This important role

---

31. Johns, *Lamb Christology*, 204.

32. Rev 5:6.

33. The crisis involved no one being able to open the seven-sealed book. This crisis moved John to tears, "then I began to weep greatly because no one was found worthy to open the book or to look into it" (Rev 5:4).

Conclusion

demonstrates that Christ is central not only to salvation history past, but salvation history future.

A Christo-centric theology for the church is also supported by the Lamb's placement in the throne room. He is shown to be "between the throne (with the four living creatures) and the elders," thereby revealing his mediating position between the church and God. Soon thereafter, the Lamb moves from his position between the elders and the throne to the throne itself. He then takes the book "out of the right hand of Him who sat on the throne." Once the Lamb assumes this position next to the one on the throne, he receives worship and is literally linked to its occupant. This link is fleshed out in John's description of the new heaven and new earth. There he describes the lack of a temple and says "for the Lord God the Almighty and the Lamb are its temple."[34] Immediately following this comment, the apostle, after identifying the lack of a sun and moon says, "for the glory of God has illumined it, and its lamp is the Lamb."[35] Therefore, the Lamb's position next to the throne and close association with God the Father (which are granted to him because of his unsurpassed humility and subsequent glory) demonstrate John's Christo-centric bent—a bent that John hoped the church would appreciate, understand, and apply as they endured until the end. The Christo-centric focus is further reiterated by the prolific use of the term ἀρνίον in a variety of contexts within Revelation.[36]

Implications for Revelation Studies

Though it was not central to the conclusions reached, this argument assumed that John, the apostle, is the author of Revelation. However, now that a better understanding of the Lamb of the Apocalypse has been provided, there is another argument to be made that supports the idea that the beloved disciple did, in fact, write the last book of the Canon. John's gospel is the only other NT work to use a form of ἀρνίον for Lamb.[37] Also,

---

34. Rev 21:22.

35. Rev 21:23.

36. Worship contexts (Rev 5:8, 12; 7:10; 13:8; 15:3), judgment contexts (Rev 6:1, 7, 9, 16; 14:10), leadership/victory contexts (Rev 7:14, 17; 12:11; 14:1, 4; 17:14; 19:7, 9), and celestial glory contexts (Rev 21:14, 23, 27; 22:2–3).

37. John 21:15, "So when they had finished breakfast, Jesus said to Simon Peter, 'Simon, son of John, do you love me More than these?' He said to Him, 'Yes Lord; You know that I love You.' He said to him, 'Tend My lambs (ἀρνία).'"

The Humility and Glory of the Lamb

nowhere is the theme of the humility and glory of Christ more recognizable than in Johannine literature.[38] Therefore, one might suggest that analysis of the Lamb favors Johannine authorship for Revelation.

As this study is predominately preoccupied with the Christology of the Apocalypse and how this is informed by or expressed in John's pervasive use of a single term, the specific date of the last canonical book is of little consequence. That said, one concession made earlier in this study (based on the best evidences—see Appendix A) was that Revelation was probably written around AD 90.[39] In light of what has been learned about the Lamb, one might argue that the uniqueness of the term used and the multivalent and highly sophisticated Christology it betrays supports this late date. As ἀρνίον enjoys very little NT precedent, this word might betray an evolution of language. Had the Apocalypse been penned earlier, one might expect a more commonly used term for Lamb instead of something that appears new/unique, especially as it is employed for Christ.

Earlier it was argued that the genre of the John's Apocalypse is highly unique and complicated. Possessing attributes of a letter, prophecy, and apocalypse, this study, like many others, has chosen to argue that Revelation is an anomaly within the literary world and multi-faceted in its style. Redacting the genre down to merely one form would run the risk of misinterpreting entire sections of John's work. What has been learned about the Lamb supports this claim as this major theme and symbol, like the genre in which it is found, is not as one-dimensional as some have suggested. These and other considerations reveal that studies of major symbols, images, and themes might serve as tools that, if properly used, can inform important biblical background debates.

Also, if much has been gained from analysis of John's use of Lamb and the christological implications thereof, might there be much to gain from similar analyses of other christologically heavy phenomena in the book of Revelation? For instance, it is quite possible that a better appreciation for

38. See Rainbow, *Johannine Theology*, 183. Here, Rainbow draws parallels between "Word made flesh" and "Lamb as if slain." If appears as though John uses "Word made flesh" (John 1) to capitalize on the divinity of the son (by mixing humble flesh with a glorious logos) in his Gospel. In the apocalypse, he uses "Lamb standing as if slain" (Rev 5) to demonstrate the glory of the Son in the celestial throne room by accentuating his humility. See also John 4:34; 10:11ff; 13:5–15. In each of these passages, Jesus, either by example or by teaching (or both) places glory alongside humility.

39. That said, this study is also sympathetic to D. Warden who acknowledges the difficulty of dating the Apocalypse, ultimately conceding that an actual date is uncertain. Warden, "Imperial Persecution," 203–12.

Conclusion

Christ and his work (especially his eschatological work) would be gained by juxtaposing the Lamb and another apocalyptic characters like the beast.[40] While John casts the beast with a spirit of falsity,[41] as a member of an unholy trinity,[42] and "just like Satan who indwells and empowers him,"[43] the apostle describes the Lamb as an illuminator of truth,[44] a member of the holy Trinity,[45] and as occupying the same throne space as God.[46] A meaningful study that pits these two characters against each other might yield even more theological insights concerning the Lamb, his foe, and the followers of each.

In addition to studies performed on the Lamb and the eschatological competition the Lamb has with the beast, one might also choose to investigate the complex descriptions of Christ throughout John's Apocalypse in an effort to yield a more christologically rich understanding of what John saw in his vision. One description offered of Christ is found in Revelation 1:13–18.[47] There, the titles assigned to Christ are utilized in the introductions made to the seven churches in chapters 2–3. This renders this first description of Christ not only theologically significant, but contextually important. Another detailed delineation of Christ is found in 19:11–16.[48]

---

40. See Rev 12–13.

41. Hindson, "Antichrist," 23–26. See also 1 John 2:18–22; 4:1–3.

42. Members of this unholy trinity include the following: Satan (the father), Antichrist (the son), and the False Prophet (an antithetical Holy Spirit). See Rev 12–13.

43. Elwell and Comfort, *Bible Dictionary*, 265.

44. This is witnessed in his ability to open the scroll and reveal God's judgment. This is also witnessed in the Lamb connection with the "Word of God" in Rev 19:13 and in John 1.

45. See Rev 5:6; 22:1.

46. See Rev 5–6.

47. "I saw one like a son of man, clothed in a robe reaching to the feet, and girded across His chest with a golden sash. His head and his hair were white like white wool, like snow; and His eyes were like a flame of fire. His feet were like burnished bronze, when it has been made to glow in a furnace, and His voice was like the sound of many waters. In his right hand He held seven stars, and out of His mouth came a sharp two-edged sword; and His face was like the sun shining in it strength . . . saying, 'Do not be afraid; I am the first and the last, and the living one; and I was dead, and behold, I am alive forevermore, and I have the keys of death and of Hades.'"

48. "And I saw heaven opened, and behold, a white horse, and He who sat on it is called Faithful and True, and in righteousness He judges and wages war. His eyes are a flame of fire, and on His head are many diadems; and He has a name written on Him which no one knows except Himself. He is clothed with a robe dipped in blood and His name is called The Word of God. . . . From His mouth comes a sharp sword, so that with it

The Humility and Glory of the Lamb

This description takes place following the song that is sung to celebrate the marriage of the Warrior-Messiah (Christ), and his bride (the church).[49] However, this marriage cannot take place until victory is secured following the battle against the antichrist and his minions. This unique context informs the description of Christ in 19:11–16 as a mounted, bejeweled, armed, bloodied, and capable warrior. What might this and other lengthy descriptions of Christ have by way of christological significance?

Another integral christological label worthy of investigation is "Alpha and Omega." Found at the beginning (Rev 1:7–8) and near the end of John's Apocalypse (Rev 22:13), this title acts as an *inclusio* that houses at least one major theological consideration Revelation makes—that the end (as well as the beginning) is more about a person than it is about events. It is clear in 1:7–8[50] that although this title can be attributed both to God and Christ, the context of both passages in which this phrase is found points to the latter. Christ is the subject in verses 1–7 and, as in much of Revelation, he is equated with God.[51] This appears to be an apocalyptic continuation of the divine themes attributed to Jesus that were introduced in John and in 1 John.[52] Revelation 22:13 reiterates the same themes that are endorsed in 1:8.[53] In the context of the new creation, John, either consciously or subconsciously, suggests that in light of his second coming, Jesus is sovereign over both the beginning (when he played the role of agent in creation) and the end of time (when he will serve as the agent of a new creation).

He may strike down the nations, and He will rule them with a rod of iron; and He treads the wine press of the fierce wrath of God, the Almighty. And on His robe and on His thigh He has a name written, King of Kings and Lord of Lords."

49. See Rev 19:1–8.

50. Rev 1:8, "'I am the Alpha and the Omega' says the Lord God, 'who is and who was and who is to come, the Almighty.'"

51. Thomas, *Revelation*, 80.

52. John 1:1, "In the beginning was the Word, and the Word was with God and the Word Was God." 1 John 1:1, "What was from the beginning, what we have heard, what we have seen with our eyes, what we have looked at and touched with our hands, concerning the Word of Life."

53. Rev 22:13, "I am the Alpha and the Omega, the first and the last, the beginning and the end."

Conclusion

These potential studies and the completed analysis of the Lamb of Revelation in this present work demonstrate that John's Apocalypse is saturated with christological content—content that has been in many ways historically overlooked and/or underappreciated. Although this project has successfully cultivated one area of the clearing in the christological forest, much remains undone by way of utilizing Revelation for all that it has to offer. John's Apocalypse is not just a prophecy of coming events; it is a christological treatise that is highly interested in *who* is returning. As John sought to encourage the churches to which he was writing as they endured their brave new world, he was given a vision not only of future events, but of a Lamb whose character (equal parts humble and glorious) and eschatological work can inspire any community of believers and encourage perseverance among its saints.

Appendix A
A Word on Revelation's Date and Authorship in Connection with the Apocalyptic Lamb

WHO GAVE US REVELATION? When was it given? What is Revelation, anyway? These are the kinds of questions that are typically answered before any interpretation and/or analysis of biblical literature can be reached. In considering these inquiries as applied to the Book of Revelation, what follows in this appendix is a brief survey of biblical background issues that is intent on highlighting any relationship such considerations may have for a better understanding of Revelation's christological program. It will be concluded from this presentation that while these background considerations are integral to understanding Revelation itself, ultimately they prove peripheral to the discussion contained in this work, especially as it pertains to apocalyptic Christology in general and the Lamb Christology in particular.

An Examination of Revelation's Authorship in Relation to the Lamb Christology

According to Revelation 1, the Apocalypse does not emerge as a pseudonymous document. In fact, the author clearly identifies himself as "John" no less than four times in this work.[1] This indicates that the author is using his identity to legitimize his role as witness to the revelatory visions he narrates.[2] However, the question "which John?" has been the subject of much debate throughout the millennia. Although issues surrounding the specific identity of the author have failed to maintain the interest of a growing

---

1. Rev 1:1, 4, 9; 22:8.
2. Aune, *Revelation*, xlix.

number of scholars in recent years,[3] the debate still exists as several possible authors are alleged. These include but are not limited to the following: John, the son of Zebedee and the disciple of Jesus Christ; John the elder; John Mark; another John; John the Baptist; Cerinthus; and someone using the name of John the Apostle as a pseudonym.[4]

At least three of these choices possess little, if any, real merit. First, Dionysius the Great, bishop of Alexandria in the mid-third century, suggested that John Mark (the youth who accompanied Paul and Barnabas on the first missionary journey) could have been the author of Revelation. However, he retracted his position shortly after positing the idea on the grounds that John Mark returned to Jerusalem instead of going with Paul and Barnabas into Asia (the very region that housed the churches addressed in Revelation 2–3).[5] Additionally, there are few significant literary similarities between Mark's Gospel and Revelation. The only one to have argued that John the Baptist authored Revelation was J. M. Ford.[6] However,

---

3. Aune believes that the loss of interest in identifying the specific author of Revelation appears be a result of the following: (1) the fact that many books in both the Old and New Testaments are anonymous and not a lot is offered by way of linking these works to historical figures; (2) the preoccupation with Revelation's authorship from the mid-second century on has proven more theologically motivated than historically rooted; (3) ancient authors appear to have understood their role as author–editor more than merely an author; (4) many written works appear to have gone through several stages of rewriting, rendering the isolation of the original author tenuous; (5) Many books in the New Testament have been written under the names of people more prominent than the actual author; (6) so little can be known for sure about the authors themselves, even if they are identified, calling into question the merits of this pursuit from the beginning; (7) the author is not divorced from his/her audience and context and therefore cannot be understood in isolation anyway; and (8) the implied author and audience has usurped the actual author/audience as the predominant supervening force behind a text, its meaning, and application. *Revelation*, xlvii–xlix.

4. List derived from Osborne, *Revelation*, 2. Osborne's list is more exhaustive than Aune's, who only lists five possibilities: John the apostle, John the Elder, Cerinthus, John Mark, and John the Baptist. See Aune, *Revelation*, l. Still others delimit the list down even further. Paige Patterson in his commentary only acknowledges John the apostle, John the Elder, another John, and John the Baptist. See Patterson, *Revelation*. Beale is only willing to take three possibilities seriously: John the apostle, another John (sometimes referred to as John the Elder), and someone else using "John" as a pseudonym. Beale, *Book of Revelation*, 34.

5. See Mounce, *Revelation*, 9. See also Eusebius, *Hist. Eccl.*, 7.25.

6. Ford, *Revelation*, 28–37. Her view argues that John the Baptist and his followers produced Revelation in three stages: chapters 4–11 as visions given to John before Jesus' ministry began, chapters 12–22 that were completed by one of John's disciples sometime before 70 AD, and chapters 1–3 by a final editor.

A Word on Revelation's Date and Authorship

Ford's position appears to be just that—her position and hers alone.[7] Also, the possibility of Cerinthus was only offered by two early groups that were motivated primary by an opposition to Montanism (and, by proxy, Revelation itself, which was heavily endorsed by the Montanists). However, no serious connection between the gnostic Cerinthus is witnessed in Revelation, especially when one considers how un-gnostic the Apocalypse appears in many passages.[8]

The next least compelling choice, according to R. H. Charles, is the view that someone wrote the work while using the name of John the Apostle as a pseudonym. In what is argued to be the most comprehensive discussion on Apocalyptic authorship debate,[9] Charles claims that there is not "a shred of evidence" or "the shadow of a probability for such a hypothesis,"[10] especially when one considers that the reasons for using pseudonymity were no longer valid after the emergence of Christianity.[11] Upon observing the author's distinct claims of prophet status and reticence concerning apostleship, Charles's own position was that a prophet named John (not the apostle John), wrote the Apocalypse. However, this view has never metastasized into a viable option as the author of the Apocalypse appears to have the kind of authority over the Asian churches that New Testament prophets did not know.[12] This authority, along with a myriad of other considerations (widespread circulation, early acceptance, etc.), calls into question any position that claims some other John or a "Johannine school" is responsible for writing this work.[13]

---

7. Osborne believes that most find it difficult to explain how a book brought about by a community of John the Baptist's disciples would have ever been accepted into the Canon. Osborne, *Revelation*, 2. Aune concurs with Osborne in saying that few if any have accepted this possibility. Aune, *Revelation*, l.

8. See Revelation 19's portrayal of God's interaction with the physical world, Revelation 20's prophecy concerning the resurrection of the body, and Revelation 21–22's description of a renewed earth and physical paradise as evidences against gnostic-leaning teachings.

9. Patterson, *Revelation*, 18.

10. R. H. Charles, *A Critical and Exegetical Commentary*, xxxix.

11. Mounce, *Revelation*, 9.

12. Mounce, *Revelation*, 9.

13. For an example of this position see J. N. Sanders's view that some Sadducean aristocrat is responsible for having edited Revelation. Sanders, "St. John on Patmos," 75–85. Therein, Sanders concludes that while the exact identity of the author cannot be determined, much of his social identity can from the text itself. For a response to this view and others like it, see Carson, Moo, and Morris, *Introduction*, 367–71; Guthrie, *New*

Appendix A

The two remaining options for Revelation's authorship—John the Apostle and John the Elder—are not only the most compelling, but also the most widely held. Historically, the former garnered a great deal of early support. In the mid-second century, Justin Martyr affirmed that the apostle John was the author of the Apocalypse[14] and this appeared to be the accepted view among other early church fathers.[15] However, Marcion rejected this view at around the same time (mid-second century). Thereafter, Dionysius, Eusebius, Cyril of Jerusalem, and Chrysostom followed suit. It was Eusebius who believed that he discovered the answer to Revelation's authorship in Papias, who refers to someone called "John the Elder."[16] Ever since this view emerged, different schools have pulled from various data sets in an effort to argue their respective positions.

In addition to the testimony of the early church fathers, those in favor of John the Apostle acknowledge that there are plenty of similarities both textually and theologically between the Gospel of John and the Apocalypse of John. For instance, Osborne claims that these are the only two New Testament books that argue for the deity of Christ on the basis of the "oneness motif" between God and Jesus. These two texts are also unique in their shared theme of mission via repentance.[17] Mounce also reveals that both John's Gospel and the Apocalypse quote Zech. 12:10[18] "using the same Greek verb (ἐκκεντέω), which in turn is not used by the LXX and is found nowhere else in the NT."[19] Additionally, C. G. Ozanne has uncovered a list of terms that are common to the Gospel of John and the Apocalypse. These include the following: "conquer," "keep the word," "keep the commandments," "dwell," "sign," "witness," and "true."[20] Furthermore, Guthrie asks, how can one account for such a bold departure from the apocalyptic

---

Testament Introduction, 1011–28; and Ellis, "Pseudonymity and Canonicity," 212–24.

14. Justin Martyr, *Dial.*, 81.4.

15. Irenaus, *Against Heresies*, 4.20.11; Tertullian, *Against Marcion*, 3.14.3; Clement of Alexandria, *Paedagogus*, 2.108; Origen, *Princ.*, 1.2.10.

16. Eusebius, *Hist. eccl.*, 3.39.2–4.

17. Osborne, *Revelation*, 5.

18. See John 19:37; Rev 1:7.

19. Mounce, *Revelation*, 14.

20. Ozanne, "Language of the Apocalypse," 3–9. Ozanne has also identified common themes like the shepherd, manna, living water, and life and light. Findings such as these are sympathetic to conclusions reached earlier by H. B. Swete when he argues that the linguistic/grammatical data favor an authorial connection between the Gospel of John and Revelation. See Swete, *Apocalypse*, cxxx.

tradition in which he dispenses with the device of pseudonymity and identifies himself by name under the conviction that the spirit of prophecy had once again become active, except to say that the apostle John wrote these words?[21]

Those arguing for John the Elder highlight many idiosyncrasies in Revelation that are not in John's Gospel or other writings—variations and anomalies that seem to overwhelm points of convergence. In his brief compendium of grammatical nuances that are unique to the Apocalypse, Guthrie says that the author "places nominatives in opposition to other cases, irregularly uses participles, constructs broken sentences, adds unnecessary pronouns, mixes up genders, numbers and cases and introduces several unusual constructions."[22] Such findings are no doubt sympathetic to what Ben Witherington has discovered in his own study. For a whole host of grammatical/syntactical reasons,[23] Witherington concludes that "the difference in diction rather strongly favors the conclusion that the person who produced the final form of Revelation did not also produce the final form of the Gospel of John." One such anomaly that Witherington and others highlight is especially pertinent to the present argument at hand—"The author of Revelation frequently uses different words than the gospel writer does to refer to the same concept."[24] One example of this phenomena is the author's use of ἀρνίον. Nowhere else in the New Testament, let alone in John's Gospel, is this word used in this form. However, it is used some twenty-nine times in the Apocalypse.

In addition to these distinctions, many who argue against apostolic authorship are quick to remind readers that the author of Revelation never refers to himself as an apostle—he delimits his office to prophet.[25] Not only

---

21. Guthrie, *Introduction*, 256–58.

22. Guthrie, *Introduction*, 939.

23. Witherington, *Revelation*, 2. These discrepancies between John's Gospel and the Apocalypse include the following: in Revelation ἄξιος is followed by the infinitive while in the Gospel it is followed by ἵνα, the construction of participles differs greatly in the two works, ἀρνίον is used for lamb in Revelation instead of ἀμνός, the spelling of Jerusalem differs, Revelation uses ἰδού for exclamations while the Gospel uses ἴδε, and Revelation uses καλέω when something is being called or named while the Gospel uses λέγω.

24. Witherington, *Revelation*, 2. See also Osborne, *Revelation*, 4. See also Williamson, *Revelation*, 19.

25. Witherington, *Revelation*, 3. "Were he John the son of Zebedee it is passing strange that he does not identify himself as an apostle or as an original disciple of Jesus in the letter portion of Revelation, where credentials were important and would have contributed to the rhetorical establishment of the author's authority in relationship to

Appendix A

that, but many accentuate theological differences between the Gospel and the Apocalypse in an effort to aid this position. Osborne and others find these arguments unconvincing, citing the different genres involved in these respective books as a main source for their varied peculiarities.[26] These also identify major theological similarities between the Gospel of John and the Apocalypse of John: the theology of the "Word,"[27] christological titles, use of "Son of Man," the activity of the Holy Spirit,[28] and eschatological nuances.[29] These evidences argue against the claim that John the Apostle is somehow not responsible for this final canonical work.[30]

That both of these possibilities make a compelling case is witnessed in the ambivalence of some who do not claim either side. For instance, G. K. Beale concludes the following: "While the Apostle may well have written the book, another author John also could have written it. The issue is not important to settle since it does not affect the message of the book."[31] Stephen S. Smalley barely awards the issue of authorship with much of a discussion at all.[32] Perhaps these voices reveal that answering the authorship debate is not as absolutely necessary as one might initially think, even as one seeks a robust interpretation of Revelation's contents in general and specific words therein in particular. That said, this argument has chosen to join the rather large chorus of those who accept Johannine authorship—that is, the Apostle John—and will, to that end, refer to the author as John.[33]

---

the audience."

26. Osborne, *Revelation*, 4. Carson, *Gospel According to John*, 149. Smalley, "John's Revelation," 549–71.

27. See John 1:1; Rev 19:13.

28. See John 16:8–15; Rev 2:7.

29. While it appears as though John's Gospel advances a realized eschatology, John 5:28–29 and 14:2–3 suggest that the eschatology present in John is not without a final aspect that seems to be satisfied in the presentation found in Revelation.

30. Smalley, "John's Revelation and John's Community," 549–71.

31. Beale, *Revelation*, 35.

32. Smalley, *Revelation*, 2–3. For his part, Smalley addresses the issue of authorship briefly in an introductory comment on the origin of Revelation and says "Throughout this commentary, the author of the Apocalypse and its prophet-seer will be described as 'John'. Although my own contention is that this name is synonymous with John the apostle, its use is not intended to foreclose discussion of the authorship issue."

33 This is sympathetic to the conclusions reached by Osborne, *Revelation*, 5–6. "In short, the internal evidence supports the external witness of the earliest fathers; and of the options noted . . . Johannine authorship makes the best sense." See also Mounce, *Revelation*, 15. "Since internal evidence is not entirely unfavorable to apostolic authorship

A Word on Revelation's Date and Authorship

This survey on the authorship of the Apocalypse does not yield any major interpretative background information that actively supervenes over the case that is made in this book. However, this discussion has indirectly betrayed the uniqueness of the term that will preoccupy this study. Regardless of whether John the Apostle, John the Elder, a Johannine school, or some other John is responsible for the Apocalypse, the use of ἀρνίον is unique and pervasive enough to merit special attention. This prolific term was important enough to someone and, as Peter Williamson reminds us "regardless of whether he [John] is the apostle John, the Church receives the book of Revelation as divinely inspired and canonical Scripture."[34]

A Discussion on the Date of Revelation in Relation to John's Use of Lamb

As for when the Lamb of Revelation emerged onto the literary scene, Carson, Moo, and Morris suggests four possible dates.[35] These dates correspond to who ruled as emperor over Rome: Claudius (41–54),[36] Nero (54–68),[37] Domitian (81–96),[38] and Trajan (98–117).[39] Though there appear to be four predominant views on Revelation's date that all enjoy at least some early evidence, Osborne and Aune observe that most contemporary scholars opt for dates during the time of Nero or Domitian.[40] Therefore, most of the

---

and external evidence is unanimous in its support, the wisest course of action is to accept as a reasonable hypothesis that the Apocalypse was written by John the apostle, son of Zebedee disciple of Jesus." See also Patterson, *Revelation*, 21. "In the end, as is the case with most books from antiquity, establishing proof of authorship is not possible. What may be safely affirmed is that the cases for all other proposed authors are so unimpressive that there appears to be no substantial reason to reject the nearly universal confidence of the church through the ages that Revelation is the final, preserved written scroll of John the apostle."

34. Williamson, *Revelation*, 21.
35. Carson, Moo, and Morris, *Introduction*, 474.
36. Early support for this date is found in Epiphanius, *Haer.* 51.12.
37. See Syriac versions of Revelation.
38. See Irenaeus, *Haer.*, 5.30.3; Victorinus, *Apoc.*, 10.11; Eusebius, *Hist. eccl.*, 3.18; Clement of Alexandria, *Quis div.* 42.
39. Carson, Moo, and Morris, *Introduction*, 474.
40. Osborne, *Revelation*, 6. Aune, *Revelation*, lvii. Here Aune reveals that while the Domitianic date prevailed from the second through the eighteenth centuries and again in the twentieth century, the Neronic date was most conceded in the nineteenth century. For others who believe that these two dates are most to be considered see Wilson,

Appendix A

discussion on the date of John's apocalypse appears to be preoccupied with these two choices. In an effort to choose between the two, many have discussed the following socio-historical situations that are not only present in the text itself, but also correspond to what was going on in the author's *sitz im leben*: emperor worship, the acuity of persecution the church faced, and the sophistication of the church in general and in Asia Minor in particular.

John's Apocalypse assumes that Christians living during the period in which this work was written were being required to participate in some form of emperor worship/imperial cult.[41] In fact, history demonstrates that the requirement of emperor worship is something that was already in place even before the reign of Domitian.[42] During the regimes of Julius Caesar, Augustus, Claudius, and Vespasian, the common practice was to deify the emperor after he died, rather than when he lived. However, at the time of Nero, there is some evidence which suggests that this particular emperor desired to be deified before he perished. However, Nero's efforts largely failed.[43] In contrast to Nero and his predecessors, Suetonius states clearly that Domitian stressed his deity, ordering that he be called *dominus et deus* ("lord and god").[44] That said, Beale argues that "hard evidence for persecuting Christians for refusing to acquiesce to legal requirements for emperor worship comes in 113 AD. during the reign of Trajan in a letter written by Pliny to Trajan and in Trajan's response."[45] Therefore, one could say that what was established in some figurative way before Domitian grew more acute during his reign and even more emphatic during the later reign of Trajan.

This growing demand to worship the emperor is witnessed in the persecution that was dealt the church in its early history. As it pertains to the date of Revelation, many suggest that it was penned in a time in which

---

"Revelation," 246, "the writing of Revelation has been placed either in the decade of the 60s or the 90s of the first century A.D." See also Beale, *Revelation*, 4ff. Here, Beale bifurcates his discussion on the date between two categories—the early date and the late date (though not in that order). These two categories correspond roughly to what Carson, Moo, and Morris refer to as Nero and Domitian dates respectively.

41. See Rev 13:4, 15–16; 14:9–11; 15:2; 16:2; 19:20; 20:4. See discussion on imperial cult worship requirements in Mounce, *Revelation*, 33.

42. See discussion in Price, *Rituals and Power*, 28.

43. Osborne, *Revelation*, 6.

44. Suetonius, *Dom.*, 13.

45. Beale, *Revelation*, 5. Pliny the Younger, *Ep.*, 10.96–7.

A Word on Revelation's Date and Authorship

Christians were being persecuted in a relatively profound way.[46] However, others argue that as far as the Apocalypse is concerned, most of the opposition the church is said to encounter had yet to transpire and that very little persecution was actually taking place.[47] Given what has already been said about the imperial cult, it would appear as though a later date in which persecution for withholding emperor worship might make more sense than an earlier date in which this was not yet a formal requirement. However, Carson, Moo, and Morris suggest that persecution of Christians under Nero (54–68 AD) is clear and irrefutable, making it possible that persecution of Christians was taking place during his regime in Rome and elsewhere.[48] Although this might indicate an early date, Beale argues that there is no evidence that Nero's persecution of Christians in Rome extended to Asia Minor (where the churches addressed in the Apocalypse are located)[49] as the persecution in question was primarily predicated on blame for the great fire of Rome and directed toward local followers of Christ. In fact, investigations made by S. R. F. Price have concluded that in Asia Minor (the region addressed in the Apocalypse), public expressions of loyalty to the imperial cult were not emphasized until the time of Domitian.[50] During his reign, a myriad of mandates handed down by local authorities in this region demanded demonstrations of allegiance to the emperor, especially during times of celebrations and festivals. This is why many concede that the Domitianic date is more sympathetic to the whole body of acquired

---

46. See Carson, Moo, and Morris, *Introduction*, 474. See also Hagner, *New Testament*, 772ff. Here, Hagner states, "The main clue to the date of the Apocalypse is the evidence of the persecution presently being experienced by the readers or imminently expected." These use the following tests in support of this position: Rev 1:9; 2:3, 10, 13, 19; 3:2, 8, 10; 6:9, 11; 12:11; 17:6; 18:24; 19:2; 20:4, 6.

47. Osborne, *Revelation*, 8; Aune, *Revelation*, lxiv–lxix; Collins, *Crisis and Catharsis*, 69–73; Thompson, *Book of Revelation*, 105–9; Barr, *Tales of the End*, 165–69. These cite the following texts to support their position: 6:9–11; 12:11; 13:7, 10; 16:6; 17:6; 19:2; 20:4.

48. Carson, Moo, and Morris, *Introduction*, 474. "We have no evidence that Nero's persecution extended beyond Rome, but if we are looking for a period when Christians in Asia Minor were likely to be persecuted, a time during which Christians were being persecuted elsewhere is more likely than a time when we are not sure that they were being persecuted at all." See also C. Wilson, "Problem of the Comitian Date," 376–93.

49. Beale, *Book of Revelation*, 12. Osborne agrees with this saying, "But the Neronian persecution was limited to Rome as far as the data tells us, and there is no evidence for it extending to the province of Asia at that time." Osborne, *Revelation*, 8.

50. Price, *Rituals and Power*, 78–124, 155–66, 207–22.

Appendix A

historical data, at least as it pertains to the emperor worship and persecution against Christians that characterizes this period.

However, at least one more consideration is worth entertaining as it corresponds to the issues of Revelation's date—the sophistication of the church as it is portrayed in Revelation 2-3. Hemmer, Guthrie, Aune, and Osborne identify several events/situations connected to the churches mentioned in these chapters that favor a date later than the 60s AD. For instance, the recovery of Laodicea in 3:17 best fits the reconstruction of the region around AD 80 following a great earthquake.[51] If the city was destroyed by an earthquake in AD 60-61, it would have taken some time to come back and, subsequently, be described as it is in Revelation 3.[52] These same commentators argue that the phrase "do not harm the oil and the wine"[53] later in John's work most likely refers to an edict of Domitian in AD 92 restricting the growing of vines in Asia.[54] Those sympathetic to a later date also believe that the "synagogues of Satan"[55] are best understood as situated in struggles that took place under Domitian.[56] Not only that, but there is no evidence that the church of Smyrna existed in the 60s AD.[57] Added to these, many believe the mature stagnation witnessed in several of the churches of Revelation 2-3 is proof that certain issues in these localities had been allowed to fester over a long period of time. Finally, the lack of any mention of Paul (who had labored in Ephesus, possibly until 64 AD) favors a date far removed from Paul's ministry.

The only argument early date adherents have that is in any way connected to a place of worship involves a literal reading of Revelation 11:1-2 in which the temple is in view. If the temple of 11:1-2 is to be taken literally,

---

51. Hemmer, *Letters to the Seven Churches*, 4-5; Guthrie, *Introduction*, 948-55, and Aune, *Revelation*, lx-lxv.

52. Rev 3:17, "Because you say, 'I am rich, and have become wealthy, and have need of nothing,' and you do not know that you are wretched and miserable and poor and blind and naked."

53. Rev 6:6.

54. Hemmer, *Letters to the Seven Churches*, 4-5; Guthrie, *Introduction*, 948-55; Aune, *Revelation*, lx-lxv.

55. Rev 2:9; 3:9.

56. Hemmer, *Letters to the Seven Churches*, 4-5; Guthrie, *Introduction*, 948-55; Aune, *Revelation*, lx-lxv. See also Osborne, *Revelation*, 9.

57. Hemmer, *Letters to the Seven Churches*, 4-5; Guthrie, *Introduction*, 948-55; Aune, *Revelation*, lx-lxv. See also Osborne, *Revelation*, 9. See also Carson, Moo, and Morris, *Introduction*, 475. There, these argue that the church may not have existed until 60-64.

it could favor a pre-70 AD date (when the temple of Jerusalem was still standing). Therefore, as there is widespread early support for a later date for John's Apocalypse (as witnessed in the works of Irenaeus, Eusebius, Clement of Alexandria, and Origen), emperor worship appears to be a serious concern in the text, the scope of the persecution seems to have reached Asia minor (the direct recipients of Revelation), and the church is described in this work as relatively sophisticated (both positively and negatively), understanding this text as written during the reign of Domitian (circa 81–96 AD) seems most appropriate.[58]

Though the study found in this work assumes a late date for Revelation, it also recognizes the warning provided by D. Warden who acknowledges the difficulty of dating the Apocalypse, ultimately conceding that an actual date is uncertain.[59] As this argument is predominately preoccupied by the Christology of the Apocalypse and how this is informed by or expressed in John's pervasive use of Lamb, the specific date of the last canonical book is of little consequence. In fact, even if an early date is conceded (mid-60s AD), the writing of Revelation would still be thirty or more years removed from the crucifixion, lending ample time for the author to develop the sophisticated and unique Christology contained within. That said, one might argue that the uniqueness of the term used for Lamb (ἀρνίον) may support a later date. As this word is not found in the gospels or Paul's letters, ἀρνίον might betray an evolution of language as this term enjoys very little, if any, New Testament precedent. Had the Apocalypse been penned earlier, one might expect a more commonly used term for Lamb, not something that appears new/unique, especially as it is employed for Christ. In either case (early or late), the date of Revelation does not suffer compelling implications for what is argued about the Lamb Christology in this work.

Conclusion

Ultimately, this appendix has illustrated that while each of these background considerations informs apocalyptic Christology in general and the Lamb

---

58. See Giesen, *Die Offenbarung des Johannes*, 41–42. See also Osborne, *Revelation*, 9; Carson, Moo, and Morris, *Introduction*, 476; Achtemeier, Green, and Thompson, *Introducing the New Testament*, 572–3; M. Wilson, "Revelation," 246; Beale, *Book of Revelation*, 27; Keener, *IPV Bible Background Commentary*, 724; and Lea and Black, *The New Testament*, 581.

59. Warden, "Imperial Persecution," 203–12.

Appendix A

Christology in particular in cursory ways, these more historical–critical investigations do not supervene on the conclusions this book hopes to reach. In other words, what is more important to this argument than identifying the specific author is understanding what the author (whoever he may be) meant by "Lamb" and how this connects to his christological presentation. Again, this prolific term was important enough to someone to be used as often and as consistently as it is employed in John's Apocalypse to merit special analysis. What is more important than affirming a specific date for Revelation is that a relatively unique term for Jesus (ἀρνίον) was endorsed at some point to say something significant.

That said, for the purposes of discussion and based on the analysis represented in this appendix, this work has chosen to assume that John the Apostle wrote Revelation around 90–95 AD. This commitment is not given to make a strong case for any one of these conclusions, but in an effort to establish precedent regarding terms and to promote consistency as an interpretation for the Lamb in Revelation is reached and as an explanation for how this Lamb informs an apocalyptic Christology is pursued.

Appendix B
Diagrammatical Analysis of Revelation 5:6–10

(5:6)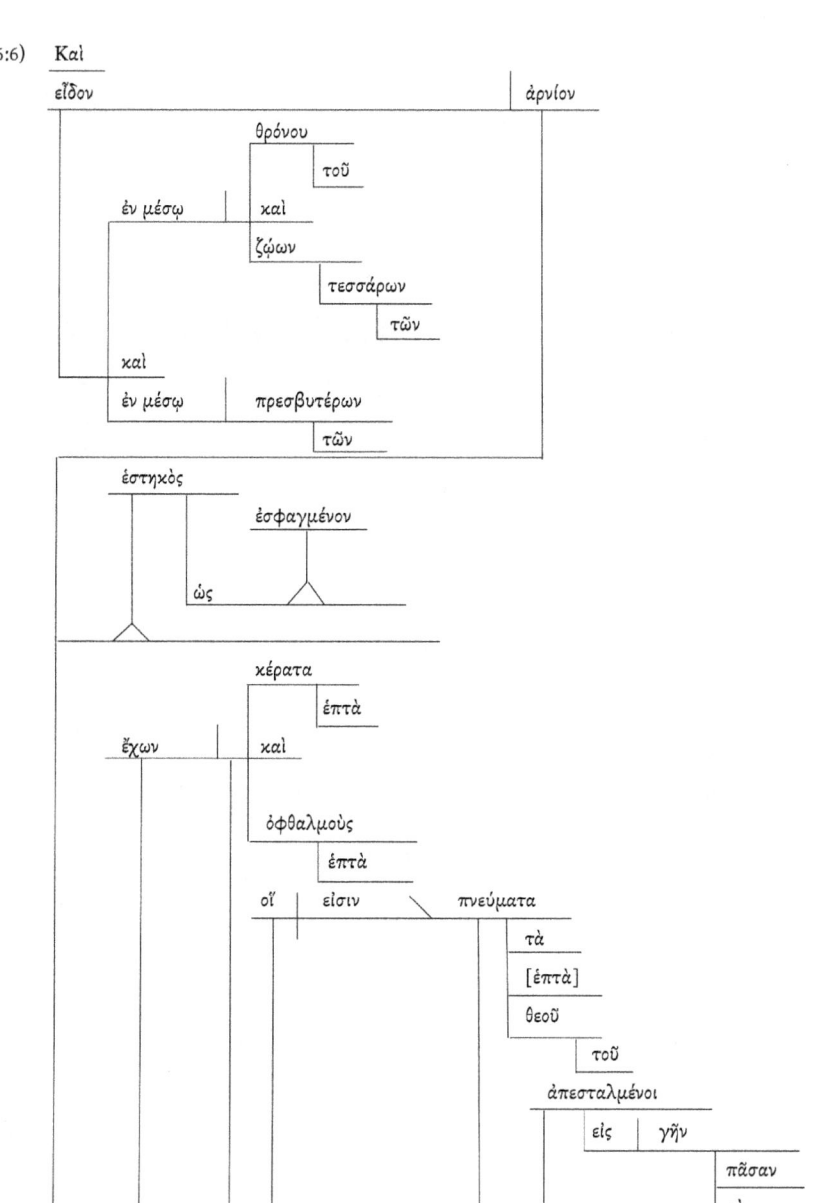

(5:7)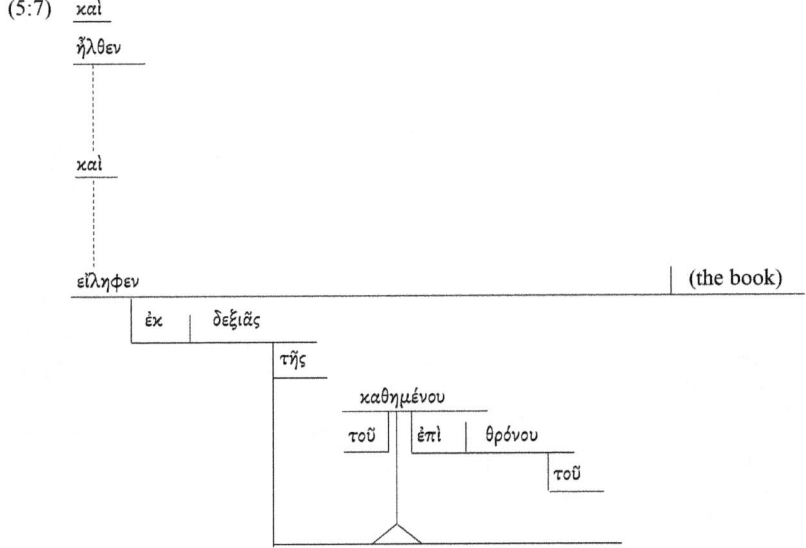

(5:8) Καὶ
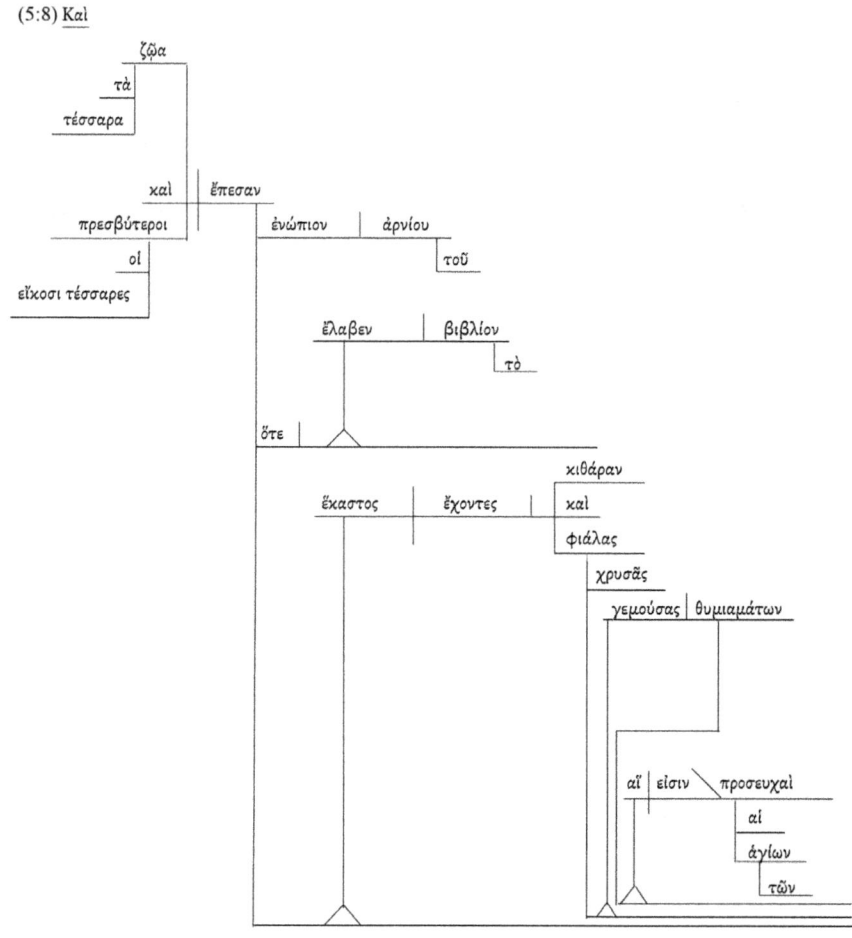

(5:9)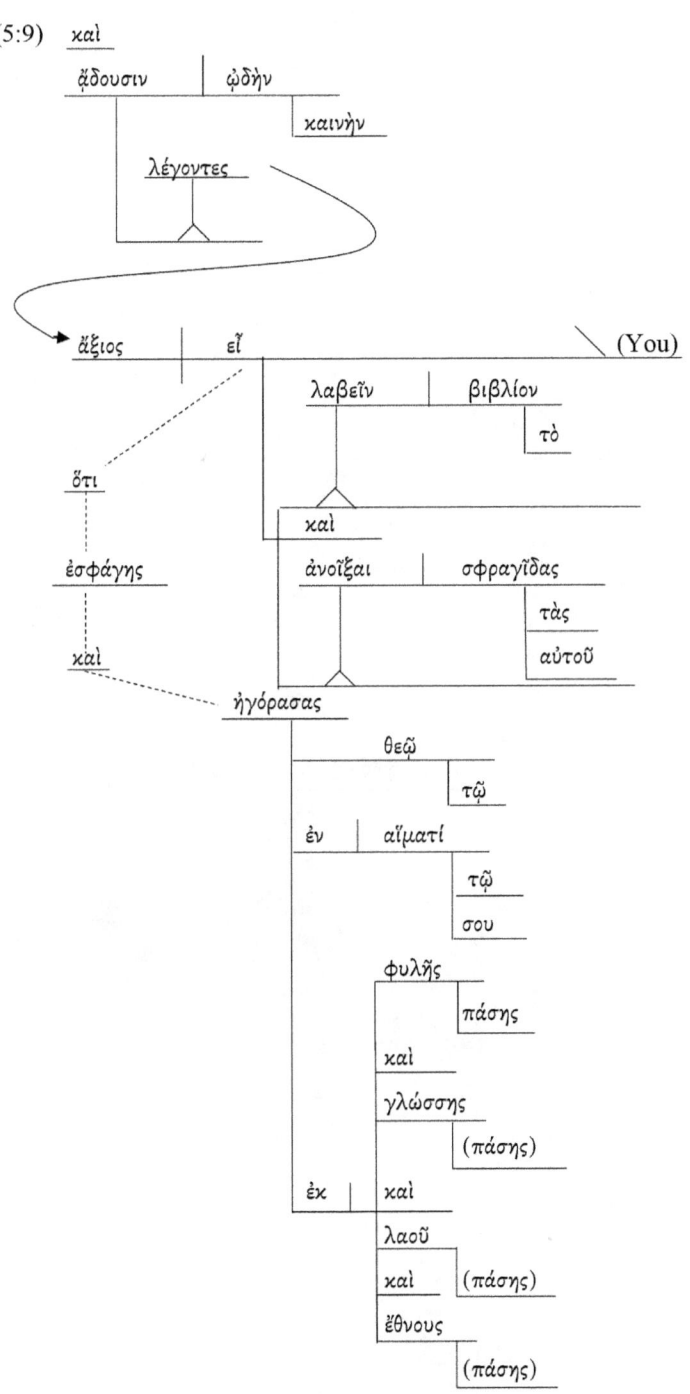

(5:10) καὶ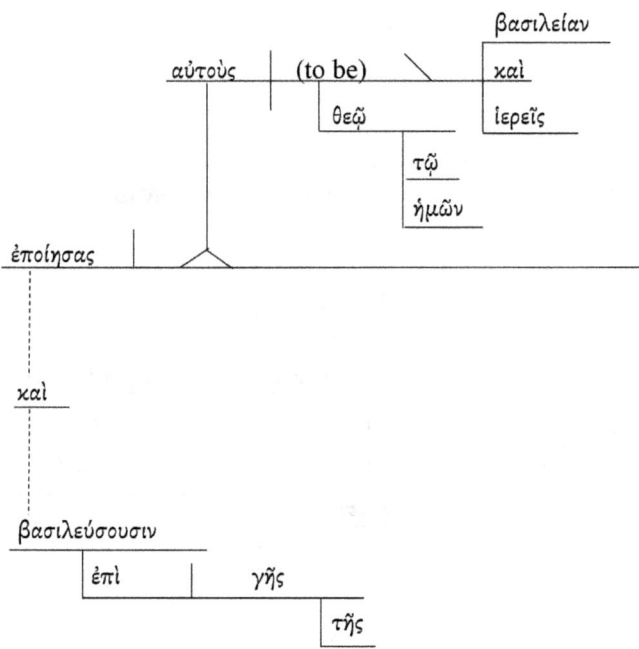

Bibliography

Abbott, Thomas Marks. "Paul's Christology in Romans." PhD diss., Drew University, 1989.

Ables, Travis E. "The Word in which All Things Are Spoken: Augustine, Anselm, and Bonaventure on Christology and the Metaphysics of Exemplarity." *Theological Studies* 76 (June 2015) 280–97.

Achtemeier, Paul J., Joel B. Green, and Marianne Meye Thompson. *Introducing the New Testament, Its Literature and Theology*. Grand Rapids: Eerdmans, 2001.

Albright, W. F. "A Biblical Fragment of the Maccabaen Age: The Nash Papyrus." *Journal of Biblical Literature* 56 (1937) 145–76.

Alford, Henry. *The Greek Testament*, 4 vols. London: Longmans, Green, 1903.

Allison, Gregg R. *Historical Theology: An Introduction to Christian Doctrine*. Grand Rapids: Zondervan, 2011.

Anderson, Paul N. *The Christology of the Fourth Gospel*. Tubingen: Mohr, 1996.

Aquinas, Thomas. *Summa Theologica: Complete English Edition in Five Volumes*, Vol. 4. Translated by Fathers of the English Dominican Province. New York: Benziger Bros., 1981.

Augustine. "Sermon 263.2." In *Works of St. Augustine: A Translation for the Twenty-First Century*, Vol. 3, edited by J. E. Rotelle. Hyde Park, NY: New City, 1995.

———. "Sermon 375." In *Works of St. Augustine: A Translation for the Twenty-First Century*, Vol. 3, edited by J. E. Rotelle. Hyde Park, NY: New City, 1995.

———. *The Trinity*. Translated by Edmund Hill and John E. Rotelle. Hyde Park, NY: New City, 2015.

Aune, David. *Revelation 1–5*, Word Biblical Commentary. Dallas, TX: Word, 1997.

———. *Revelation 17–22*, Word Biblical Commentary. Grand Rapids: Zondervan, 1998.

———. "Stories of Jesus in the Apocalypse of John." *Contours of Christology in the New Testament*, edited by Richard N. Longenecker, 292–319. Grand Rapids: Eerdmans, 2005.

Barr, D. L. *Tales of the End: A Narrative Commentary on the Book of Revelation*. Santa Rosa, CA: Polebridge, 1998.

Barth, Karl. *Der Römerbrief*, 8th ed. Zurich: Zollikon, 1947.

———. *Epistle to the Romans*. 6th ed. Translated by E. C. Hoskyns. Oxford: Oxford University Press, 1933.

———. *Evangelische Theologie im 19. Jahrhundert*. Zurich: Evangelischer Verlag, 1957.

Barthellos, Demetrios. *The Byzantine Christ: Person, Nature, and Will in the Christology of Saint Maximus the Confessor*. Oxford: Oxford University Press, 2004.

Bibliography

Bauckham, Richard. *Gospel of Glory: Major Themes in Johannine Theology.* Grand Rapids: Baker, 2015.

———. *Jesus and the God of Israel: God Crucified and Other Studies on the New Testament's Christology of Divine Identity.* Grand Rapids: Eerdmans, 2009.

———. "Joining Creation's Praise of God." *Ecotheology* 7 no. 1 (2002) 45–59.

———. *Jude, 2 Peter.* Word Biblical Commentary. Waco, TX: Word, 1983.

———. "Monotheism and Christology in the Gospel of John." In *Contours of Christology in the New Testament,* edited by Richard N. Longenecker, 148–68. Grand Rapids: Eerdmans, 2005.

———. *New Testament Theology: The Theology of the Book of Revelation.* Cambridge: Cambridge University Press, 1993.

———. *The Climax of Prophecy: Studies on the Book of Revelation.* Edinburgh: T. & T. Clark, 1993

———. *The Theology of the Book of Revelation.* Cambridge: Cambridge University Press, 1993.

———. "The Worship of Jesus in Apocalyptic Christianity." *New Testament Studies* 27 (1981) 322–41.

Beale, G. K. *John's Use of the Old Testament in Revelation.* Sheffield, UK: Sheffield Academic, 1998.

———. *The Book of Revelation, A Commentary on the Greek Text.* Grand Rapids: Eerdmans, 1999.

Beale, Gregory K. *We Become What We Worship: A Biblical Theology of Idolatry.* Downers Grove, IL: IVP, 2009.

Beasley, G. R. *The Book of Revelation.* London: Marshall, Morgan & Scott, 1974.

Beckelhymer, Hunter. "The Place of Preaching in Worship: A theological Rationale." *Encounter* 44 (Summer 1983) 277–89.

Beckwith, Isbon T. *The Apocalypse of John.* New York: Macmillan, 1919.

Blevins, James L. "The Genre of Revelation." *Review and Expositor* 77 (Summer 1980) 393–408.

Blevins, William L. "The Demand Motif in Synoptic Christology." PhD diss., New Orleans Baptist Theological Seminary, 1966.

Boring, Eugene. *Revelation,* Introduction: A Bible Commentary for Teaching and Preaching. Louisville: Westminster John Knox, 1989.

———. *Sayings of the Risen Jesus: Christian Prophecy in the Synoptic Tradition.* New York: Cambridge University Press, 1982.

———. "The Theology of Revelation, 'The Lord Our God the Almighty Reigns.'" *Interpretation* 40 (July 1986) 257–69.

Brown, Harold O. J. *Heresies: Heresy and Orthodoxy in the History of the Church.* Peabody, MA: Hendrickson, 2015.

Brown, James. *Subject and Object in Modern Theology.* London: SCM, 1955.

Brown, Raymond. *Introduction to the New Testament Christology.* New York: Paulist, 1994.

———. *The Birth of the Messiah.* Garden City, NY: Doubleday, 1977.

Brownlee, William. "Comparison of the Covenanters of the Dead Sea Scrolls with Pre-Christian Jewish Sects." *Biblical Archaeologist* (1950) 49–72.

Bultmann, Rudolph. *History and Eschatology.* Edinburgh: University Press, 1957.

———. *Kerygma und Mythos,* Vol. I. Hamburg: Reich & Henrich, 1948.

———. *Marburger Predigten.* Tubingen: Mohr, 1956.

Bibliography

———. *New Testament & Mythology and Other Basic Writings*. Philadelphia: Fortress, 1984.

———. *Theologie des Neuen Testaments*. Tubingen: Mohr, 1954.

Burba, K. *Die Christologie in Luthers Liedern*. Gutersloh: Carl Bertelsmann, 1956.

Caird, G. B. *The Revelation of St. John the Divine*. New York: Harper & Row, 1966.

Calvin, John. *Calvin's New Testament Commentaries,* 12 vols. D. W. Torrance and T. F. Torrance, eds. Grand Rapids: Eerdmans, 1959–72.

———. *Institutes of the Christian Religion*, 2 vols. Edited by J. T. McNeill and translated by F. L. Battles. Philadelphia: Westminster, 1960.

Cameron, A. *Christianity and the Rhetoric of Empire: The Development of Christian Discourse*. Berkley: University of California Press, 1991.

Carey, Greg. *Ultimate Things: An Introduction to Jewish and Christian Apocalyptic Literature*. St. Louis: Chalice, 2005.

Carrell, Peter. *Jesus and the Angels: Angelology and the Christology of the Apocalypse of John*. Cambridge: Cambridge University Press, 1997.

Carson, D. A. *Exegetical Fallacies*. 2nd ed. Grand Rapids: Baker Academic, 1996.

———. *The Gospel According to John*, Pillar Commentary Series. Grand Rapids: Eerdmans, 2016.

———. *The Gospel According to John*. Grand Rapids: 1991.

Carson, D. A., and Douglas J. Moo. *An Introduction to the New Testament*. 2nd ed. Grand Rapids: Zondervan, 2005.

Carson, D. A., Douglas J. Moo, and Leon Morris. *An Introduction to the New Testament*. Grand Rapids: Zondervan, 1992.

Casey, P. M. *From Jewish Prophet to Gentile God*. Louisville: Westminster John Knox, 1991.

Caspi, Mishael Maswari, and Sascha Benjamin Cohen. "The Binding [Aqedah] and Its Transformation in Judaism and Islam: The Lamb of God." In *Mellen Biblical Press Series* No. 32. Lewiston, NY, 1995.

Charles, J. Daryl. "An Apocalyptic Tribute to the Lamb (Rev 5:1–14)." *Journal of the Evangelical Theological Society* 34 (December 1991) 461–73.

Charles, R. H. *A Critical and Exegetical Commentary on the Revelation of St. John*. Vol. 1. Edinburgh: T. & T. Clark, 1920.

Cho, Sukmin. *Jesus as Prophet in the Fourth Gospel*. Sheffield, UK: Sheffield Phoenix, 2006.

Collins, A. Yarbro. *Crisis and Catharsis: The Power of the Apocalypse*. Philadelphia: Westminster, 1984.

Collins, J. *The Apocalyptic Imagination: An Introduction to the Jewish Matrix of Christianity*. New York: Crossroad, 1984.

Conley, J. Drew. "The Christology of the Gospel of Mark: Portrait of the Suffering Sovereign." PhD diss., Bob Jones University, 1991.

Cook, Stephen. *The Apocalyptic Literature*. Nashville: Abingdon, 2003.

Crossley, J. G. *The Date of Mark's Gospel: Insight form the Law in Earliest Christianity*. New York: T. & T. Clark, 2004.

Cullmann, Oscar. "Significance of the Qumran Texts for Research into the Beginnings of Christianity." *Journal of Biblical Literature* 74 (1955) 213–26.

Cyril of Alexandria. *On the Unity of Christ*. Translated by J. A. McGuckin. Crestwood, NY: St. Vladimir's Seminary Press, 2000.

Dahl, Nils Alstrup. *Jesus in the Memory of the Early Church*. Minneapolis: Augsburg, 1976.

Danby, Herbert, ed. *The Mishnah*. Oxford: Clarendon, 1933.

Bibliography

Davies, B., and G. R. Evans, eds. and trans. *Anselm of Canterbury: The Major Works*. Oxford: Oxford University Press, 1998.

Deichgraber, R. *Gotteshymnus und Christushymnus in der fruhen Christenheit*. Gottingen: Vandenhoeck & Ruprecht, 1967.

DeSilva, David A. *Seeing Things John's Way: The Rhetoric of the Book of Revelation*. Louisville: Westminster John Knox, 2009.

Dodd, C. H. *The Interpretation of the Fourth Gospel*. Cambridge: Cambridge University Press, 1953.

Donaldson, Terrence L. "The Vindicated Son: A Narrative Approach to Matthean Christology." In *Contours of Christology in the New Testament*, edited by Richard N. Longenecker, 100–121. Grand Rapids: Eerdmans, 2005.

Dorner, I. A. "Die deutsche Theologie une ihre dogmatischen und ethischen Aufgaben in der Gegenwart." In *Gesammelte Schriften aus dem Gebiet der systematische Theologie, Exegese und Geschichte*. Berlin: Weimer, 1883.

———. *System der Christlichen Glaubenslehre*, Vol. I. Berlin: Hertz, 1879–91.

Douglas, J. D., gen. ed. *New Bible Dictionary*. 2nd ed. Downers Grove, IL: InterVarsity, 1982.

Dunn, James D. G. *Unity and Diversity in the New Testament: An Inquiry into the Character of Earliest Christianity*. London: SCM, 1977.

Edwards, O. C., Jr. *A History of Preaching*. Nashville: Abingdon, 2004.

Ehrman, Bart. *Did Jesus Exist? The Historical Argument for Jesus of Nazareth*. New York: HarperOne, 2012.

———. *How Jesus Became God: The Exaltation of a Jewish Preacher from Galilee*. New York: HarperOne, 2014.

———. "The Text as Window: New Testament Manuscripts and the Social History of Early Christianity." In *The Text of the New Testament in Contemporary Research: Essays on the Status Quaestionis*, edited by Bart D. Ehrman and Michael W. Holmes, 361–79. Boston: Brill, 2014.

Elliott, Mark W. "Christology in the Seventeenth Century." In *The Oxford Handbook of Christology*, edited by Francesca Aran Murphy, 297–314. Oxford: Oxford University Press, 2015.

Ellis, E. E. "Pseudonymity and Canonicity of the New Testament Documents." In *Worship, Theology and Ministry in the Early Church: Essays in Honour of Ralph P. Martin*, edited by Michael J. Wilkins and Terence Paige, 212–20. New York: Bloomsbury, 1992.

Elwell, Walter A., gen. ed. *Baker Encyclopedia of the Bible*, Vol. 2. Grand Rapids: Baker: 1998.

Elwell, Walter A., and P. W. Comfort. *Tyndale Bible Dictionary*. Wheaton, IL: Tyndale, 2001.

Eno, R. B. "Authority and Conflict in the Early Church." *Eglise et Theologue* 7 (1976) 41–60.

Ewing, Ward. *The Power of the Lamb: Revelation's Theology of Liberation for You*. Eugene, OR: Wipf and Stock, 2006.

Fee, Gordon D. *Pauline Christology: An Exegetical-Theological Study*. Peabody, MA: Hendrickson, 2007.

Fennema, David A. "Jesus and God according to John: An analysis of the Fourth Gospel's Father-Son Christology." PhD diss., University of Michigan, 1979.

Fiorenza, Elizabeth. *The Book of Revelation: Justice and Judgment*. Philadelphia: Fortress, 1985.

Bibliography

Fish, Stanley. *Is There a Text in This Class?* Cambridge: Harvard University Press, 1980.
Ford, J. Massyngberde. *Revelation,* AB 38. Garden City, NJ: Doubleday, 1975.
Freedman, D. N., ed. *Anchor Bible Dictionary,* 6 vols. New York: Doubleday, 1992.
Fuller, Reginald H. *The Foundations of New Testament Christology.* New York: Scribner's, 1965.
Galot, Jean. *Who Is Christ?: A Theology of the Incarnation.* Chicago: Franciscan Herald, 1981.
Gathercole, Simon J. *The Pre-existent Son: Recovering the Christologies of Matthew, Mark, and Luke.* Grand Rapids: Eerdmans, 2006.
Giesen, H. *Die Offenbarung des Johannes,* Regensburger Neus Testament. Regensburg: Friedrich Pustet, 1997.
Gorman, Michael J. *Reading Revelation Responsibly: Uncivil Worship and Witness: Following the Lamb into the New Creation.* Eugene, OR: Cascade, 2011.
Gregory of Nazianzus. "The Third Theological Oration—On the Son 17." In *Christology of the Later Fathers,* edited by Edward R. Hardy. Philadelphia: Westminster, 1981.
Grikalis, A. *Images of the Divine: The Theology of Icons at the Seventh Ecumenical Council.* Leiden: Brill, 2005.
Grillmeier, Aloys. *Christ in Christian Tradition Vol. I: From the Apostolic Age to Chalcedon (451).* Atlanta: John Knox, 1964.
Grindheim, Sigurd. *Christology in the Synoptic Gospels: God or God's Servant?* New York: T. & T. Clark, 2012.
Gruenler, Royce Gordon. *New Approaches to Jesus and the Gospels: A Phenomenological and Exegetical Study of Synoptic Christology.* Grand Rapids: Baker, 1982.
Guthrie, Donald. *New Testament Introduction.* Downers Grove, IL: InterVarsity, 1990.
———. "The Lamb in the Structure of the Book of Revelation." *Vox Evangelica* 12 (1981) 64–71.
Hagner, Donald A. *The New Testament: A Historical and Theological Introduction.* Grand Rapids: Baker, 2012.
Hahn, Ferdinand. *The Titles of Jesus in Christology.* New York: World, 1969.
Hall, Stuart George, ed. *Jesus Christ Today: Studies of Christology in Various Contexts.* New York: de Gruyter, 2009.
Hanson, R. P. C. *The Search for the Christian Doctrine of God: The Arian Controversy 318–381.* Grand Rapids: Baker Academic, 2007.
Hardy, Edward R. "Athanasius." In *Christology of the Later Fathers,* edited by Edward R. Hardy, 41–110. Philadelphia: Westminster, 1981.
Harnack, Adolf Von. *Das Wesen des Christentums.* Leipzig: Hinrichs, 1906.
———. *History of Dogma,* Vol. I. Edinburgh, 1894–9.
Harris, W. Hall, III. "Apocalyptic Genre." In *Interpreting the New Testament Text: Introduction to the Art and Science of Exegesis,* edited by Darrell L. Bock and Buist M. Fanning, 241–54. Wheaton, IL: Crossway, 2006.
Harrison, Everett F. *Introduction to the New Testament.* Grand Rapids, MI: Eerdmans, 1964.
Hector, Kevin. "Christology After Kant." In *The Oxford Handbook of Christology,* edited by Francesca Aran Murphy, 315–27. Oxford: Oxford University Press, 2015.
Hedley, George. *Christian Worship.* New York: Macmillan, 1953.
Hegel, G. W. F. *Lectures on the Philosophy of Religion One-Volume Edition: The Lectures of 1827.* Edited and translated by P. C. Hodgson. New York: Oxford University Press, 2006.

Bibliography

———. *Vorlesungen uber die Philosophie der Religion*, 18 vols. Berlin: Dunker und Humblot, 1832–45.

Hellholm, David. "The Problem of Apocalyptic Genre and the Apocalypse of John." In *Society of Biblical Literature Seminar Papers*, edited by Kent Harold Richards, 157–98. Chico, CA: Scholars, 1982.

Hemmer, C. J. *The Letters to the Seven Churches of Asia in Their Local Setting*. Sheffield: JSOT, 1986.

Henderson, Suzanne Watts. *Christology and Discipleship in the Gospel of Mark*. New York: Cambridge University Press, 2006.

Hendrickson, William. *More Than Conquerors: An Interpretation of the Book of Revelation*. Grand Rapids: Baker, 1967.

Herrmann, Wilhelm. *The Communion of the Christian with God*. London: Williams and Norgate, 1895.

Hindson, Ed. "Antichrist." In *The Popular Encyclopedia of Bible Prophecy*, edited by Tim Lahaye and Ed Hindson. Eugene, OR: Harvest House, 2004.

Hoekema, Anthony. *The Bible and the Future*. Grand Rapids: Eerdmans, 1979.

Hogg, David S. "Christology: The *Cur Deus Homo*." In *The Oxford Handbook of Christology*, edited by Francesca Aran Murphy, 199–215. Oxford: Oxford University Press, 2016.

Hok, Gosta. *Die Elliptische Theologie Albrecht Ritschls*. Uppsala: Lundequista, 1942.

Hooker, Morna D. "'Who Can This Be?' The Christology of Mark." In *Contours of Christology in the New Testament*, edited by Richard N. Longenecker, 79-99. Grand Rapids: Eerdmans, 2005.

Hoskins, Paul M. "Deliverance from Death by the True Passover Lamb: A Significant Aspect of the Fulfillment of the Passover in the Gospel of John." *JETS* 52 No. 2 (June 2009) 285–99.

Hurst, L. D., and N. T. Wright, eds. *The Glory of Christ in the New Testament: Studies in Memory of George Bradford Caird*. London: Oxford University Press, 1987.

Hurtado, Larry W. *At the Origins of Christian Worship: The Context and Character of Earliest Christian Devotion*. Grand Rapids: Eerdmans, 1999.

———. "First-Century Jewish Monotheism." *Journal for the Study of the New Testament* 71 (1998) 3–26.

———. *How on Earth Did Jesus Become a God?: Historical Questions about Earliest Devotion to Jesus*. Grand Rapids: Eerdmans, 2005.

———. *Lord Jesus Christ: Devotion to Jesus in Earliest Christianity*. Grand Rapids: Eerdmans, 2003.

———. *One God, One Lord: Early Christian Devotion and Ancient Jewish Monotheism*. New York: T. & T. Clark, 1998.

Hylen, Susan E. "Lamb." In *The New Interpreter's Dictionary of the Bible*, Vol. 3, edited by Katherine Doom Sakenfeld. Nashville: Abingdon, 2008.

Issel, Ernst. *Die Lehre von Reich Gottes im Neuen Testaments*. Leiden: Brill, 1891.

Jackson, Gregory L. "Christology of Mark." PhD diss., Waterloo Lutheran Seminary, 1972.

Johns, Loren L. *The Lamb Christology of the Apocalypse of John: An Investigation into Its Origins and Rhetorical Force*. Eugene, OR: Wipf and Stock, 2014.

Johnson, Keith E. "Augustine, Eternal Generation, and Evangelical Trinitarianism." *Trinity Journal* 32 (Fall 2011) 141–163.

Johnson, N. B. *Prayer in the Apocrypha and Pseudepigrapha: A Study of the Jewish Concept of God*. Philadelphia: Society of Biblical Literature, 1948.

Bibliography

Kant, Immanuel. "Critique of Practical Reason (1788)." In *Practical Philosophy*. Edited and translated by P. Guyer and A. W. Wood. New York: Cambridge University Press, 1996.

———. *Critique of Pure Reason*. Edited and translated by P. Guyer and A. W. Wood. New York: Cambridge University Press, 1998.

———. "Religion with the Boundaries of Mere Reason (1793)." In *Religion and Rational Theology*. Edited by A. W. Wood and G. di Giovanni and translated by G. di Giovanni. New York: Cambridge University Press, 2006.

Karrer, M. *Die Johannesoffenbarung als Brief: Studien zu ihrem literatischen, historischen und theologischen Ort*. Gottingen: Vandenhoeck & Ruprecht, 1986.

Keener, Craig S. *The IVP Bible Background Commentary*. 2nd ed. Downers Grove, IL: InterVarsity, 2014.

Kelly, J. N. D. *Early Christian Doctrines*. 5th rev. ed. London: Black, 1977.

Kelly, William. *The Revelation*. London: Thomas Weston, 1904.

Kingsbury, Jack Dean. *The Christology of Mark's Gospel*. Philadelphia: Fortress, 1983.

Knox, John. *The Humanity and Divinity of Christ*. Cambridge: Cambridge University Press, 1967.

Knox, W. L. *St. Paul and the Church of the Gentiles*. Cambridge: Cambridge University Press, 1961.

Kodell, Jerome. *The Eucharist in the New Testament*. Wilmington, DE: Glazier, 1988.

Kohler-Rollesfson, Ilse U. "Sheep." In *HarperCollins Bible Dictionary*. Edited by Paul J. Achtemeier. San Francisco: HarperCollins, 1996.

Köstenberger, Andreas. *John*, Baker Exegetical Commentary on the New Testament. Grand Rapids: Baker, 2004.

———, L. Scott Kellum, and Charles L. Quarels. *The Lion and the Lamb: New Testament Essentials from the Cradle, the Cross, and the Crown*. Nashville: B. & H., 2012.

Kraybill, J. Nelson. *Apocalypse and Allegiance: Worship, Politics, and Devotion in the Book of Revelation*. Grand Rapids: Brazos, 2010.

Labahn, Michael, and Outi Lehtipun, eds. *Imagery in the Book of Revelation*. Walpole, MA: Peeters, 2011.

Ladd, G. E. *A Commentary on the Revelation of John*. Grand Rapids: Eerdmans, 1972.

———. "Why Not Prophetic-Apocalyptic?" *Journal of Biblical Literature* 76 (1957) 192–200.

Lam, Joseph C. Q. "Revelation, Christology and Grace in Augustine's anti-Manichean and anti-Pelagian Controversies." *Phronema* 28 (2013) 131–49.

Lea, Thomas D., and David Alan Black. *The New Testament: Its Background and Message*. 2nd ed. Nashville: B. & H., 2003.

Leaver, R. *Luther's Liturgical Music: Principles and Implications*. Grand Rapids: Eerdmans.

Letham, Robert. *The Holy Trinity: In Scripture, History, Theology, and Worship*. Phillipsburg, NJ: P. & R., 2004.

Lietzmann, Hans. *Mass and Lord's Supper: A Study in the History of the Liturgy*. Translated by D. H. G. Reeve. Leiden: Brill, 1979.

Longenecker, Richard N, ed. *Contours of Christology in the New Testament*. Grand Rapids: Eerdmans, 2005.

Louw, Johannes P., and Eugene A. Nida, eds. *Greek-English Lexicon of the New Testament Based on Semantic Domains Vol. 1: Introduction & Domains*. New York: United Bible Societies, 1988.

Lucke, F. *Die Offenbarung Des Johannes*. Charleston, SC: Nabu, 2010.

Bibliography

Lugioyo, Brian. "Martin Luther's Eucharistic Christology." In *The Oxford Handbook of Christology*, edited by Francesca Aran Murphy, 267-83. Oxford: Oxford University Press, 2015.

Luther, Martin. *Luther's Works*, 55 vols. J. Pelikan and H. T. Lehman, eds. Philadelphia: Fortress, 1955-72.

———. *The Works of Martin Luther*, Vol. 6. Translated by Henry Eyster Jacobs and Adolph Spaeth. Philadelphia: Mulenberg, 1932.

Lyons, Georg, "Pursuing an Ontology of Attunement through St Augustine's Christology." *Wesleyan Theological Journal* 45 (Spring 2010) 179-96.

Macgregor, Kirk R. "1 Corinthians 15:3b-6a, 7 and the Bodily Resurrection of Jesus." *Journal of the Evangelical Theological Society* 49 (June 2006) 225-34.

MacLeod, Donald. "The Christology of Chalcedon." In *The Only Hope Jesus: Yesterday, Today, Forever*, edited by Mark Elliot and John McPake, 203-19. Fearn, UK: Christian Focus, 2001.

———. "The Lion Who Is a Lamb: An Exposition of Revelation 5:1-7." *Bibliotheca Sacra* 164 No. 655 (Summer 2007) 323-40.

Maier, Gerhard. "Die Johannesoffenbarung und die Kirche." *Wissenschaftliche Untersuchungen zum Neuen Testament* 25. Tubingen: Moher, 1981.

Mansi, J. D. *Sacrorum conciliorum nova et amplissima collection*. Graz: Akademische Druck- u. Verlagsanstalt, 1960.

Marshall, I. Howard. "The Christology of Luke's Gospel and Acts." In *Contours of Christology in the New Testament*, edited by Richard N. Longenecker, 122-47. Grand Rapids: Eerdmans, 2005.

———. *The Last Supper and Lord's Supper*. Grand Rapids: Eerdmans, 1980.

———. *The Origins of New Testament Christology*. Downers Grove, IL: InterVarsity, 2005.

Martin, Ralph P. "The Christology of the Prison Epistles." In *Contours of Christology in the New Testament*, edited by Richard N. Longenecker, 193-218. Grand Rapids: Eerdmans, 2005.

McDonald, Patricia M. "Lion as Slain Lamb: On Reading Revelation Recursively." *Horizons* 23 (Spring 1996) 29-47.

McGrath, Alister. *The Making of Modern German Christology*. Oxford: Blackwell, 1986.

McGrath, James F. *John's Apologetic Christology: Legitimation and Development in Johannine Christology*. New York: Cambridge University Press, 2001.

Michaels, Ramsey. *Interpreting the Book of Revelation*. Grand Rapids: Baker, 1992.

Middleton, Paul. *The Violence of the Lamb: Martyrs as Agents of Divine Judgments in the Book of Revelation*. New York: Bloomsbury, 2018.

Milbank, Alison. "Seeing Double: The Crucified Christ in Western Medieval Art." In *The Oxford Handbook of Christology*, edited by Francesca Aran Murphy, 215-32. Oxford: Oxford University Press, 2016.

Moo, Douglas. "The Christology of the Early Pauline Letters." In *Contours of Christology in the New Testament*. Edited by Richard N. Longenecker. Grand Rapids: Eerdmans, 2005.

Mounce, Robert H. *The Book of Revelation*, New International Commentary on the New Testament. Grand Rapids: Eerdmans, 1997.

———. "The Christology of the Apocalypse." *Foundations* 11 (Spring 1968) 42-45.

Murphy, Francesca, ed. *Oxford Handbook of Christology*. Oxford: Oxford University Press, 2016.

Bibliography

Murphy, Frederick James. *Apocalypticism in the Bible and its World.* Grand Rapids: Baker Academic.

Mussies, G. *The Morphology of Koine Greek as Used in the Apocalypse of John.* Leiden: Brill, 1971.

Nakhro, Mazie. "The Manner of Worship According to the Book of Revelation," *Bibliotheca Sacra* 158 no. 629 (January—March 2001) 165–80.

Neill, Stephen, and Tom Wright. *The Interpretation of the New Testament: 1861-1986.* Oxford: Oxford University Press, 1988.

Newsom, Carol. *Songs of the Sabbath Sacrifice: A Critical Edition.* Atlanta: Scholars, 1985.

Nichols, Aidan. "Image Christology in the Age of the Second Council of Nicaea." In *The Oxford Handbook of Christology,* edited by Francesca Aran Murphy, 169–82. Oxford: Oxford University Press, 2016.

Nicoll, W. Boertson. *The Lamb of God: Expositions in the Writings of St. John.* New York: Macmillan, 1883.

Origen. *Commentary on the Gospel of John,* 6.273–74. *Fathers of the Church: A New Translation.* Washington, DC: Catholic University of America Press, 1947.

Osborne, Grant. *Revelation,* Baker Exegetical Commentary on the New Testament. Grand Rapids: Baker, 2008.

Ozanne, C. G. "The Language of the Apocalypse." *Tyndale House Bulletin* 16 (1965) 3–9.

Pannenberg, Wolfhart. *Jesus—God and Man.* Translated by L. L. Wilkins and D. A. Priebe. Philadelphia: Westminster, 1977.

———. *Revelation as History.* Edited by Wolfhart Pannenberg. Translated by E. Quinn. New York: Macmillan, 1968.

Parvis, Sara, and Paul Fosters, eds. *Justin Martyr and His Worlds.* Minneapolis: Fortress, 2007.

Patterson, Paige. *Revelation,* New American Commentary Series. Nashville: B. & H., 2012.

Paulien, John. "Recent Developments in the Study of the Book of Revelation." *Association of University Summer Sessions* 26 (1988) 159–70.

Percer, Leo R. "The War in Heaven: Michael and Messiah in Revelation 12." PhD diss., Baylor University, 1999.

Perronet, Edward. "All Hail the Power of Jesus' Name."

Petersen, David L. *Zechariah 9-14 and Malachi.* Louisville: Westminster John Knox, 1995.

Peterson, David. *Engaging with God: A Biblical Theology of Worship.* Downers Grove, IL: IVP, 2004.

Pippin, Tina. *Death and Desire: The Rhetoric of Gender in the Apocalypse of John: Literary Currents in Biblical Interpretation.* Louisville: Westminster John Knox, 1992.

Pollard, T. E. *Johannine Christology and the Early Church.* Cambridge: Cambridge University Press, 1970.

Price, S. R. F. *Rituals and Power: The Roman Imperial Cult in Asia Minor.* Cambridge: Cambridge University Press, 1984.

Rainbow, Paul A. *Johannine Theology: The Gospel, the Epistles, and the Apocalypse.* Downers Grove, IL: InterVarsity, 2014.

———. "Jewish Monotheism as the Matrix for New Testament Christology: A Review Article." *Novum Testamentum* 33 (1991) 78–91.

———. "Monotheism and Christology in 1 Corinthians 8:4-6." PhD diss., Oxford University, 1987.

Reicke, B. I. "Traces of Gnosticism in the D.S.S.?" *New Testament Studies* 1 (1954-5) 130–140.

Bibliography

Ritschl, Albrecht. *Die christliche Lehre vonder Rechtfertigung und Versohnung*, Vol. I. Bonn: Marcus, 1870-74.

Robbins, Vernon K. "The Christology of Mark." PhD diss., University of Chicago, 1969.

Robertson, A. T. *Word Pictures in the New Testament*, 6 vols. Nashville: B. & H., 1933.

Roloff, Jurgen. *The Revelation of John*. Minneapolis: Fortress, 1993.

Rowland, Christopher. *The Open Heaven*. London: Society for Promoting Christian Knowledge, 1982.

Sanders, E. P. *Judaism: Practice and Belief, 63 B.C.E.-667 C.E.* London: SCM, 1992.

Sanders, J. N. "St. John on Patmos." *New Testament Studies* 9 (1962-63) 75-85.

Sanders, Fred. "Chalcedonian Categories for the Gospel Narrative." In *Jesus in Trinitarian Perspective*, edited by Fred Sanders and Klaus D. Issler, 1-43. Nashville: B. & H., 2007.

Schaff, R. *The Creeds of Christendom, with a History and Critical Notes*, Vol. 2. New York: Harper, 1877.

Schillebeeckx, Edward. *Christ: The Christian Experience in the Modern World*. London: SCM, 1980.

Schleiermacher, F. *The Christian Faith*. Berkeley, CA: Apocryphile, 2011.

Schmidt, J. M. *Die judische Apokalyptik: Die Geschichte ihrer Erforschung von den Anfangen bis zu den Textfunden von Qumran*. Neukirchen: Neukirchenner, 1963.

Schmoller, Otto. *Die Lehre vom Reich Gottes in den Schriften des Neues Testaments*. Leiden: Brill, 1891.

Schweitzer, Albert. *The Quest of the Historical Jesus*. Translated by W. Montgomery. London: Black, 1910.

Smalley, Stephen. "John's Revelation and John's Community." *Bulletin of the John Ryland's Library* 69 (1988) 549-71.

———. *The Revelation of John: A Commentary on the Greet Text of the Apocalypse*. London: Society for Promoting Christian Knowledge, 2005.

Smith, D. Moody. *John Among the Gospels*. 2nd ed. Columbia: University South Carolina Press, 2001.

Smith, Morton. "The Common Theology of the Ancient Near East." *Journal of Biblical Literature* 71 (1952) 135-147.

Spitta, Friedrich. *Streitfragen der Geschichte Jesu*. Gottingen: Vandenhoeck und Ruprecht, 1907.

Stefano, Troy A. "Christology after Schleiermacher: Three Twentieth-Century Christologists." In *The Oxford handbook of Christology*, edited by Francesca Murphy, 362-76. Oxford: Oxford University Press, 2016.

Stegner, Richard. "The Ancient Jewish Synagogue Homily." In *Greco-Roman Literature and the New Testament*, edited by David E. Aune. Atlanta: Scholars, 1988.

Steinsaltz, Adin. *The Talmud: The Steinsaltz Edition: A Reference Guide*. New York: Random House, 1989.

Streett, Matthew. *Here Comes the Judge: Violent Pacifism in the Book of Revelation*. London: T. & T. Clark, 2012.

Strohl, Jane E. "Luther's Eschatology." In *The Oxford Handbook of Martin Luther's Theology*, edited by Robert Kolb, et al., 353-64. Oxford: Oxford University Press, 2014.

Stuckenbruck, Loren T. "Revelation 4-5: Divided Worship or One Vision?" *Stone-Campbell Journal* 14 no. 2 (2011) 235-48.

Swete, Henry Barclay. *The Apocalypse of St. John*. London: Macmillan, 1906.

Bibliography

Swetnam, James. *Jesus and Isaac: A Study of the Epistle to the Hebrews in the Light of the Aqedah*. Rome: Biblical Institute, 1981.

Tabbernee, William, and John M. Imbler. *A Passion for Christian Unity: Essays in Honor of William Tabbernee*. St. Louis: Chalice, 2009.

Talbert, Charles H. *The Development of Christology during the First Hundred Years and Other Essays on Early Christian Christology*. Boston: Brill, 2011.

Tenney, Merrill. *Interpreting Revelation*. Grand Rapids: Eerdmans, 1957.

Thomas, Robert L. *Revelation*, An Exegetical Commentary, 2 vols. Chicago: Moody, 1992.

Thompson, L. *The Book of Revelation*. New York: Oxford, 1990.

Tilling, Chris. *Paul's Divine Christology*. Grand Rapids: Eerdmans, 2015.

Towner, Philip H. "Christology in the Letters to Timothy and Titus." In *Contours of Christology in the New Testament*, edited by Richard N. Longenecker, 219–46. Grand Rapids: Eerdmans, 2005.

Trevett, Christine. "Apocalypse, Ignatius, Montanism: Seeking the Seeds." *Vigilae Christianae* 43 (December 1989) 313–338.

Van Belle, Gilbert, J. G. Van der Watt, and P. J. Maritz. *Theology and Christology in the Fourth Gospel: Essays by the Members of the SNTS Johannine Writings Seminar*. Leuven: Leuven University Press, 2005.

Vanhoozer, Kevin J. *Is There Meaning in This Text?* Grand Rapids: Zondervan, 2009.

Von Balthasar, H. U. *Theo-Drama Volume V the Last Act*. Translated by G. Harrison. San Francisco: Ignatius, 1998.

Wallace, Daniel B. *Greek Grammar: Beyond the Basics*. Grand Rapids: Zondervan, 1996.

Warden, D. "Imperial Persecution and the Dating of 1 Peter and Revelation." *Journal of the Evangelical Theological Society* 34 (June 1991) 203–12.

Wawrykow, Joseph. "The Christology of Thomas Aquinas." In *The Oxford Handbook of Christology*, edited by Francesca Aran Murphy, 233–49. Oxford: Oxford University Press, 2016.

Weber, Has-Ruedi. *The Way of the Lamb: Christ in the Apocalypse*. Geneva: World Council of Churches, 1988.

Weiss, Johannes. *Jesus' Proclamation of the Kingdom of God*. London: SCM, 1971.

Wellum, Stephen. *God the Son Incarnate: The Doctrine of Christ*. Wheaton, IL: Crossway, 2016.

Whale, Peter. "The Lamb of John: Some Myths about the Vocabulary of the Johannine Literature." *Journal of Biblical Literature* 106 (1987) 289–95.

Wheelwright, Philip. *The Burning Fountain: A Study in the Language of Symbolism*. 2nd ed. Bloomington, IN: University of Indiana Press, 1968.

Williamson, Peter S. *Revelation*. Catholic Commentary on Sacred Scriptures. Grand Rapids, MI: Baker, 2015.

Williett, Michael E. *Wisdom Christology in the Fourth Gospel*. San Francisco: Mellen Research University Press, 1992.

Wilson, C. "The Problem of the Comitian Date of Revelation." *New Testament Studies* 39 (1993) 587–605.

Wilson, Mark. "Revelation." *Zondervan Illustrated Bible Backgrounds Commentary*, Vol. 4. Grand Rapids: Zondervan, 2002.

Witherington, Ben. *The Christology of Jesus*. Minneapolis: Fortress, 1990.

———. *Revelation*. Cambridge: Cambridge University Press, 2003.

———. *We Have Seen His Glory: A Vision of Kingdom Worship*. Grand Rapids: Eerdmans, 2010.

Bibliography

Wright, N. T. *The Climax of the Covenant: Christ and the Law in Pauline Theology.* Minneapolis: Fortress, 1991.

Yoder, John Howard. *The War of the Lamb: The Ethics of Nonviolence and Peacemaking.* Grand Rapids: Brazos, 2009.

Young, Richard A. *Intermediate New Testament Greek: A Linguistic and Exegetical Approach.* Nashville: B. & H., 1994.

Zachman, Randall C. "The Christology of John Calvin." In *The Oxford Handbook of Christology,* edited by Francesca Aran Murphy, 284–96. Oxford: Oxford University Press, 2015.

Zahn-Harnack, Agnes von. *Adolf von Harnack.* 2nd ed. Berlin: de Gruyter, 1951.

www.ingramcontent.com/pod-product-compliance
Lightning Source LLC
Chambersburg PA
CBHW051935160426
43198CB00013B/2156